MW00616051

GEOCRITICISM AND SPATIAL LITERARY STUDIES

Series Editor:

ROBERT T. TALLY JR., Texas State University

Geocriticism and Spatial Literary Studies is a new book series focusing on the dynamic relations among space, place, and literature. The spatial turn in the humanities and social sciences has occasioned an explosion of innovative, multidisciplinary scholarship in recent years, and geocriticism, broadly conceived, has been among the more promising developments in spatially oriented literary studies. Whether focused on literary geography, cartography, geopoetics, or the spatial humanities more generally, geocritical approaches enable readers to reflect upon the representation of space and place, both in imaginary universes and in those zones where fiction meets reality. Titles in the series include both monographs and collections of essays devoted to literary criticism, theory, and history, often in association with other arts and sciences. Drawing on diverse critical and theoretical traditions, books in the Geocriticism and Spatial Literary Studies series disclose, analyze, and explore the significance of space, place, and mapping in literature and in the world.

Robert T. Tally Jr. is an associate professor of English at Texas State University, USA. His work explores the relations among narrative, representation, and social space in American and world literature, criticism, and theory. Tally has been recognized as a leading figure in the emerging fields of geocriticism, spatiality studies, and the spatial humanities. Tally's books include *Fredric Jameson: The Project of Dialectical Criticism*; *Poe and the Subversion of American Literature: Satire, Fantasy, Critique*; *Utopia in the Age of Globalization: Space, Representation, and the World System*; *Spatiality*; *Kurt Vonnegut and the American Novel: A Postmodern Iconography*; and *Melville, Mapping and Globalization: Literary Cartography in the American Baroque Writer*. The translator of Bertrand Westphal's *Geocriticism: Real and Fictional Spaces*, Tally is the editor of *Geocritical Explorations: Space, Place, and Mapping in Literary and Cultural Studies*; *Kurt Vonnegut: Critical Insights*; and *Literary Cartographies: Spatiality, Representation, and Narrative*.

Titles to date:

Cosmopolitanism and Place: Spatial Forms in Contemporary Anglophone Literature
By Emily Johansen

Literary Cartographies: Spatiality, Representation, and Narrative
Edited by Robert T. Tally Jr.

The Geocritical Legacies of Edward W. Said: Spatiality, Critical Humanism, and Comparative Literature
Edited by Robert T. Tally Jr.

Also by Robert T. Tally Jr.

Fredric Jameson: The Project of Dialectical Criticism

Literary Cartographies: Spatiality, Representation, and Narrative (editor)

Poe and the Subversion of American Literature: Satire, Fantasy, Critique

Spatiality

Utopia in the Age of Globalization: Space, Representation, and the World-System

Geocritical Explorations: Space, Place, and Mapping in Literary and Cultural Studies (editor)

Kurt Vonnegut and the American Novel: A Postmodern Iconography

Kurt Vonnegut: Critical Insights (editor)

Melville, Mapping, and Globalization: Literary Cartography in the American Baroque Writer

The Geocritical Legacies of Edward W. Said

Spatiality, Critical Humanism, and Comparative Literature

Edited by

Robert T. Tally Jr.

First published in 2015 by
PALGRAVE MACMILLAN®
in the United States—a division of St. Martin's Press LLC,
175 Fifth Avenue, New York, NY 10010.

Where this book is distributed in the UK, Europe and the rest of the
World, this is by Palgrave Macmillan, a division of Macmillan Publishers
Limited, registered in England, company number 785998, of
Houndmills, Basingstoke, Hampshire RG21 6XS.

Palgrave Macmillan is the global academic imprint of the above
companies and has companies and representatives throughout the world.

Palgrave® and Macmillan® are registered trademarks in the United
States, the United Kingdom, Europe and other countries.

ISBN: 978–1–137–48979–1

Library of Congress Cataloging-in-Publication Data

The geocritical legacies of Edward W. Said : spatiality, critical humanism,
and comparative literature / edited by Robert T. Tally Jr.
    p. cm.
Includes bibliographical references and index.
ISBN 978–1–137–48979–1 (hardback)
    1. Said, Edward W.—Criticism and interpretation.
    2. Said, Edward W.—Influence. 3. Geocriticism. 4. Space in
literature. 5. Place (Philosophy) in literature. 6. Geographical
perception in literature. 7. Geography and literature. I. Tally,
Robert T., Jr., editor. II. Title: Spatiality, critical humanism,
and comparative literature.
PN75.S25G46 2015
801′.95092—dc23   2014029407

A catalogue record of the book is available from the British Library.

Design by Integra Software Services

First edition: January 2015

10 9 8 7 6 5 4 3 2 1

Transferred to Digital Printing in 2015

For Mélanie Heydari

CONTENTS

SERIES EDITOR'S PREFACE

The spatial turn in the humanities and social sciences has occasioned an explosion of innovative, multidisciplinary scholarship. Spatially oriented literary studies, whether operating under the banner of literary geography, literary cartography, geophilosophy, geopoetics, geocriticism, or the spatial humanities more generally, have helped to reframe or to transform contemporary criticism by focusing attention, in various ways, on the dynamic relations among space, place, and literature. Reflecting upon the representation of space and place, whether in the real world, in imaginary universes, or in those hybrid zones where fiction meets reality, scholars and critics working in spatial literary studies are helping to reorient literary criticism, history, and theory. *Geocriticism and Spatial Literary Studies* is a book series presenting new research in this burgeoning field of inquiry.

In exploring such matters as the representation of place in literary works, the relations between literature and geography, the historical transformation of literary and cartographic practices, and the role of space in critical theory, among many others, geocriticism and spatial literary studies have also developed interdisciplinary or transdisciplinary methods and practices, frequently making productive connections to architecture, art history, geography, history, philosophy, politics, social theory, and urban studies, to name but a few. Spatial criticism is not limited to the spaces of the so-called real world, and it sometimes calls into question any too facile distinction between real and imaginary places, as it frequently investigates what Edward Soja has referred to as the "real-and-imagined" places we experience in literature as in life. Indeed, although a great deal of important research has been devoted to the literary representation of certain identifiable and well-known places (e.g., Dickens's London, Baudelaire's Paris, or Joyce's Dublin), spatial critics have also explored the otherworldly spaces of literature, such as those to be found in myth, fantasy, science fiction, video games, and cyberspace. Similarly, such criticism is interested in the relationship between spatiality and such different media or genres as film or television, music, comics, computer programs, and other forms that may supplement, compete with, and potentially problematize literary representation. Titles in the *Geocriticism and Spatial Literary Studies* series include both monographs and collections of essays devoted to literary criticism, theory, and history, often in association with other arts and sciences. Drawing on diverse critical and theoretical traditions, books in the series reveal, analyze, and explore the significance of space, place, and mapping in literature and in the world.

The concepts, practices, or theories implied by the title of this series are to be understood expansively. Although geocriticism and spatial literary studies represent a relatively new area of critical and scholarly investigation, the historical roots of spatial criticism extend well beyond the recent past, informing present and future work. Thanks to a growing critical awareness of spatiality, innovative research into the literary geography of real and imaginary places has helped to shape historical and cultural studies in ancient, medieval, early modern, and modernist literature, while a discourse of spatiality undergirds much of what is still understood as the postmodern condition. The suppression of distance by modern technology, transportation, and telecommunications has only enhanced the sense of place, and of displacement, in the age of globalization. Spatial criticism examines literary representations not only of places themselves, but of the experience of place and of displacement, while exploring the interrelations between lived experience and a more abstract or unrepresentable spatial network that subtly or directly shapes it. In sum, the work being done in geocriticism and spatial literary studies, broadly conceived, is diverse and far-reaching. Each volume in this series takes seriously the mutually impressive effects of space or place and artistic representation, particularly as these effects manifest themselves in works of literature. By bringing the spatial and geographical concerns to bear on their scholarship, books in the *Geocriticism and Spatial Literary Studies* series seek to make possible different ways of seeing literary and cultural texts, to pose novel questions for criticism and theory, and to offer alternative approaches to literary and cultural studies. In short, the series aims to open up new spaces for critical inquiry.

Robert T. Tally Jr.

Acknowledgments

Edward W. Said's literary criticism, scholarship, and advocacy have supplied a seemingly inexhaustible resource for further study and action, and his work continues to make possible new research in comparative literature, in the humanities, and in the wider world. In organizing, arranging, and editing this volume, I have found inspiration in Said's work, particularly in his steadfast commitment to literature, criticism, and theory as necessary components of socially conscious, politically engaged, and altogether worldly critical practices in our time and place.

This project first took shape as a seminar on geocriticism and the legacies of Edward Said at the American Comparative Literature Association's 2013 convention in Toronto. The theme of the meeting, "Global Positioning Systems," was especially well suited to our seminar topic, all the more so given that the ACLA that year also honored the memory of Said on the tenth anniversary of his death with a plenary session devoted to his work and influence. Several of the contributors to this volume—among them, Cameron Bushnell, Jeffrey Hole, Kristine Kelly, Elizabeth Syrkin, Emel Tastekin, Darwin Tsen, and Charlie Wesley—presented early versions of their chapters at this event, and we have all benefited from the enthusiastic comments of the participants and audience. I am particularly grateful to the ACLA's excellent officers, organizers, and staff, who make possible such enlivening and important critical discussions. The association's commitment to comparative literature, underscoring the intrinsic value of literary criticism, history, and theory, well reflects Said's own critical legacies, which demonstrate just how crucial these apparently old-fashioned concepts and practices are for any project that hopes to engage productively with the all-too-real world in which we live.

I want to thank all of the contributors for their excellent essays. I would also like to thank various scholars whose insightful comments and encouragement have helped me in organizing this collection. These include Susan Z. Andrade, Paul A. Bové, Simon C. Estok,

Mélanie Heydari, Daniel O'Hara, Youngmin Kim, Cóilin Parsons, Luca Raimondi, Sangeeta Ray, Henry Schwarz, Steven Tötösy de Zepetnek, Agnieska Tuszynska, Bertrand Westphal, and Pei-Ju Wu. I am grateful to Brigitte Shull for her enthusiastic support both for the *Geocriticism and Spatial Literary Studies* series and for comparative literary studies in general. An earlier version of Chapter 10 appeared in *Transnational Literature* 3.2 (May 2011), and I thank the journal's readers and editor, Gillian Dooley, for their helpful comments. Much of my work on this project was done while on developmental leave at Texas State University, and I am grateful to that institution's Faculty Senate for its commitment to research, teaching, and service. My colleagues in the English Department and my students have been supportive, sometimes inspirational. And, as always, my family has been there for me. In particular, I want to thank Reiko Graham, whose love and understanding make all of this stuff worthwhile.

By definition, a legacy presupposes a powerful connection with the past, but legacies clearly belong to the present and, in the best cases, provide for an improved future. I hope that *The Geocritical Legacies of Edward W. Said* honors Said's immense contributions to twentieth-century cultural criticism, largely by demonstrating their continuing significance in contemporary critical practices, but ultimately by suggesting some of the ways in which this work may be of use to the literary criticism, history, and theory to come. Amid the shifting spaces of a complex geopolitical, transnational, and multicultural world system, emerging scholars and critics are perhaps best suited to the task of making sense of the ways in which we try to make sense of our world, thereby also, occasionally and with no small amount of luck, making that world a better place.

Introduction: The World, the Text, and the Geocritic

Robert T. Tally Jr.

The concepts of, as well as practices related to, space, place, and mapping have become key elements of literary and cultural studies in the past few decades. What some have called the *spatial turn* in recent critical theory has highlighted the significance of spatiality in comparative and world literature, among other areas, as the relations between geographical knowledge and cultural productions have been subject to greater scrutiny by scholars in various disciplinary fields. Geocriticism, literary cartography, and the spatial humanities more generally have introduced new approaches to and interpretations of literature, while also drawing from the spatially oriented interventions of scholars not necessarily associated with these emergent discourses. Among the most influential of these scholars, Edward W. Said represents an important figure in the development of spatially oriented cultural criticism. Although it would be misleading and anachronistic to characterize him as a geocritic, Said remains a powerful precursor whose writings on a vast range of subjects and *topoi* offer indispensable resources for geocritics and other scholars interested in the relations among spatiality, representation, and cultural forms. In his commitment to a critical approach that gave due attention to the geographical and historical registers of both narrative and lived experience, Said was an early trailblazer for critics now working in spatial literary studies. Additionally, Said's thoroughly engaged criticism has become a model for socially relevant and politically active intellectual labor. What is more, in his unflagging support for comparative literature, literary criticism, history, and theory, Said embodied the spirit of critical humanism, and he remains a crucial presence in the ongoing defense and promotion of the humanities in the present era.

A decade after his untimely death, Said is still one of the most influential literary and cultural critics in the world. A towering figure in postcolonial studies and an ardent activist on behalf of Palestine, among other causes, Said may be equally well regarded for his scholarship in comparative literature, critical theory, and intellectual history. Less commonly known, perhaps, is Said's extraordinary influence on geocriticism or spatial literary studies. In my *Spatiality*, I identified Said as a significant force in the development of literary geography, broadly conceived, someone who with seeming ease could connect narrative representation in a nineteenth-century novel to the most complicated conundrums of contemporary *Realpolitik*, extending a project like that of Raymond Williams's *The Country and the City* into a global approach to international languages and literatures.[1] In works such as *Orientalism* and *Culture and Imperialism*, Said directly undertakes what he referred to as a "geographical inquiry into historical experience,"[2] but his less overtly geographical or political texts, such as *Beginnings* or *Musical Elaborations*, also raise valuable questions for geocritical or spatial literary studies. In such writings, Said persistently demonstrates the human (all-too-human) need for a sort of figurative mapping, most often in the form of aesthetic productions, of the social, historical, and cultural spaces in which we live and struggle. *The Geocritical Legacies of Edward W. Said: Spatiality, Critical Humanism, and Comparative Literature* brings together a variety of essays, which, each in its own way, highlight the significance of Said's work for contemporary spatial criticism.

Partly in order to bring attention to this tremendous influence on spatial literary studies and partly to honor his memory on the tenth anniversary of his death, I organized a seminar titled "Geocriticism and the Legacies of Edward W. Said," which took place at the annual convention of the American Comparative Literature Association in Toronto in April 2013. Seven of the contributors to this volume presented talks at the seminar, and another contributor was an active participant in the discussion as a member of the audience. The seminar itself provided a lively forum in which to discuss a variety of topics more or less covered by the seminar's expansive title. The participants' work, here supplemented by three additional essays, ranged from studies of individual books and articles by Said to explorations of his ideas in new contexts and to applications of his theories to entirely different texts. Accordingly, in their revised, expanded, and sometimes thoroughly reconceived form, the chapters in this volume cover wide swaths of Said's already eclectic and extensive critical projects, from matters of aesthetics and interpretation to questions of history, geography, political theory, and social criticism. The essays included here work closely with a number of Said's well-known books, such as *Beginnings, Orientalism, The World, the Text, and the Critic, Culture and Imperialism, Out of Place: A Memoir, Reflections on Exile and Other Essays, Humanism and Democratic Criticism,* and *On Late Style,* while also establishing innovative theses and arguments for the present, twenty-first-century situation, in both local and global contexts. It is my hope that this collection of essays will be useful both to students of Said's own career and to those interested in geocriticism, literary cartography or geography, geoaesthetics, the spatial humanities, and other related fields or practices. I also hope that these diverse essays demonstrate the degree to which the study of literature and other cultural productions remains, as Said himself never tired of averring, an invaluable institution, one that is crucial for any attempt to comprehend the protean, complex, and vast constellations of social and spatial relations, of power and knowledge, in the present world system.

SAID'S SPATIAL CRITICISM

In recent years, as part of what has been referred to as the *spatial turn* in the arts, humanities, and social sciences, literary scholars have focused greater attention on the relations among space, place, or mapping and literature.[3] A number of critics have drawn attention to the ways in which narratives produce maps of the real and imaginary places represented in them, and this cartographic function operates with respect to both form and content. Although Said himself is not generally thought of as a geocritic, or even primarily as a spatially oriented critic, his work has been extremely influential to geocritics and to others interested in the relations of space, place, and mapping to literary and cultural studies. From his earliest writings on Joseph Conrad and literary theory to his monumental studies of orientalism and postcolonial criticism, Said always paid attention to the spatial and geographical registers of literary art, history, and representation. The significance of both spatiality and geography is apparent, though understated, even in Said's first book, *Joseph Conrad and the Fiction of Autobiography.* Originally written as his PhD dissertation at Harvard (and first published by Harvard University Press in 1966), Said's study subtly assesses the spatial form as well as the geographical and historical content of Conrad's letters and short fiction. For example, Said notes that "Writing and life were, for him, like journeys without maps, struggles to win over and then claim unknown ground. [...] As the physical and moral geography of Europe changed, he changed too."[4] Whether speaking more or less metaphorically about *l'espace littéraire* or focusing attention on the all-too-real geography of territorial conquest, Said's entire body of work is infused with a keen sense of the spatial.

Said is perhaps best known for his contributions to postcolonial studies, which as an interdisciplinary field has been at the forefront of geocritical or spatial literary theory.[5] Postcolonial critics like José Rabasa and Ricardo Padrón have provided significant deconstructive readings of geographical discourses surrounding New World colonization,[6] and such geographers as J. B. Harley and Derek Gregory have demonstrated how cartographic practices frequently served imperialist programs, whether or not the cartographers involved were aware of it.[7] Mark Monmonier, in *How to Lie with Maps*, has shown how even the mathematical projections used in mapmaking came to serve ideological purposes, often in ways that supported colonial practices. Speaking of the Mercator projection, which distorts the represented areas of space by aggrandizing those located further from the equator, Monmonier writes that "The English especially liked the way the Mercator flattered the British Empire with a central meridian through Greenwich and prominent far-flung colonies like Australia, Canada, and South Africa."[8] And Said, particularly in influential books like *Orientalism*, has made clear the ways that both literary and scientific productions in the eighteenth and nineteenth centuries functioned as means of abetting the spread and consolidation of imperialism.

Today, in the wake of such postcolonial and critical theory, we are less surprised to hear that maps, or any other "scientific" device or discourse, for that matter, are also ideological, that they are imbedded within and often serve the interests of structures of power or domination. But this is partly because the ascension of cartography in the early modern era made the map the primary way of viewing the world, which in turn became the mode by which power was exercised in the world. As Harley has noted, cartography is "thoroughly enmeshed with the larger battles which constitute our world. [...] Since the Renaissance they have changed the way in which power is exercised. In colonial North America, for example, it was easy for Europeans to draw lines across the territories of [American] Indian nations without sensing the reality of their political identity."[9] Among the most significant effects of the rise and dominance of cartography is that the view afforded by the map enables the viewer to detach himself or herself from the phenomena studied, as with a military leader poring over maps rather than trudging through the battlefields, and this abstraction necessarily alters the underlying reality, and certainly has rather pertinent effects on the people who actually occupy the places that are so abstractly represented and understood.

Furthermore, the imagery on the map projects far more than the pictorial depiction of geographical information. In Conrad's novel *Heart of Darkness*, for example, Marlowe describes the thrill he felt when looking at the "blank spaces" on his map, especially the central part of Africa, since those were relatively unknown places to be explored. Later, as he looks at a colonial map of the Belgian Congo, Marlowe notices how the blankness has been filled in with "all the colours of a rainbow. There was a vast amount of red—good to see at any time, because one knows that some real work is done in there, a deuce of a lot of blue, a little green, smears of orange, and, on the East Coast, a purple patch to show where the jolly pioneers of progress drink the jolly lager-beer."[10] In "Geography and Some Explorers," Conrad ridiculed the "fabulous geography" of the Age of Discovery, which had filled in the unexplored spaces with sea monsters and other fanciful illustrations, preferring the "blank spaces" of "honest" modern maps: "From the middle of the eighteenth century on, the business of mapmaking had been growing into an honest occupation registering the hard won knowledge but also in a scientific spirit recording the geographical ignorance of its time."[11] The need to "fill in" those blank spaces, to inscribe toponyms or to paint them with colors that indicate "activity"—and, sometimes, thereby ignoring the place-names already in use by, not to mention the activities of, the inhabitants of these spaces—is itself both a principal aim and an inevitable effect of colonization.

In *Orientalism*, Said shows how the "imaginative geography" represents different spaces and types of space according to the rather arbitrary distinctions made by individuals or groups. As he puts it, the "practice of designating in one's mind a familiar space which is 'ours' and an unfamiliar space which is 'theirs' is a way of making geographical distinctions that can be quite arbitrary. [...] It is enough for 'us' to set up these boundaries in our own minds; 'they' become 'they' accordingly, and both their territory and their mentality are designated as different from 'ours'."[12] Drawing upon Gaston Bachelard's arguments in *The Poetics of Space*, Said then notes that "space acquires emotional and even rational sense by a kind of poetic process, whereby the vacant and anonymous reaches of distance are converted into meaning for us here."[13] Just as the "country" and the "city" emerged, in different ways, as models for organizing the domestic spaces of Great Britain and, eventually, the world, the ancient dichotomy of "our land—barbarian land" translates into a basic structure with which to organize the spaces of one's imaginative geography.[14] For Said, this lies at the heart of the orientalism that develops in and alongside European culture, especially during the nineteenth and early twentieth centuries.

In *Culture and Imperialism*, Said takes as a starting point that "none of us is completely free from the struggle over geography," a struggle that is not only about imperial armies and direct conquest, but also "about ideas, about forms, about images and imaginings."[15] Indeed, narrative is as much the contested "territory" that Said wishes to explore as are the physical spaces of the earth. As he observes, "The main battle in imperialism is over land, of course; but when it came to who owned the land, who had the right to settle and work on it, who kept it going, who won it back, and who now plans its future—these issues were reflected, contested, and even for a time decided in narrative."[16] Clearly, material interests such as the profit motive and the geopolitical balance of power inspired the expansion of colonial empires, but Said rightly emphasizes the cultural aspects of imperialism (which itself is distinct from, though obviously related to, colonialism) that "allowed decent men and women to accept the notion that distant territories and their native peoples *should* be subjugated" and "these decent people could think of the *imperium* as a protracted, almost metaphysical obligation to rule subordinate, inferior, or less advanced peoples."[17] In his examination of the topic in *Geographical Imaginations*, Gregory alludes to this as "dispossession by othering," whereby an identifiable "they" can be deemed unfit to govern themselves, which allows the colonizers to adopt the humanitarian stance of the "civilizing mission."[18] Once a kind of *mission civilisatrice* is accepted, taken for granted even, it becomes the duty of those in the metropolitan center to "look out for" their colonized populations on the periphery. Both cartography and narrative played significant roles in establishing these cultural attitudes.

Said points out that the so-called "age of empire" coincides neatly with "the period in which the novel form and the new historical narrative become preeminent," but he insists that "most cultural historians, and certainly all literary scholars, have failed to remark the *geographical* notation, the theoretical mapping and charting of territories that underlies Western fiction, historical writing, and philosophical discourse of the time."[19] A proper analysis would require greater attention to the spatiality of empire, to the geographical and cartographical aspects of the imperial mission and its multifarious effects. An example of the type of work Said has in mind can be found in Paul Carter's magnificent book, *The Road to Botany Bay*, an extended essay on "spatial history" that explores the polyvalent uses of myth, history, geography, and mapping in the colonization of Australia.[20]

Such narrative representation is not limited to the great realist tradition of the nineteenth-century novel, historiography, and ethnography. In a "note on modernism" in *Culture and Imperialism*, Said suggests that the new aesthetic forms reflect a growing apprehension of the irony of imperialism, of the overlapping territories of the "other" in the metropolitan centers. This sentiment is enunciated by Marlowe in Conrad's *Heart of Darkness* (originally published in 1899) when, regarding England itself from the Thames River, he observes that "this also has been one of the dark places on the earth," thus suggesting the degree to which Europe's supposed superiority is itself contingent and ephemeral. "To deal with this," writes Said, "a new encyclopedic form became necessary," and the features of the modernist novel would include "a circularity of structure, inclusive and open at the same time" (as, for example, in the stream-of-consciousness narrative technique in Joyce's *Ulysses*), and whose "novelty [is] based on a reformulation of old, even outdated fragments drawn self-consciously from disparate locations, sources, and cultures."[21] Writing of the same historical situation from an explicitly Marxist perspective, Fredric Jameson has argued that the age of imperialism or of monopoly capitalism brought about a schism between "truth" and "experience," where the material conditions for the possibility of an individual's lived experience in a metropolitan center, for instance, are actually to be found in the far-flung colonial elsewhere. "The truth of that limited daily experience of London lies, rather, in India or Jamaica or Hong Kong; it is bound up with the whole colonial system of the British Empire that determines the very quality of the individual's subjective life."[22] For Jameson, the stylistic innovations of literary modernism were attempts to deal with this existential condition, effectively operating as strategies of containment that repressed the historical and political content of the novels.[23] However, for Said, this aesthetic of modernism was a reaction to the impending breakdown of the imperial system, as the artist attempted to hold an imaginary reality together which was no longer feasible in the "real world." As Said concludes, "Spatiality becomes, ironically, the characteristic of an aesthetic rather than of political domination, as more and more regions—from India to Africa to the Caribbean—challenge the classical empires and their cultures."[24]

In this process of resistance and decolonization, postcolonial writers and theorists have challenged the dominance of an ideological and geographical representation of the world still based on early modern cartography. In Africa and Asia, for example, the anticolonial revolutions sometimes included reverting to indigenous names or inventing new toponyms (e.g., in renaming a nation-state, such as Rhodesia's becoming Zimbabwe). Also, for example, mapmakers in Australia, Canada, and the Americas have introduced aboriginal place names to revisionary maps, and a famous "upside-down" or "corrective" world map, centered at the international date line and with New Zealand prominently near the top, has become a popular poster. The work of postcolonial critics and writers to de-naturalize the ways we tend to think of space and geography has led to a greater appreciation of the cultural and ideological underpinnings of the cartographic art and science. With new, critical mapmaking techniques and dramatic changes in geographical, travel, and communication technologies in the era of globalization, the cartographic revolutions of the fifteenth and sixteenth centuries take on even greater historical significance, even as their results and repercussions are challenged, reassessed, and overturned. The spatial turn in the humanities and social sciences, which has been motivated in part by the work of postcolonial theory, has placed greater emphasis in recent years on literary geography, literary cartography, and geocriticism, enabling critical interventions into these fields and suggesting new possibilities for them.[25] Said's wide-ranging literary criticism, cultural history, and political activism have been, and remain, extremely influential on such work.

Said's Geocritical Legacies

The contributors to *The Geocritical Legacies of Edward W. Said* bring the critic's work to bear on a variety of issues, some of which more obviously concern the spatial humanities than others, but all of which have significance for spatially oriented critics today. Each essay engages with some aspect of Said's critical project, as some contributors offer new readings of individual works by Said, while others follow Said's own lead in producing novel readings of different literary and social texts. Focusing on the institutions of literature and literary criticism, as well as problems of exile, imperialism, transnationality, and geopolitics, these essays offer innovative readings of Said's work while suggesting ways in which Said's ideas can be extended into different areas of geocritical inquiry. All address key elements of Said's *oeuvre* in ways that demonstrate the value of spatiality in comparative literary studies. *The Geocritical Legacies of Edward W. Said* thus provides a representative sample of cultural criticism being done in the wake of Said's multifaceted and enormous body of work.

In "Said, Space, and Biopolitics: Giorgio Agamben's and D. H. Lawrence's States of Exception," Russell West-Pavlov begins by exploring possible resonances between the work of Said—in particular, his sustained engagement with the plight of his Palestinian compatriots—and the theory of biopolitics pioneered by Michel Foucault, Giorgio Agamben, and Roberto Esposito. Much of Said's polemical writing on Palestinian issues can be identified as a form of biopolitical critique *avant la lettre*. Conversely, Said's interest in spatial issues, especially his attention to "imaginative geographies" (in *Orientalism*) and to "contrapuntal reading" (in *Culture and Imperialism*), can be deployed to reinforce the latent potential of "topological" thought in biopolitical analysis. Said's attention to the concrete aspects of spatial politics in the Israeli occupation of Gaza and the West Bank may challenge the abstraction of topological thought in Agamben's work and offer possibilities for analyzing the neocolonial configurations of a global biopolitical regime whose "topography" encompasses erstwhile metropolitan centers and colonial peripheries. West-Pavlov explores these global connections by analyzing the opposed but entangled metropolitan and colonial poles of early-twentieth-century biopolitics laid bare in D. H. Lawrence's somewhat neglected Australian novel *Kangaroo* (1923), which provides an exemplary narrative for discerning the biopolitical and spatial aspects of Said's engaged criticism.

Emel Tastekin, in "Orient Within, Orient Without: Said's 'Hostipitality' towards Arnoldian Culture," examines Said's seemingly harsh critique of Matthew Arnold in *The World, the Text, and the Critic*, where Arnold appears as both the instigator of a narrow, national, and hegemonic canon of English literature and the founder of a concept of national culture. Tastekin argues that Said's judgment is based on Arnold's location in relation to the Orient: Arnold was "at home" within the discourse of the West that stood in an imperial relation to the Muslim Orient. Once viewed from the perspective of Europe's Jewish minorities as the Semitic Orientals within, Tastekin argues, Said's own minority "struggle for geography" becomes more apparent. Locating Arnold strictly on the side of Western or Anglo-Saxon orientalism and, institutionally, as the proleptic figure of a New Critical tradition in literary criticism allows Said to map himself strategically as an Arab-Palestinian scholar and as a "worldly" critic within his own disciplinary history and discourse. His silence on the nineteenth-century Jewish emancipation movement, which Arnold supported, is an aspect of this strategy. Tastekin reads Arnold's dialectic of the Hebrew and the Hellene as a supportive response to the granting of rights to Britain's Jewish minorities; she goes on to examine Arnold's appreciative reception by Lionel Trilling, Said's mentor and a Jewish literary scholar who experienced pre–World War II anti-Semitism. Supplementing the insights provided by the field of geocriticism with Jacques Derrida's concept of deconstructive hospitality, Tastekin shows that Arnold's concept of culture complicates and destabilizes the positions of the host and guest in the ethical relation to the Other, which in turn affects the way we might interpret Said's secular criticism.

In "Edward W. Said, the Sphere of Humanism, and the Neoliberal University," Jeffrey Hole examines Said's work in the context of the global economic experiments taking root in the late 1970s and 1980s under Thatcher and Reagan, which have since reshaped the political landscape of our present geopolitical situation. For those whose academic formations have coincided with the influences and forces of neoliberalism in the university, Said's thinking provides important lessons, as well as materials for those attempting to ensure the survival of the humanities. The creation of what Said called the "sphere of humanism," Hole argues, requires sustained historical memory over and against neoliberalism's propensity toward willful amnesia. It requires the prioritizing of curiosity over the anxieties induced by the psychology of an inhuman market, of careful, attentive reading over the arrogance associated with the "cult of expertise," and of the precision of language over the professional jargon and the idioms of finance now shaping worldviews almost everywhere. Following Said, Hole emphasizes the necessity of humanistic criticism as a counterforce to modes of neoliberal managerialism currently reorganizing, even destroying, heterogeneous orders of life on the planet.

While Said's political writings understandably garner a great deal of attention from his admirers and opponents alike, it must never be forgotten just how significant a *literary* critic, scholar, and theorist Said always was. Said never decamped from his committed position within comparative literature and literary studies, and some of his most important writings are devoted to questions associated with a properly literary critical discourse. In "Back to *Beginnings*: Reading Between Aesthetics and Politics," Daniel Rosenberg Nutters attempts to think through Said's conception of "critical reading," especially as exhibited in Said's 1975 masterpiece, *Beginnings: Intention and Method*. Nutters notes that Said's current legacy seems to be as the founder of postcolonial criticism and the harbinger of the cultural studies orthodoxy of our current-day academy, but, by situating *Beginnings* in relation to Said's posthumously published "The Return of Philology,"

Nutters suggests that such a legacy belies the innovative and rigorous demands that Said makes on the critic in the act of reading: "to apprehend a text is to begin to find intention and method in it [...] to construct the field of its play, its dispersion, its distortion."[26] Said's early work sought to clear a space within a deconstructive orthodoxy that "risk[ed] becoming wall-to-wall discourses, blithely predetermining what they discuss," as he put it in *The World, the Text, and the Critic*.[27] Rather than repudiate such modes of reading, Said drew upon the same phenomenological tradition that authorized them. The process of "constructing" that "field of play" allows Said simultaneously to "apprehend" a text's worldliness without sacrificing its aesthetic integrity, the root of its textual "distortion." These days worldliness seems synonymous with culture or history and might be pitted against the return of the text or of the aesthetic, the new formalism, or the fate of close reading. Nutters contends, however, that such distinctions are inimical to intellectual endeavors. To this end, this chapter describes how Said, throughout his career, sought to avoid the pitfalls of a pure historicism or pure aestheticism while, at the same time, linking close critical reading to scholarly praxis.

Focusing on Said's influential essay "Secular Criticism," a rich collection of orientations that advocate a situational position "between culture and system" while avoiding a programmatic or clearly defined methodology, Darwin H. Tsen and Charlie Wesley seek to trace the anti-authoritarian ideas undergirding Said's theory, both in that particular essay and in such other works as *Orientalism, Culture and Imperialism*, and *Humanism and Democratic Criticism*. In "Revisiting Said's 'Secular Criticism': Anarchism, Enabling Ethics, and Oppositional Ethics," Tsen and Wesley discuss the ways in which Said's ideas about institutions and human agency engender what they refer to as an "ethics of enablement and opposition." Ever critical of orthodoxy and dogma, Said's larger body of work blends a geospatial conception of the work the individual critical consciousness with a notion of collective action inherent in his anti-colonialist critiques. While some readers have sensed affiliations with Marxism in Said's famous essay, Tsen and Wesley argue that Said's political argument is based on an ethics that allied with, but not clearly connected to, the rival tradition of anarchism. This distinction, they argue, helps to critically resituate Said's seemingly contradictory critique of nationalism and his apparent advocacy for a nationalist identity as a Palestinian. In view of this enabling and oppositional ethics, Said may be reconsidered as a critic affiliated with the concerns of the anarchist tradition, partially represented by the work of Noam Chomsky.

Such anarchism pays attention to how institutions limit, govern, create or enable the possibilities for its members. While Said does not engage anarchist thinkers directly, his notions of humanism, pleasure, and secular criticism all echo anarchist concerns about the state and its institutions.

In "Transnational Identity in Crisis: Re-reading Said's *Out of Place*," Sobia Khan critically reexamines Said's memoir, looking at the ways that his self-identification as an "exile" breaks down, while arguing that his personal identity was distinctively transnational. In *Out of Place*, Said surveys the multiple homes he has occupied in his life, including Jerusalem, Cairo, Lebanon, and the United States. Speaking as a displaced and a homeless subject, Said interrogates his nomadic life all over the globe. Khan argues that Said's sense of displacement illuminates larger questions of identity for transplanted, displaced, dislocated, and relocated individuals, whom she labels *transnational*. In his memoir, Said presents a chronicle of his transnational existence, but it also becomes the space through which he tries to find a "place" to belong. Khan reads Said's nomadic transnational identity as one which never quite settled in the geographical spaces he occupied, resulting in his always remaining an outcast and never being "at-home." Furthermore, Khan argues that being out of place is the rough equivalent to being a transnational, which in turn is disastrous to any attempt to form a stable sense of identity, be it personal, cultural, or national. Khan re-reads Said's memoir, not as that of an exilic writer, but that of a transnational writer mired in the depths of despair because of his displaced or dislocated life postcolonization. In an attempt to locate a particular "place" to belong, lacking his "true" homeland (Palestine), Said grounds his identity in two non-national and nongeographical institutions: schools or universities and his own mother. As Khan reads them, these two "spaces" are also imbued with multiple contradictions, for Said received a colonial education and had a tempestuous relationship with his mother. Despite finding a home of sorts in these areas, Said at the end of his life remained in a state of crisis, owing to his constant displacements and dislocations in a postcolonial world system.

Cameron Bushnell's "De-Orienting Aesthetic Education" takes as its subject the identification, description, and analysis of a geography of aesthetic education, paying closest attention to what she views as the spatial coordinates of literary imagination. Focusing specifically on the concept of *cardinality* to suggest that orientation by standard compass technology is a presupposition, Bushnell calls into question the scientific value of ordering the world into East, West, North, and South. Drawing upon Said's studies of orientalism, she looks at how the East, coded as the Orient, is an ideologically laden experience of direction. Spatial coordinates ground judgments of others vis-à-vis our own self-positioning, and we find it difficult to throw off the geographical frames of reference in which we operate. However, Bushnell shows how two novels, Moshin Hamid's *The Reluctant Fundamentalist* and Salman Rushdie's *The Ground Beneath Her Feet*, demonstrate the desirability of locating other systems of orienting ourselves. These texts offer strategies not only for negotiating conflicting instructions from multiple geographies, what Gayatri Chakravorty Spivak calls the *double bind*, but also for questioning the assumptions of "orientation" itself. Specifically, Bushnell argues, Hamid and Rushdie present situations of catastrophe, serial heterotopia, and refigured orientation-markers, conditions that suspend normal senses of direction, triggering periods of what Bachelard identifies as "non-knowing," and licensing other conceptions of orientation that alter the spatial relations through which we understand ourselves and others in the world.

In "Reflections on Exile," Said reminds us that, "Just beyond the frontier between 'us' and the 'outsiders' is the perilous territory of not-belonging: this is to where in a primitive time peoples were banished, and where in the modern era immense aggregates of humanity loiter as refugees and displaced persons."[28] As Kristine Kelly argues in "Dangerous Insight: (Not) Seeing Australian Aborigines in the *Narrative of James Murrells*," Said's description of exile resonates with studies in colonial emigration and investigations of the ways in which British travelers and emigrants learned to navigate the "perilous territory" of the colonies. For such exiles, the shift from home to colony entailed a choice between radical transformation and resistance to cultural changes. In this chapter, Kelly argues that narrative representations of individuals' negotiations between transformation and resistance offer insight into how colonists, especially in Australia, inhabited and claimed the in-between colonial space in which they found themselves. In particular, Kelly investigates the ways in which spectacular stories about castaways, like James Murrells (lost at sea and found in 1863 after living 19 years among Queensland Aborigines), represent the dangerously transformative nature of colonial travel. Castaway narratives offer a counterpoint to colonial adventure stories by writers like emigration advocate Samuel Sidney, whose stories were regularly published in *Household Words* in the 1850s and who presented Australian settler life as a space of resistance to cultural and geographical transformation. These nineteenth-century narratives of exile and the dynamics of resettlement inform contemporary expressions of shame in regard to colonial history and motivate national gestures of reconciliation. Kelly traces how colonial settlement in Australia was not only a story about aggressively claiming land and resources but also a study of the politics of identity beyond the protection of national order.

In "Exilic Consciousness and Alternative Modernist Geographies in the Work of Olive Schreiner and Katherine Mansfield," Elizabeth Syrkin considers the ways in which the exportation of the rigid boundaries and domestic standards of Victorian England to the empire's peripheries fostered an exilic consciousness in Katherine Mansfield and Olive Schreiner, two expatriate writers from the British colonies who became pioneers of the feminist and modernist movements. Their writing emanates out of the spaces they inhabited and the "outsider" critical dispositions these fostered, a perspective evocative of what Said theorizes as the enabling "spiritual detachment *and* generosity necessary for true vision." Invoking Said's theories on exile, space, and empire, Syrkin brings into sharp relief the myriad echoes and complexities connecting the work of two colonial writers rarely thought together. Syrkin focuses specifically on Schreiner's *The Story of an African Farm* and the allegorical tale "Three Dreams in a Desert: Under a Mimosa Tree," as well as Mansfield's "In the Botanical Gardens," "The Woman at the Store," and "Prelude." The striking parallels in their writing suggest how modernist and feminist themes developed not only within an alternative geographic space, but also as an alternative to a particular kind of colonial reality.

The collection concludes with my own essay, "*Mundus Totus Exilium Est*: Reflections on the Critic in Exile," in which I examine Said's famous "Reflections on Exile" in the broader context of the vocation of the literary critic, using as exemplary figures not only Said himself, but such important precursors as Erich Auerbach, Georg Lukács, and Theodor W. Adorno. In his elegant examination of the philology of world literature, Auerbach cites the wisdom of a twelfth-century monk, who understood that while the "tender beginner" cleaves to nationality, in the well-developed human being, "the whole world is a foreign country [*mundus totus exilium est*]." What Auerbach means is that a critic must detach himself or herself from the native soil, from the local prejudices and comforts, and adopt the persona of a stranger or exile, who can thereby map such spaces critically without the distortions caused by undue familiarity. Just as many literary artists have been exiles, émigrés, nomads, renegades, and refugees, so criticism may benefit from the exile's vantage, as may be seen in the work of a number of the century's most astute scholars of comparative literature. In an era of globalization, in which the project of literature is fundamentally transnational, the critic who can view the entire world as a foreign land is perhaps best suited to make sense of the postnational condition. Said's "Reflections on Exile" is, in my view, an exemplary text that points to the fundamental vocation of secular criticism in the present world-historical situation, with its inconceivably complex, global network of social and spatial relations. In augmenting and refining the cultural cartography of this world system, Said's geocritical legacies demonstrate the persistent value of comparative literary studies in the twenty-first century.

NOTES

1. See my *Spatiality* (London: Routledge, 2013), 90–95.
2. Edward W. Said, *Culture and Imperialism* (New York: Knopf, 1993), 7.
3. For examples of the range of work currently underway in the literary humanities, see my recent edited collections, *Geocritical Explorations: Space, Place, and Mapping in Literary and Cultural Studies* (New York: Palgrave Macmillan, 2011); and *Literary Cartographies: Spatiality, Representation, and Narrative* (New York: Palgrave Macmillan, 2014). For examples that explore disciplines beyond literary studies, I also recommend the wide-ranging collection edited by Michael Dear, Jim Ketchum, Sarah Luria, and Doug Richardson, *GeoHumanities: Art, History, Text at the Edge of Place* (London: Routledge, 2011).
4. Said, *Joseph Conrad and the Fiction of Autobiography* (New York: Columbia University Press, 2008 [1966]), 63.
5. This section draws upon my discussion of "Cartography and Navigation," in *Blackwell Encyclopedia of Postcolonial Studies*, ed. Sangeeta Ray and Henry J. Schwarz, 3 vols. (Malden, MA: Blackwell, forthcoming 2015).
6. See José Rabasa, *Inventing America: Spanish Historiography and the Formation of Eurocentrism* (Norman, OK: University of Oklahoma Press, 1993); Ricardo Padrón, *The Spacious Word: Cartography, Literature, and Empire in Early Modern Spain* (Chicago: University of Chicago Press, 2004).
7. See J. B. Harley, *The New Nature of Maps: Essays in the History of Cartography*, ed. Paul Laxon (Baltimore: Johns Hopkins University Press, 2001); Derek Gregory, *Geographical Imaginations* (Oxford: Blackwell, 1994).
8. Mark Monmonier, *How to Lie with Maps* (Chicago: University of Chicago Press, 1991), 96.

9. Harley, *The New Nature of Maps*, 167.
10. Joseph Conrad, *Heart of Darkness* (New York: Bantam, 1969), 11, 14–15.
11. Conrad, "Geography and Some Explorers," in *Last Essays*, ed. Richard Curle (London: J. M. Dent, 1921), 19.
12. Said, *Orientalism* (New York: Vintage, 1978), 54.
13. Ibid., 55; see also Gaston Bachelard, *The Poetics of Space*, trans. Maria Jolas (Boston: Beacon, 1969).
14. See Raymond Williams, *The Country and the City* (Oxford: Oxford University Press, 1973).
15. Said, *Culture and Imperialism*, 7.
16. Ibid., xii–xiii. See also Homi K. Bhabha, ed., *Nation and Narration* (London: Routledge, 1990).
17. Said, *Culture and Imperialism*, 7.
18. Gregory, *Geographical Imaginations*, 179.
19. Said, *Culture and Imperialism*, 58.
20. Paul Carter, *The Road to Botany Bay: An Exploration of Landscape and History* (Minneapolis: University of Minnesota Press, 2010 [1987]).
21. Said, *Culture and Imperialism*, 189.
22. Fredric Jameson, *Postmodernism, or, the Cultural Logic of Late Capitalism* (Durham, NC: Duke University Press, 1991), 411. See also my *Fredric Jameson: The Project of Dialectical Criticism* (London: Pluto, 2014), 95–111.
23. On "strategies of containment," see especially Jameson, *The Political Unconscious: Narrative as a Socially Symbolic Act* (Ithaca, NY: Cornell University Press, 1981).
24. Said, *Culture and Imperialism*, 190.
25. See my *Spatiality*, 11–17.
26. Said, *Beginnings: Intention and Method* (New York: Columbia University Press, 1985 [1975]), 59.
27. Said, *The World, the Text, and the Critic* (Cambridge, MA: Harvard University Press, 1983), 26.
28. Said, *Reflections on Exile and Other Essays* (Cambridge, MA: Harvard University Press, 2000), 177.

CHAPTER 1

SAID, SPACE, AND BIOPOLITICS: GIORGIO AGAMBEN'S AND D.H. LAWRENCE'S STATES OF EXCEPTION

Russell West-Pavlov

The almost photographic memory Edward W. Said was reputed to possess has been ascribed, in a recent assessment, to a "topographic" mnemonic mode that recalls the early modern techniques of memory based upon "common places" or imagined geographies.[1] Yet, once brought together in autobiographical form, Said's memories transpired to be less rooted in place than in a sense of being "out of place,"[2] or, to put it more accurately, the formative experience of dislocation perhaps informed all Said's subsequent attention to the politics of place and space, which a later school of literary reading might well describe as a geocriticism.[3] In this chapter, I suggest that the double vision arising out of the experience of being "outside in the teaching machine,"[4] to purloin the expression of one of Said's most famous colleagues, may endow his work with many features in common with another contemporary thinker, Giorgio Agamben.

Agamben's sustained attention to what has come to be known as "biopolitics" has constant recourse to the notion of being "outside within the system." My analysis will take the leitmotif of the blurring of inside/outside locations to suggest a number of parallels between Said's interest in spatiality and the contemporary field of biopolitical analysis represented by the work of Agamben and Roberto Esposito.

Beginning with a comparison of Said's analyses of the Palestinian question and the central *topoi* of Agamben's biopolitical theories, I propose that two of Said's concepts for the spatial analysis of literary texts, those of "imaginative geographies" and of "contrapuntal reading" may be helpful in rendering more concrete the manifest spatial abstraction of Agamben's biopolitical "topologies." To this extent, Said's work may contribute to the urgent ethical and political task of grounding and contextualizing Agamben's already intensely relevant, if controversial, biopolitical analyses. In order to illustrate my points, I will turn to an oft-neglected text of literary modernism, D. H. Lawrence's Australian novel *Kangaroo* (1923), to show how the "contrapuntal reading" of "imaginative geographies" of modern biopolitics may lay bare the global reach of such strategies of control and oppression, based upon the entangled relationships of metropolitan and colonial biopolitics.

SAID AND BIOPOLITICS?

Said's descriptions of the plight of his Palestinian compatriots in the occupied territories may have an ominously familiar ring to them for those scholars working in the field of "biopolitics." For those critical humanities researchers implementing the instruments of "biopolitical" analysis invented by Foucault in his late lectures and developed by Giorgio Agamben's multi-volume *Homo Sacer* series,[5] Said's polemical interventions into the condition of the stateless Palestinian people, from *The Question of Palestine* (1979)[6] onwards, have all the hallmarks of an interrogation of biopolitics *avant la lettre*. It is paradoxical that those survivors of the *Lager* that Agamben has so controversially identified as the paradigm of biopolitical modernity[7] in turn instigated the establishment of a network of (refugee) camps and set up a system of camp-like zones (the Gaza strip or the West Bank enclaves) that strongly resembled the geography of the *univers concentrationnaire*.[8] Said's portrayal of the desperate situation of the Palestinian people since 1948 is redolent of the panoply of biopolitical strategies enumerated by Agamben in his influential recasting of Foucault:

> Until 1966, the Arab citizens of Israel were ruled by a military government exclusively in existence to control, bend, manipulate, terrorize, tamper with every facet of Arab life from birth virtually to death. After 1966 the situation is scarcely better [...] the Emergency Defense regulations were used to expropriate tens of thousands of acres of Arab lands [...] Any Palestinian can tell you the meaning of the Absentee's

Property Law of 1950, the Land Acquisition Law of 1953, the Law for Requisitioning of Property in Time of Emergency (1949), the Prescription Law of 1958. Moreover, Arabs were and are forbidden to travel freely, to lease land from Jews, or ever to speak, agitate, be educated freely.[9]

What is striking is the way that Said's description of the tribulations of Palestinians in Israel or in the occupied territories segues from "biopolitical" interventions to the politics of spatial expropriation and back again, remaining at all times brutally specific in its attention to the concrete detail of Palestinian experience.

Said notes that the "present security situation on the West Bank gives the military governor the power to censor everything written; to deport, detain, and destroy the houses of suspected subversives; to take virtually any action whose purpose is to protect the state of Israel."[10] Summing up, he concludes that "every Arab is subject to military regulations," evoking the "martial law and the state of siege" that legislates the lawless zone of the camp, and state of "legal civil war" that according to Agamben has characterized the state of exception in its twentieth-century manifestations around the globe.[11] Said's evocation of the way in which the "the non-Jew in Israel represents a permanent banishment from his as well as all *other* past, present, and future benefits in Palestine"[12] echoes Agamben's semantics of the ban, and recalls explorations of the tendency of the state of exception not only to expand to a global phenomenon, but to become a permanent state of affairs: "Palestinian autonomy will give the Israeli government and army the right to continue this state of affairs more or less indefinitely. [. . .] [D]etention, deportation and collective punishment will continue since the army will remain on the West Bank."[13] Said's commentaries on the "separation wall," which cordons off hundreds of Palestinian enclaves from their inhabitants' places of work, and from each other, throw up striking resemblances to the zones of exclusion within the polity, an exterior at the interior of the state "[a]t once excluding bare life from and capturing it within the political order", for which Agamben proposes the camp as the paradigmatic model.[14] Finally, the experience of Said's Palestinian family—"To have lived as a member of society [. . .] one day, and then suddenly on another day not to be able to do that, was [. . .] a living death"— echoes in its phrasing Agamben's description of those consigned and resigned to death, the "living dead of the camps."[15] This accumulation of conceptual and even phraseological similarities between Said's polemics about the Palestinian situation and Agamben's mapping of twentieth-century biopolitics points toward salient resemblances that have not gone unnoticed by other theoreticians. Thus Žižek in *Welcome to the Desert of the Real* can claim that "Palestinians in the occupied territories are reduced to the status of *Homo sacer*, the object of disciplinary measures and/or even humanitarian help, but not full citizens."[16] Mbembe sees in the Gaza strip and the occupied territories the exercise of "necropower," the deathly face of an administrative biopolitics.[17]

Yet at the same time, Said's insistent repetition of the crucial *topos* of place in postcolonial studies—"The main battle in imperialism is over land,"[18] as he puts it in *Culture and Imperialism*—which translates into a sustained attention to the loss of territory suffered by the Palestinian people, distinguishes the focus of Said's analyses from those of Agamben. "In a very literal way," Said observes, "the Palestinian predicament since 1948 is that to be a Palestinian at all has been to live in a utopia, a nonplace, of some sort [...] the Palestinian struggle today is profoundly topical [...] it is focussed on the goal of getting a place, a territory, on which to be located nationally." Said concludes, "Palestinian self-determination has come to rest by and large on the need for a liberated part of the original territory of Palestine."[19] All subsequent struggle has aimed toward the "restoration of Palestinian identity and of actual land";[20] the former is defined by the latter, by the "Palestinian impulse to stay on the land."[21] This salient aspect of Said's writing on the Palestinian issue may be salutary in correcting a curious spatial blind spot within biopolitical theory.

Agamben's analyses return constantly to the *topos* of the blurred inside/outside border. "Bare life" is on the border between life and death; it is excluded from the polity (abandoned by the law) while being exposed to the full force of a lawless law; the camp concretizes this anomalous situation as "the space that is opened when the state of exception begins to become the rule."[22] The camp is a domain that is either inside the state geographies but outside its jurisdiction (as in Auschwitz, or in the detention centers for asylum seekers in international airports, or the Australian government's 2001 excision of offshore "immigration zones" to deprive illegal immigrants of the right to demand asylum),[23] or outside the state boundaries but within the purview of the state to suspend the law (as in Guantánamo); the state of exception itself constitutes a zone of juridical undecidability, which is simultaneously included within juridical power yet beyond its boundaries.[24]

Yet Agamben deliberately eschews a spatial analysis that is too concrete in its applicability:

The simple topographic opposition (inside/outside) implicit in these theories seems insufficient to account for the phenomenon that it should explain. If the state of exception's characteristic property is a (total or partial) suspension of the juridical order, how can such a suspension be contained within it? [. . .] In truth, the state of exception is neither external nor internal to the juridical order, and the problem of defining it concerns precisely a threshold, or a zone of indifference, where inside and outside do not exclude each other but rather blur with each other. [. . .] Hence the interest of those theories that [. . .] complicate the topographical opposition into a more complex topological relation, in which the very limit of the juridical order is at issue.[25]

Thus the inside/outside "topology" of "bare life" and the "state of exception," appears to displace more concrete issues of "topography." Agamben's demand for complexity is one of the most powerful and suggestive components of his analysis, yet its benefits come at the risk of abstraction. Agamben's neglect of real spaces, from those of the micrological camp to those of macrological geopolitics, is puzzling, given, for instance, the salience of "territory" as one of the key terms within Foucault's early working-out of a theory of biopower.[26] This neglect also explains one of the main weaknesses of Agamben's theory, namely its tendency to "superimpose Nazi thanatopolitics too directly over contemporary biopolitics."[27] Agamben fails to articulate the more complex imbrications between the extreme instances of the Nazi concentration camps, Guantánamo, or other "spaces of exception," and endemic global biopolitics, a "banality" of everyday power, for which he also makes powerful claims, remains to be addressed.[28] There have been some attempts to render biopolitical analysis more concretely spatial in its orientation, for instance in Battista's study of American geoimperial inscriptions of Indigenous space, Perera's analyses of refugee internment camps and detention centers in Australia from the 1990s onwards, or Minca's analyses of the police shootings of putative terrorists in London in 2005,[29] but in general biopolitical analysis requires more sustained spatial investigation. This spatial lacuna is even more striking when one notes the absence of postcolonial spatial analysis within the area of biopolitical analysis. A theory that can combine the "topologies" of the inside/outside distinction and the real spaces of (postcolonial) geopolitics is urgently necessary. I suggest that Said's notion of a "contrapuntal reading" of "imaginative geographies" may provide just such a theory.

The work of Said may thus contribute much to addressing these lacunae within biopolitical theory. Because the point at which

Said's work appears to share most common ground with Agamben's biopolitics is the issue of Palestinian dispossession, one only needs to conceptualize Israel as the most recent of the settler colonies[30] (whence its strategic closeness, for instance, to South Africa under apartheid)[31] to glimpse the broader postcolonial ramifications of biopolitics. The role of biopolitics in the colonies and in the postcolony has gone largely unnoticed until recently; the work of Achille Mbembe is a notable exception.[32] Two of Said's central *topoi* of literary geocriticism, "contrapuntal reading" and "imaginative geographies," may be helpful in cementing such a revisionist reading of biopolitics.

CONTRAPUNTAL READING AND IMAGINATIVE GEOGRAPHIES

Responding to a range of critiques of *Orientalism*, which in various guises highlighted the monovocalism of the concept (e.g., no voice for the Orient, a monolithic concept of the Orientalist project, etc.), Said modified his model to make the notion of Western/non-Western engagements more dialogical, an undertaking reflected already in the dual title of the successor volume, *Culture and Imperialism*. One element of his response was to coin the notion of "contrapuntal reading," a method of textual analysis that sought to be always at least bifocal, including metropolitan and peripheral or colonial perspectives.[33] It is significant that the thumbnail sketch Said presents for this methodology very early on in *Culture and Imperialism*, a brief commentary on Dickens's *Great Expectations*, highlights the manner in which the colonial project, embodied in the person of Magwitch the escaped convict ("a man started up," a "fearful man"), is seen to resurge on the margins of the metropolitan text.[34] "Contrapuntal reading" offers a way of locating metropolitan texts within a history of "a wider experience between England [or other metropolitan, imperial centers] and its overseas colonies."[35] This doubly focused method of literary analysis, though coined in the 1990s, in fact described what Said had been doing for several decades: namely, mapping the connections between European Orientalism and colonial conquest, between the American academy and Cold War imperialism,[36] between the interests of the American media and oil lobby and Israel's occupation of Palestine and other Western geopolitical action in the Middle East.[37] Said's project here provides a methodological template for a postcolonial account of biopolitics that combines "contrapuntal reading" and "imaginative geographies." Both elements, I propose, are crucial to the project of biopolitical analysis,[38] but have been largely neglected until now in the central work of Agamben. My reading seeks to take up these two elements of Said's work so as to propose a revision of Agamben's theory of biopolitics. Let me enumerate their respective significance for a postcolonial recalibration of biopolitical analysis.

Said's earlier notion of "imaginative geographies" was a central part of the project of *Orientalism*.[39] It allowed him to articulate the relationship between ideologically motivated stereotypes and the broader representational structures of Orientalism, and the geopolitical processes of conquest, occupation, and exploitation that were buttressed and legitimized by such images. From the outset, though, such "imaginative geographies" were always inherently double, linking us and them, here and there, metropolis and colony, center and periphery, ideology and power, theory and practice, and ultimately conquest and resistance, in multiple and mutually imbricated ways, as Said explained retrospectively:

> If there is anything that radically distinguishes the imagination of anti-imperialism, it is the primacy of the geographical element. Imperialism is after all is an act of geographical violence through which virtually every space in the world is explored, charted, and finally brought under control. For the native, the history of colonial servitude is inaugurated by loss of the locality to the outsider; its geographical identity must thereafter be searched for and somehow restored. Because of the presence of the colonizing outsider, the land is recoverable at first only through the imagination.[40]

The very notion of "imaginative geographies" thus anticipates and calls forth the later notion of "contrapuntal reading." Even though "contrapuntal reading" was part of a retrospective correction of the apparent shortcomings of *Orientalism*, the earlier term of "imaginative geographies" had already invoked its successor and would recur in Said's responses to his critics.[41]

Though Said's literary analyses of "imaginative geographies" often fail to do justice to the "overpowering materiality" of the "struggle for control over territory" mentioned in the "Afterword" to the 1995 reprint of *Orientalism*,[42] in his work on the Palestinian question those geographies nonetheless become intensely real. Those analyses evidenced Said's acute awareness of the spatial politics of settler nations and the fate of the indigenous inhabitants dislocated by such (neo)colonial projects of settlement. The potential of Said's work may be helpful in recalibrating Agamben's suggestive notion of the blurred, intertwined inside/out "topologies" of bare life. Indeed,

I will suggest that Said's doubling of the literary critical optic in "contrapuntal reading" may properly realize the entangled topologies of Agamben's biopolitics.

It is significant that though Agamben insists upon the camp as the concretization of these topologies, it is offered as a "paradigm", that is, as a theoretical blueprint, and less as a material realization of a specific biopolitics.[43] It is for this reason, perhaps, that Agamben appears to overlook in his work on Auschwitz the concrete spatial networks that made up the military-industrial complex of biopolitical "dispositifs." By contrast, as Giacarria and Minca claim, "what will eventually become the most infamous extermination camp was [...] not located in a void; quite the contrary, it was fully embedded within the broader spatialities and territorialities that were implemented by the Nazi imperial project."[44] Said's insistence on "imaginative geographies" inflected by the lived biopolitical realities of the Palestinian fate allows one to push Agamben's analysis much further toward the "topographies" that he so high-handedly dismisses.

In particular, Said's concept of "contrapuntal reading" is salutary in correcting what one might term a Eurocentric blind spot in Agamben's work. I propose that Said's form of contrapuntal reading can be used to lay bare constitutive relationships between metropolitan "inside" and colonial "outside," which tend to become entangled and reversed. First, however, I would like to put Said's "contrapuntal reading" to a more theoretical use: namely, to insert Agamben's biopolitics within a metropolitan–colonial relationship. As is well known, Agamben draws heavily upon the work of the right-wing German legal and political theorist Carl Schmitt in sketching his theory of "bare life," which is exposed to the arbitrary force of "sovereign law" under the "state of exception." Schmitt himself proposed a genealogy of the state of exception in his work *The Nomos of the Earth*, which couched the state of exception in geopolitical terms, seeing in the so-called "New World" a template for a zone outside the purview of the rule of law, a domain of the "state of exception" in which the "amity lines" of international law evaporated into the lawless "frontiers" of the conquered colonial space.[45] Agamben responds to Schmitt's geopolitical intimations by acknowledging the colonial predecessors of the concentration camps, especially in the concentration camps of the South African War (formerly known as the Boer War).[46] But because Agamben's claims for the concentration camp make it a paradigmatic "blueprint" for modernity, he tends to reduce such adumbrations of the colonial origins of metropolitan biopolitics to a merely metaphorical status, while recognizing their conceptual validity. But in fact, the historical connections between the colony and the metropolis may be far more concrete than Agamben's vague gestures suggest. Much has been made of Nazi interest in European colonialism as a model for the so-called "colonization" of Eastern Europe.[47] These connections are less direct and more complex than it might appear at first glance.[48] Nonetheless, they do tend to substantiate Schmitt's somewhat abstract notion that the state of exception is in the first instance an invention of European colonial politics, which then reappears at the metropolitan center of the imperial world. Fascism has been interpreted, in the words of Robert Young, as "European colonialism brought home to Europe by a country that had been deprived of its overseas empire after World War I."[49] Anticolonial critics such as Aimé Césaire or Franz Fanon read Nazism as Europe's shocked encounter, on its own continent, of colonial practices hitherto only known elsewhere: what Europe "cannot forgive Hitler for is not *crime* in itself, *the crime against man*, it is not *the humiliation of man as such*, it is the crime against the white man, the humiliation of the white man, and the fact that he applied to Europe colonialist procedures which until then had been reserved exclusively for the Arabs of Algeria, the coolies of India, and the blacks of Africa."[50] In Mbembe's gloss, "colonies are zones in which war and disorder, internal and external figures of the political, stand side by side or alternate with each other. As such, the colonies are the location par excellence where the controls and guarantees of judicial order can be suspended—the zone where the violence of the state of exception is deemed to operate in the service of 'civilization'."[51] In other words, it may be plausible to suggest that colonial practices reveal the "obscene underside" of a putatively more civilized or simply elided metropolitan (bio)politics.[52] Indeed, the topologies of blurred inside and outside describe the multiple overlaps of the colony as the space in which an external war is waged against internal subjects, and in which the external state of exception is invented, tested, perfected in a process by which it is then introjected into the core self-understanding of the metropolitan state. In other words, the center of metropolitan biopolitics lies on its peripheries, its formative inside transpires to be outside. The fused inside/outside relationships that Agamben locates variously in the status of "bare life," the camp, and in the state of exception that reign there, can be projected back onto the geopolitical relationships (metropolitan center–colonial periphery), which map the emergence of biopolitics in its global genealogy. In the process, however, the non-European genesis of such biopolitical strategies may be forgotten. The West "turns away" from the traumas it has wreaked upon its others, forgetting its own past and others' suffering.[53] With the help of Said's notion of "contrapuntal reading," it may then become possible to construct a bifocal analysis of biopolitics that makes a genuine contribution to understanding how metropolitan and colonial practices of spatial power have been intimately imbricated in one another from the inception and exception of the colonial undertaking.

ENGLISH BIOPOLITICS IN LAWRENCE'S *Kangaroo*

In order to substantiate this claim, I wish now to proceed to a reading of D. H. Lawrence's somewhat maligned Australian novel *Kangaroo*.[54] In my reading I propose that the biopolitics of a state of quasi-martial law in World War I, Britain finds itself refracted across the politics of a "state of exception" by Lawrence's fictive right-wing plot to establish a proto-fascist regime in post–World War I Australia. The plot, both political and narratological, fizzles out, and Lawrence's English protagonists leave Australia for South America, not without the text gesturing to another, biopolitical history, the erstwhile genocidal reduction of Australia's Indigenous inhabitants to "bare life," which it cannot directly articulate. Lawrence's text makes no explicit reference to the violent process of dispossession, which cemented the colonial invasion and occupation of the continent; indeed, by the 1920s, public discourse had almost completely erased traces of the still-recent collective memory of the genocide and displacement from its banal to brutal manifestations over the previous century. Nonetheless, Lawrence's text is replete with a sense of symptomatic half-hidden meanings that gravitate toward an intuition of a concealed truth within the landscape, toward something "which seems to lurk just beyond the range of our white vision. You feel you can't *see*—as if your eyes hadn't the vision in them to correspond with the outside landscape. The landscape is so unimpressive, like a face with little or no features, a dark face. It is so aboriginal, outside of our ken, and it hangs back so aloof" (87). Thus Lawrence's *Kangaroo* offers, albeit in a purely implicit manner, a "contrapuntal" view of a metropolitan biopolitics of modern industrial warfare, which is connected, at several removes, to a biopolitics of colonial settlement and genocide now hardly visible to the eye of the outside observer. Despite the invisibility of the still-recent genocide, which by the 1920s was modulating into a state-sponsored form of eugenics, biopolitical social engineering, which sought to eliminate, in the name of racial hygiene, the mixed-races or "half-castes," the text is clear about the connection between the two forms of biopolitics: "Richard Lovat wearied himself to death struggling with the problem of himself and calling it Australia" (33). Or, to reverse the terms, one might say that the problem of Australia holds the keys to an emergent biopolitics at the heart of the European self.

Lawrence's couple, Richard Lovat Somers and his wife Harriet, are fleeing a traumatic experience of victimization as conscience objectors during World War I. Lawrence's novel offers a personalized, subjective perspective upon the measures set in place by the Defence of the Realm Acts of 1914 onwards, which were then revised by the Emergency Powers Act of 1920 and invoked on frequent occasions in subsequent decades.[55] The historical era that Lawrence commemorates in his novel is significant, because "World War One coincided with a permanent state of exception in the majority of warring countries."[56] Within Agamben's account of the state of exception, World War I has a watershed status, because it inaugurates a sustained, blanket suspension of normal legal proceedings that "has continued to function almost without interruption from World War One, through fascism and National Socialism, and up to our own time. Indeed, the state of exception today has reached its maximal worldwide deployment."[57] Lawrence's tactic of creating a fictive north–south geography in which the wartime state of emergency is remembered in an Antipodean context, is an incipient theorization of the global state of emergency, which began to become visible in World War I.

Almost immediately after the outbreak of World War I, the British government passed the Defence of the Realm Act (DORA), whose scope was expanded by several successive emendations during the course of the war. The DORA gave extensive emergency powers to the authorities, including the establishment of military tribunals to try civilian offenders. *Kangaroo* registers in some detail civilian subjection to what it calls "the stay-at-home military who had all the authority in England" (279) and the effects of the importing of the conditions of an overseas war into the domestic domain, in other words, the de facto establishment of "a legal civil war."[58] The extensive suspension of civil rights is indexed in Harriet's complaint to a policemen searching the Somers's house, "Have we no rights at all?" (268). Harriet articulates an outraged bewilderment at being "to be persecuted like this, for nothing [. . .] And not even openly accused" (269). The shift from *de jure* to *de facto* authority[59] is evinced by the police officers' refusal to divulge the reasons for the repeated searches and summons (268–269). The state of exception as the importing of war and martial

law into the civilian world, and the establishment of extralegal measures within the jurisdiction of law, are given spatial expression by the
looming specter of the camp: Harriet's "horror had always been that
she should be interned in one of the horrible camps" (274).

If the Somers, as the object of the emergency legislation, find
themselves in a zone of legal indistinction and opacity, their own
relationship to themselves as private individuals with a civil status
undergoes the same transformation. The body, as the seat of an
enclosed, private realm, is penetrated in much the same way as the
civilian home is searched by military authorities. The private body,
"the only body that would carry my particular self," as Somers puts
it (245), is subsumed to the public realm of de facto law, just as the
outside of the law takes its place within the law's jurisdiction. This
is exemplified in the nudity, the stripping of the private body down
to "nude life,"[60] literally so, inasmuch as an American visitor to the
Somers is "arrested, and conveyed to Scotland Yard: there examined,
stripped naked, his clothes taken away. Then he was kept for a night
in a cell—next evening liberated and advised to return to America"
(249). At Somers's final humiliating army medical examination, a "big
stark-naked collier was being measured: a big, gaunt, naked figure,
with a gruesome sort of nudity" (280).

Somers's own examination represents the acme of reduction of
the civil person, with its discrete realm of bodily privacy, to exposure to the law. An examining officer, significantly, fully dressed "in a
navy blue serge" and thus clad in the opacity of the uniform, "came
forward close to him [. . .] holding back a little as if from the conta-
gion of the naked one. He put his hand between Somers's legs, and
pressed upwards, under the genitals" (281). Somers is told to bend
over forwards, further and further: the officer "was standing behind
him looking into his anus" (282). The innermost spaces of the body
are exposed to the eye of the law. Lawrence's micro-genealogy of the
state of exception pinpoints the manner in which the inside and outside of the law blur into a zone of indistinction, the public political
existence and the private individual domain are fused into a space of
surveillance, *bios* stripped down to *zoē* only to then be discarded.[61]

The scrutiny of the most intimate recesses of the body, the turning
inside out of the bodily interior can also be read, however, as synec-
doche for the inside/out relationships between metropolitan/colonial
states of exception. Travelling to the "new world" does not release
the protagonists from the trauma of the "state of exception," but
merely allows the "nightmare" of their wartime tribulations to return
to haunt them. The Antipodes merely present a reversed mirror-image

of the state of exception, not an alternative to it. Lawrence's bi-hemispheric narrative demands a "contrapuntal reading" of a Saidian variety that reveals the elided interdependences at work in imperial "imaginative geography."

In Australia, the Somers make the acquaintance of Ben Cooley, nicknamed Kangaroo, an Australian lawyer, who aims to topple the postwar democracy to restore Australian society to a lost vitality. The discourse of biopolitical threat justifying a state of exception is instantiated in Kangaroo's rhetoric of life and its protection when he imagines a looming "[m]alignant resistance to the life principle. And it uses the very life-force itself against life and sometimes seems as if it were absolutely winning" (127). The language is that of disease, and armed combat against disease. The continuity with the wartime state of exception is underscored by the fact that Kangaroo has recruited a private army of returned soldiers, the Diggers (the slang term for the Australian soldiers in World War I, referring of course to the Australian gold rush of the 1850s). Such right-wing proto-fascist, quasi-military organizations did indeed exist in Australia in the 1920s, seeking the sort of antidemocratic political powers invested in the Australian wartime government in imitation of DORA.[62] The vocabulary of vitalism and antivitalism echoes the examinations of naked bodies "moved about like a block of meat" (280), the healthy to be separated from the unhealthy and then fed into the military machine in defense of the realm. The anticipations of an Antipodean state of exception proved to be unfounded. Kangaroo and his Diggers, it seems, are a mere decoy distracting attention from something that the text can only gesture at in an inarticulate manner. Kangaroo's incipient fascism, foreclosed in the plot, is not a secondary, peripheral spin-off of European biopolitics; on the contrary, it points to an earlier colonial origin of metropolitan biopolitics, the core of the matter.

AUSTRALIAN BIOPOLITICS IN LAWRENCE'S *Kangaroo*

The real object of this vaguely sensed "biopolitics" of corporeal abandonment to a violent law is an ambient politics of the native land, expressed vaguely by Somers when he says, "this land always gives me the feeling that it doesn't *want* to be touched, it doesn't *want* men to get hold of it" (306). In a chain of metaphors, the white Australian possession of the continent is imagined as the possession of "the land's body" (20), in which it is reduced to a corpus that the farmers "scratch and irritate" (307). The land, reduced thus, underpins Australian suburbia, made up of "little square bungalows, each on its own oblong patch of land, with a fence between it and its neighbour," which are "close together and yet apart, like modern democracy, each one fenced round with a square rail fence" (15). Many of Lawrence's descriptions of Australia concern the bush, but the depictions of suburbia have as much, if not more, to say about twentieth-century white Australia than the stereotypical *topoi* of the empty, silent, eerie bush. Up until the very recent demographic influx back into high-density inner-city housing, Australia has been by and large a suburban society, with both its city centers and its rural margins sparsely populated. When Lawrence visited Australia, it was already one of the most suburban societies in the world. But Lawrence's observations are more complex. He connects the suburban phenomenon with a social relationship in which community is based upon an essential separateness of the citizen from her or his neighbors.

To that extent, Lawrence's suburban Australia becomes the epitome of the modern body politic, which is based upon an "equality [that] places men side by side, unconnected by any common ties," to quote de Tocqueville commenting upon democracy in America, a not dissimilar scenario.[63] In Roberto Esposito's diagnosis of modern biopolitics, the modern body politic's modernity resides precisely in its "immunitary" tendencies to protect the individual possessive self initially from the predations of communitary obligations, and subsequently the collective self from those internal and external elements that threaten its identity-driven interests.[64] The self-protective tendencies of the body politic are figured here in the insular suburban bungalow, which perfectly instantiates the protectionist isolationism of Australia enshrined in the newly federated Commonwealth's anti-Asian legislation of 1901. For Hobbes, the sovereign was invoked by the modern democratic polity to protect the interest of the one against the many. Democracy thus contains in itself the autoimmune tendencies gestured at by Lawrence in his depiction of a fascist army and its Antipodean *Führer* willingly invoked (172) to protect the polity against imaginary Asian predations ("the Japs come down this way [...] if we let in coloured labour, they'll swallow us" [101]) and the inroads of a socialism deeply rooted in the Australian labor movement: "The working people are very discontented—always threaten more strikes—always more socialism."[65] Lawrence's vignettes of Australian suburbia thus immediately reach the heart of the biopolitical nature of modern democracy, the defense of modern individualism in its "quiet self-possession" (12) against threats to the communal body-politic from within and without.[66] This description of the biopolitics of the normal democratic society is connected to the state of emergency by the occasional necessity to defend society against its enemies. Lawrence presents a narrative of emergency threatening the vitality of the Antipodean body politic, only to discredit and defuse it. By so doing, however, Lawrence redirects our attention to something elided within Australian history that expresses the nature of individualist–communitarian modernity in its essence far more acutely than its extreme manifestations in Auschwitz or Guantánamo.

Lawrence's suburban bungalows recall "temporary shacks run up in the wilderness" (31, 17), indexing thus their vulnerability to a bush that is only precariously reclaimed by civilization. The bush is, from the outset, a locus of threat. "Go into the middle of Australia and see how empty it is. [...] It may be empty. But it's wicked, and it'll kill you. Something comes out of the emptiness to kill you" (227). This is the other enemy that threatens the body politic of white Australia, but it is a mysterious one, connoted always by a spectral absence–presence. The landscape "was so phantom-like, so ghostly, with its tall pale trees" (18), it is "dark and spectral" (38). The text constantly refers to Australia as a "vast, uninhabited land" (18), to the travelers' "great sense of vacant spaces" (33); "Across was a state reserve—a bit of aboriginal Australia, with gum trees and empty spaces" (32). The last reference reveals the connections between spectrality and emptiness. It is the half-felt erstwhile Indigenous inhabitation ("You might still imagine inhuman presences moving among the gum trees" [38]) indexed in the images of ghostliness, which reveals a prior state of exception in which genocide has taken place. The land is empty because it has been emptied by force of its Indigenous inhabitants, but this emptiness never ceases to point back toward their absent presence. The usage of "Aboriginality" as an epithet connoting the land itself is evidence of a metonymic slippage of the signifier resulting from the erasure of the Indigenous referent.

The land constantly seems to be receding before the European gaze, remaining "unapproachable," presenting an "aloofness" (18) to the settler or immigrant eye: "he could not penetrate its secret. He couldn't get at it. Nobody could get at it" (19). This is not merely a problem experienced by the colonial spectator in general; compare Conrad's "The bush around said nothing and would not let us look very far either."[67] It is far more the problem of the text, which finds itself confronted with an opaque history that refuses to divulge itself. "The absence of any inner meaning" (33), which the text ascribes to the land, is the result of a process of historical erasure and willed repression. The genocide of the Indigenous people of Australia had reached its demographic end result by the turn of the nineteenth century, with a population estimated at between 500,000 and 1,000,000 at the time of British conquest in 1788 reduced to an estimated 60,000 by 1880, a level equivalent to that of the 1920s when Lawrence visited Australia.[68] By the same token, however, that genocide had been elided under a discourse of the "dying races" and a collective amnesia, which undermined public knowledge about the massacres, poisonings, disease, and decimation. There is no indication from Lawrence's letters sent from Australia between April and August 1922 that he was in any way aware of Indigenous (or "native") issues of the day.[69] The novel itself contains merely a few racist anecdotes about "Abos," ostensibly culling from the gossip pages of the Australian dailies (298–299).

The imposed silence upon the historical reality of genocide, a silence progressively dispelled only from the 1950s onwards, culminating in the "history wars" of the 1990s,[70] might be disclosed as the text's unconscious, that repressed history which it cannot say, and which all the more rigorously determines the particular logic of Lawrence's depiction of the land.[71] By the same token, that textual logic demands a symptomatic reading of the novel in order to elucidate the constant and almost obsessive attention the novel pays to the landscape. A symptomatic reading can show up the connections between Lawrence's detection of Australia's "great fascination, but also a dismal grey terror, underneath."[72] The text can only index a genocide it cannot know via an environment which is "deathly still" (18) and shows "not a sign of life—not a vestige" (19). Such epithets relay the presence of absence, the indexical evidence of death in the absence of life, as in images of "tall pale trees and many dead trees, like corpses, partly charred by bush fires" (18), which may gesture toward the massacres and the burning of corpses; here, however, the comparison foregrounds its own work as metaphor, that is, as a device that suppresses its referent. The use of the figure thus points back, symptomatically, to the repression of the literal referent that enables it, thereby unwittingly revealing and reversing the repression, the "forgetting of forgetting."

Facing the putative emptiness of the land is the emptiness of its white inhabitants. "Like his country," Jack has "a vast empty 'desert' as the centre of him" (48). The Australians are characterized by "*absentness*" (165). "The colonies make for outwardness. Everything is outward [...] the inside soul just withers and goes into the outside" (146). This "emptiness" can be ascribed to three factors. First, one can surmise a repression of the historical facts of genocide, which amounts to an emptying of the inner selves of the perpetrators, an elision of the subjectivities inscribed by those genocidal events: "the continual holding most of himself aside, out of count, makes a man go blank within his withheld self" (43). Second, this emptiness may be the internal concomitant of a refusal to read the ubiquitous residual evidence of genocide, a determination to "under-read" the world, which according to Hodge and Mishra goes hand in hand with a paranoid oversensitivity to hints at guilt, an "over-reading" of the environment.[73] Lawrence dimly recognized this under-reading: "One nice thing about these countries is that nobody asks questions. I suppose there have been too many questionable people here in the past."[74] Both of these versions of emptiness are pathological, a form of perpetrator-trauma,[75] but can be attributed to an "incapacity to mourn,"[76] which, in theory at least, could be addressed by some sort of memorial working-through.

The third possible genealogy of emptiness, however, is a more disturbing one of sovereignty. The genocidal emptying of Australia, a *de facto* state of exception in which the Indigenous people were treated as "bare life" and almost entirely removed from the continent, was the extralegal face of the legal British declaration of crown sovereignty over Australian territory in 1788. On the frontiers, away from the eyes of government authorities for whom natives were still British subjects, there arose a decisionist state of emergency, in which settlers retaliated to Indigenous resistance to conquest with a campaign of extermination, a lawless zone within British sovereignty but on its outer borders. But, if we are to believe Agamben following Schmitt, sovereignty is defined by, and reposes upon, the ability to decide on a state of exception, or at least in practice to condone its existence. Paradoxically, then, legal sovereignty thus underwrote the illegal practices within its purview in a liminal frontier zone, practices that retroactively are condoned by the fact that the possession of the continent, based on *de facto* violence, has never been called into question, as possession is coeval with white Australian sovereignty.[77] White Australian sovereignty is a decisionist sovereignty conveniently ignorant of its foundations in foundationless violence.

What is revealed here is "the Australian underdark" (18), the obscene underside of civilization that is laid bare on the global peripheries of imperial civilization, a global biopolitical version of Žižek's Lacanian principle of "the obscene superego underside [which] is, in one and the same gesture, the necessary support of the public symbolic Law and the traumatic vicious circle, the impasse that subject endeavours to *avoid* by taking refuge in public Law—in order to assert itself, public Law has to resist its own foundation, to render it invisible." Or, as he says elsewhere, "The law itself needs its obscene supplement, it is sustained by its obscene underside of the law."[78] The relationship between public law and its obscene underside is cast by Lawrence in geographical terms of center and periphery, order and chaos: "In the openness and freedom this new chaos, this litter of bungalows and tin cans scattered for miles and miles, this Englishness all crumbled into formlessness and chaos" (33). Lawrence's rhetoric is that of the colonial slackening of the European superego, which allows European barbarism to slip its chains and release its savage force. Beyond this *topos*, so beloved of Conrad and others later, such as Graham Greene, one can read a "dialectic of Enlightenment" according to which a metropolitan biopolitics reveals itself in its true brutality in the colonies where it was crafted and perfected. When Lawrence writes, "The *vacancy* of this freedom is almost terrifying" (32–33), there is a postdated unwitting acknowledgement of the existential condition of the camp, "the principle according to which 'everything is possible.'"[79] Within this zone of lawless freedom, "this Englishness [...] crumbled" not "into formlessness and chaos," but that which appears to be formless and chaotic because it seems to contradict metropolitan order, whereas in fact it founds and sanctions that order. Literally, the raw materials of the metropolitan industrial economy emerge out of the colonial economy, which itself has been founded upon the raw materials of indigenous bodies and territory.

The symbolic materials of the contemporary Australian polity also arise out of this state of exception. The right-wing historian Keith Windschuttle argued against revisionist versions of Australian history laying bare the genocide of the Indigenous peoples. In the absence of reliable documentary evidence, he claimed, no arguments could be mobilized for systematic massacres and poisoning of Indigenous groups.[80] Demanding the sort of forensic methods of historians that would stand up before a court of law, Windschuttle marked out within the realm of Australian historiographical jurisdiction a zone in which, for lack of evidence, the normal rules of historiographical procedure were suspended: here, "everything was permitted" because it could not be proved, with forensic certainty, to have occurred. The fact that much archival evidence such as perpetrators' diaries had been destroyed by settler families, or that the rules of forensic evidence simply do not function within a combat context such as that of settler massacres, was ignored by Windschuttle.[81] A rigid application of the laws of historiography allowed a "state of exception" to exist in perpetuity, thus assuring the preservation of nationalist narratives of the peaceful settlement of Australia by staunch pioneers, and thereby defending relations of ownership and sovereignty based on an originary illegality. The "air of owning the city," which Lawrence comments upon on the opening page of *Kangaroo* (11), is more properly an ownership of (sub)urban land, which concretizes the nexus between the normality of immunitary democracy in the independent colonial nation and the prior state of exception, which had reigned in much of its frontier territory. The genocidal *state of exception* segues into a contemporary *state based upon an elided exception*, just like the suburban blocks whose archaic, prior ownership Lawrence cannot not comment upon directly but which form the conditions of possibility of suburban Australian sociality even today.

Lawrence's text preempts Saidian "contrapuntal reading" in its portrayal of metropolitan/colonial "imaginative geographies." *Kangaroo* presents us with a chiastic relationship between metropolis and colony. In England, Lawrence shows us a state of emergency which can be portrayed, in part because its scope is relatively limited; for instance, under DORA jail sentences were limited to three months.[82] This is situated in contrast to one that cannot be portrayed, in part because it is unlimited, and perpetual to the extent that it constituted the founding conditions upon which the sovereignty of white Australia was premised. Here the blurred inside/outside relations that Agamben detects in both the site of *homo sacer*, an outcast within the purview of the law, and of the state of exception, in which the law institutes "a zone of *extralegal authority within the law*,"[83] importing an exterior lawlessness into the zone of its own jurisdiction, returns. The salient but limited state of exception in England has as its exterior, at the peripheries of the empire, a latent but unlimited state of exception that reveals the true nature of the state of exception at the metropolitan center; before Lawrence's novel was even conceived, the DORA had been superseded by the Emergency Powers Act of 1920 and invoked several times to quell industrial unrest. The "new, young" country furnishes the precedent for the unleashed state of emergency at the metropolitan center: " 'A colony is no younger than the parent country.' Perhaps it is even older, one step further gone" (57). By the same token, the peripheral, exterior case lays bare the latent potentiality of the core. This is the real meaning of Said's "contrapuntal reading": to display, via an interwoven textual methodology, the hidden connections of an imperial, colonial, and now global, world system in which the state of exception reigns supreme, as much in the everyday normalcy of contemporary democracy as in its spectacular exceptions.

Notes

1. Tobias Döring, "Picturing Palestine: Edward Said and the Fiction of Photography," in *Edward Said's Translocations: Essays in Secular Criticism*, ed. Tobias Döring and Mark Stein (London: Routledge, 2012), 205; Frances A. Yates, *The Art of Memory* (London: Routledge and Kegan Paul, 1966).
2. Edward W. Said, *Out of Place: A Memoir* (New York: Knopf, 1999).
3. See Bertrand Westphal, *Geocriticism: Real and Fictional Spaces*, trans. Robert T. Tally Jr. (New York: Palgrave Macmillan, 2011); Robert T. Tally Jr., ed., *Geocritical Explorations: Space, Place, and Mapping in Literary and Cultural Studies* (New York: Palgrave Macmillan, 2011); and Tally, "Geocriticism," *Spatiality* (London and New York: Routledge, 2013), 112–145.
4. Gayatri Chakravorty Spivak, *Outside in the Teaching Machine* (London: Routledge, 1993).
5. Michel Foucault, *History of Sexuality: Vol. 1: An Introduction*, trans. Robert Hurley (London: Vintage, 1990); Foucault, *Society Must Be Defended: Lectures at the Collège de France, 1975–1976*, trans. David Macey (New York: Picador, 2003); Foucault, *The Birth of Biopolitics: Lectures at the Collège de France, 1978–1979*, trans. Graham Burchell, repr. (New York: Picador, 2010); Giorgio Agamben, *Homo Sacer: Sovereign Power and Bare Life*, trans. Daniel Heller-Roazen (1995; Palo Alto: Stanford University Press, 1998); Agamben, *State of Exception*, trans. Kevin Attell (Chicago: University of Chicago Press, 2005); Agamben, *Remnants of Auschwitz: The Witness and the Archive*, trans. Daniel Heller-Roazen (New York: Zone, 1999).
6. Said, *The Question of Palestine* (1979; New York: New York Times Books, 1980).
7. Agamben, *Homo Sacer*, 117.
8. David Rousset, *L'Univers concentrationnaire* (1946; Paris: Minuit, 1981).
9. Said, *The Question of Palestine*, 105.
10. Ibid., 210.
11. Said, *The Question of Palestine*, 105–106; Agamben, *Homo Sacer*, 20; Agamben, *State of Exception*, 2.
12. Said, *The Question of Palestine*, 104.
13. Ibid., 210.
14. Said, "A Road Map to Where?" *London Review of Books* 25.12 (June 19, 2003), 3–5; see also Tanya Reinhart, *The Road Map to Nowhere: Israel/Palestine since 2003* (London: Verso, 2006),

157–173; Eyal Weizman, *Hollow Land: Israel's Architecture of Occupation*, 2nd ed. (London: Verso, 2012), 161–184; Agamben, *Homo Sacer*, 9, 20.

15. Said, "On Lost Causes," *Reflections on Exile and Other Literary and Cultural Essays* (London: Granta, 2000), 545; Agamben, *Remnants of Auschwitz*, 85.

16. Slavoj Žižek, *Welcome to the Desert of the Real* (London: Verso, 2002), 116.

17. Achille Mbembe, "Necropolitics," *Public Culture* 15.1 (2003): 27.

18. Said, *Culture and Imperialism* (New York: Knopf, 1993), xiii.

19. Said, *The Question of Palestine*, 124–125.

20. Said, "On Lost Causes," 545.

21. Said, "My Right of Return," in *Power, Politics and Culture: Interviews with Edward W. Said*, ed. Gauri Viswanathan (London: Bloomsbury, 2004), 447–448.

22. Agamben, *State of Exception*, 168–169.

23. Nikos Papastergiadis, "The Invasion Complex: The Abject Other and Spaces of Violence," *Geografiska Annaler (Series B)*, 88.4 (2006), 434–437; Anja Schwarz and Justine Lloyd, "The Pacific Solution meets Fortress Europe: Emerging Parallels in Transnational Refugee Regimes," in *Polyculturalism and Discourse*, ed. Anja Schwarz and Russell West-Pavlov (Amsterdam: Rodopi, 2007), 253–257, 270. The off-shore immigration exclusion zones established in 2001 were expanded in 2013 to encompass the entire continent: see Karen Barlow, "Parliament Excises Mainland from Migration Zone," *ABC News*, May 17, 2013. URL: http://www.abc.net.au/news/2013-05-16/parliament-excises-mainland-from-migration-zone/4693940 (retrieved December 29, 2013).

24. Agamben, *Homo Sacer*, 20, 28, 168–169; *State of Exception*, 22–25.

25. Agamben, *State of Exception*, 23.

26. Foucault, *Security, Territory, Population: Lectures at the Collège de France 1977–1978*, trans. Graham Burchell (New York: Picador, 2009).

27. Timothy Campbell, "*Bíos*, Immunity, Life: The Thought of Roberto Esposito (Translator's Introduction)," in *Bíos: Biopolitics and Philosophy*, ed. Roberto Esposito, trans. Timothy Campbell (Minneapolis: University of Minnesota Press, 2008), xxiv.

28. Mbembe, "The Banality of Power and the Aesthetics of Vulgarity in the Postcolony," *Public Culture* 4.2 (1992), 1–30. What might be the biopolitical status, for instance, of humanitarian aid? See, for instance, Eyal Weizman, *The Least of All Possible Evils: Humanitarian Violence from Arendt to Gaza* (London: Verso, 2012).

29. Suvendrini Perera, "What Is a Camp…?," *Borderlands e-journal* 1.1 (2002). URL: http://www.borderlands.net.au/vol1no1_2002/perera_camp.html (accessed December 17, 2013); Claudio Minca,

"Giorgio Agamben and the New Biopolitical *Nomos*," *Geografiska Annaler: Series B, Human Geography* 88.4 (December 2006), 387–403; Christine M: Battista, "Jefferson's Ecologies of Exception: Geography, Race, and American Empire in the Age of Globalization," in *Geocritical Explorations: Space, Place, and Mapping in Literary and Cultural Studies*, ed. Robert T. Tally Jr. (New York: Palgrave Macmillan, 2011), 107–120.

30. See Arie Boder, *The Other Israel: The Radical Case against Zionism* (New York: Anchor, 1972), 192; Rebecca Stein, "The Ballad of the Sad Café: Israeli Leisure, Palestinian Terror, and the Post/colonial Question," in *Postcolonial Studies and Beyond*, ed. Ania Loomba, Suvir Kaul, Matti Bunzl, Antoinette Burton, and Jed Esty (Durham, NC: Duke University Press, 2005), 317–336; Derek Gregory, *The Colonial Present: Afghanistan, Palestine, Iraq* (Oxford: Blackwell, 2004).

31. See Bernard Porter, "Pariahs Can't Be Choosers," *London Review of Books* 32.12 (June 24, 2010), 8–10.

32. See, for instance, Mbembe, "Necropolitics," 11–40.

33. Said, *Culture and Imperialism*, 49, 97.

34. Said, *Culture and Imperialism*, xv–xvii; Charles Dickens, *Great Expectations*, ed. Angus Calder (1861; Harmondsworth: Penguin, 1967), 36.

35. Said, *Culture and Imperialism*, xvi.

36. Noam Chomsky, *American Power and the New Mandarins* (Harmondsworth: Penguin, 1969).

37. See also Said, *Covering Islam: How the Media and the Experts Determine We See the Rest of the World* (London: Routledge & Kegan Paul, 1981).

38. See, for instance, John Masterson, "Re-fathoming the Dark of Heartness: Contrapuntal Representations of the Rwandan Genocide," in *Art and Trauma in Africa: Representations of Reconciliation in Music, Visual Arts, Literature and Film*, ed. Lizelle Bischoff and Stefanie van de Peer (London: I. B. Tauris, 2013), 192–219.

39. Said, *Orientalism* (New York: Vintage, 1978), 54–55, 57.

40. Said, *Culture and Imperialism*, 271.

41. Said, "Orientalism Reconsidered," in *Literature, Politics and Theory: Papers from the Essex Conference 1976–1984*, ed. Francis Barker, Peter Hulme, Margaret Iversen, and Diana Loxley (London: Methuen, 1986), 211.

42. Said, "Afterword," *Orientalism* (1978; Harmondsworth: Penguin, reprint 1995), 331–332; Russell West-Pavlov, "Postcolonialism and the Politics of Space: Towards a Postcolonial Analysis of Material Spatial Practices," *Anglia* 126.2 (2008), 258–277.

43. See Lelande Durantaye, *Giorgio Agamben: A Critical Introduction* (Stanford: Stanford University Press, 2009), 213–215.

44. Paolo Giacarria and Claudio Minca, "Topographies/topologies of the camp," *Political Geography* 30 (2011), 3–12.

45. Carl Schmitt, *The Nomos of the Earth in the International Law of the Jus Publicum Europaeum*, trans. G. L. Ulmen (1950; New York: Telos, 2006), 86–138.

46. Agamben, *Homo Sacer*, 36, 166.

47. Bruno Wasser, *Himmlers Raumplanung im Osten: Der Generalplan Ost in Polen 1940–1944* (Basel: Birkhäuser, 1993); Mark Mazower, *Hitler's Empire: Nazi Rule in Occupied Europe* (London: Allen Lane, 2008); for literary applications, see Niels Werber, "Effekte: Das Wissen der Literatur am Beispiel von Gustav Freytags *Soll und Haben*," in *Literatur, Wissenschaft und Wissen seit der Epochenschwelle um 1800: Theorie—Epistemologie—Komparatistische Fall Studien*, ed. Thomas Klinkert and Monika Neuhofer (Berlin: de Gruyter, 2008), 111–124.

48. See Shelley Baranowski, *Nazi Empire: German Colonisation and Imperialism from Bismarck to Hitler* (Cambridge: Cambridge University Press, 2010).

49. Robert Young, *White Mythologies: Writing, History and the West* (London: Routledge, 1990), 8.

50. Europe "ne pardonne pas à Hitler... le crime contre l'homme blanc,... d'avoir appliqué à l'Europe des procédés colonialistes dont ne relevaient jusqu'ici que les Arabes d'Algérie, les coolies de l'Inde et les nègres d'Afrique." See Aimé Césaire, *Discours sur le colonialisme* (1956; Paris: Présence africaine, 1962), 12–13; *Discourse on Colonialism*, trans. Joan Pinkham (New York: Monthly Review Press, 2000); see also Franz Fanon, *Peau noire, masques blancs*, 72–73; *Black Skin, White Masks*, 90–91.

51. Achille Mbembe, "Necropolitics," 24.

52. Achille Mbembe, *On the Postcolony* (Berkeley: University of California Press, 2001).

53. Victoria Burrows, "The Heterotopic Spaces of Postcolonial Trauma in Michael Ondaatje's *Anil's Ghost*," *Studies in the Novel* 40.1/2 (Spring/Summer 2008), 161–163 (total span: 161–177).

54. D. H. Lawrence, *Kangaroo* (1923; Harmondsworth: Penguin, 1986). References to this edition hereinafter cited parenthetically in the text.

55. Agamben, *State of Exception*, 18–18.

56. Ibid., 12.

57. Ibid., 86–87.

58. Ibid., 2.

59. Ibid., 3.

60. Compare the subtitle title of Agamben's *Homo Sacer* in its original 1995 Italian edition (Turin: Einaudi): *Il potere sovrano e la nuda vita*.

61. See Agamben, *Homo Sacer*, 187.

62. Robert Darroch, *D. H. Lawrence in Australia* (South Melbourne: Macmillan, 1981), 26, 48; John Rickard, *Australia: A Cultural History*, 2nd ed. (London: Longman, 1996), 155–157.

63. Alexis de Tocqueville, *Democracy in America*, English translation of 1862, quoted in Roberto Esposito, *Bíos: Biopolitics and Philosophy*, trans. Timothy Campbell (2004; Minneapolis: University of Minnesota Press, 2006), 76.

64. In what follows I am summarizing Roberto Esposito's arguments in Esposito, *Bíos*, and the earlier works *Communitas: The Origin and Destiny of Community*, trans. Timothy Campbell (1998, 2006; Stanford University Press, 2004); and *Immunitas: The Protection and Negation of Life*, trans. Zakiya Hanafi (2002; Cambridge: Polity, 2011).

65. Lawrence, *Letters*, IV, 249 (letter of May 28, 1922).

66. Whence Samuel McGeorges's choice of a Warhol-like multiplication of an icon of the Australian suburban bungalow as the cover motif of Russell West-Pavlov and Jennifer Wawrzinek (eds). *Frontier Skirmishes: Literary and Cultural Debates in Australia since 1992.* (Heidelberg: Winter, 2010).

67. Joseph Conrad, "Heart of Darkness," in *Youth/Heart of Darkness/The End of the Tether*, ed. Owen Knowles (Cambridge: Cambridge University Press, 2010), 81.

68. David Day, *Claiming a Continent: A New History of Australia* (Pymble NSW: HarperCollins Perennial, 2005), 113, 160; C. D. Rowley, *The Destruction of Aboriginal Society* (Harmondsworth: Penguin, 1974), 383–384; Welsh, *Great Southern Land: A New History of Australia* (London: Allen Lane/Penguin, 2004), 490.

69. D. H. Lawrence, *The Letters of D. H. Lawrence*, ed. Warren Roberts, James T. Boulton and Elizabeth Mansfield (Cambridge: Cambridge University Press, 1987), Vol. IV (June 1921–March 1924).

70. See Stuart Macintyre and Anna Clark, *The History Wars* (Carlton: Melbourne University Press, 2003); Russell West-Pavlov, "Introduction: Frontier Wars, History Wars, Word Wars," in *Frontier Skirmishes: Literary and Cultural Debates in Australia after 1992*, ed. Russell West-Pavlov and Jennifer Wawrzinek (Heidelberg: Universitätsverlag Winter, 2010), 11–44.

71. Pierre Macherey, *Pour une théorie de la production littéraire* (Paris: Maspéro, 1971), 101–110.

72. Lawrence, *Letters of D. H. Lawrence*, IV, 282 (letter of August 6, 1922).

73. Bob Hodge and Vijay Mishra, *Dark Side of the Dream: Australian Literature and the Postcolonial Mind* (Sydney: Allen and Unwin, 1991).

74. Lawrence, *The Letters of D. H. Lawrence*, IV (June 13, 1922), 262–263.

75. Instances of perpetrator-trauma, whether genuine or not, and regardless of their legitimacy, were prominent in the hearings of the Truth and Reconciliation Committee in South Africa, as in the case of Jeffrey Benzien. See Antjie Krog, *Country of My Skull*, 2nd ed. (1998; Johannesburg: Random House, 2002), 76–78.

76. I am referring here to Alexander and Margarete Mitscherlich's classic work of psychopolitical analysis of postwar German society, *Die Unfähigkeit zu trauern: Grundlagen kollektiven Verhaltens* (Munich: Piper, 1967).

77. See Henry Reynolds, *Aboriginal Sovereignty: Three Nations, One Australia?* (Crows Nest, NSW: Allen and Unwin, 1996).

78. Slavoj Žižek, *The Metastases of Enjoyment: Six Essays on Woman and Causality* (London: Verso, 1994), 61; Žižek, *How to Read Lacan* (London: Granta, 2006), 84.

79. Agamben, *Homo Sacer*, 170.

80. Keith Windschuttle, *The Fabrication of Aboriginal History: Volume One: Van Diemen's Land 1803–1847* (Sydney: Macleay Press, 2002), 165.

81. Paul Carter, *The Road to Botany Bay: An Essay in Spatial History* (London: Faber, 1987), 343; John Connor, *The Australian Frontier Wars 1788–1838* (Crows Nest, NSW: University of New South Wales Press).

82. Agamben, *State of Exception*, 19.

83. Eric L. Santner, *On Creaturely Life: Rilke, Benjamin, Sebald* (Chicago: University of Chicago Press, 2006), 13.

CHAPTER 2

ORIENT WITHIN, ORIENT
WITHOUT: SAID'S "HOSTIPITALITY"
TOWARD ARNOLDIAN CULTURE

Emel Tastekin

It is commonly assumed that Edward Said's privileging of the Oriental side of the East–West dichotomy in Western literary history has
to do with his commitment to the Palestinian liberation struggle.
Quite often, reference to Western politics in the Middle East under-
cuts his literary scholarship. His 1993 article "Nationalism, Human
Rights, and Interpretation" is a case in point. In this article, Said starts
by discussing Matthew Arnold's cultural nationalism and fleetingly
proves how Arnold constructs his hegemonic notion of "culture" and
a "deeply authoritarian and uncompromising notion of the State."[1]
He then devotes approximately half of the article to the discussion of
the Palestinian conflict and the first Gulf War. This article is a perfect
example of Said employing his disciplinary discourse to draw attention
to the current urgencies for which he is taking responsibility.

Said's critique of deconstruction is similarly based on this same
commitment for "taking responsibility." In *Humanism and Democratic Criticism* (2001) he states that "it is the avoidance of this process of taking comradely responsibility for one's reading that explains,
I think, a crippling limitation in those varieties of deconstructive readings that end (as they began) in undecidability and uncertainty."[2]
Said's intellectual concerns are dictated by his morals, and his theory
on Orientalism is foremost an ethical philosophy that draws attention

to the subaltern or non-Western "Other," particularly the Islamic Orient. But it is the location of Said's oriental Other that also cripples Said's theory and attracts the most criticism for creating a monolithic understanding of the West, particularly Europe. Perhaps this deconstructive "undecidability" that Said critiques, what I will call *deconstructive hospitality*, might remedy some of the idiosyncrasies in Said's ethics. What Said calls "secular" or "oppositional" criticism,[3] or the "strategic location"[4] of criticism, is in fact the act of siding with the Other as the suppressed guest within the powerful discourse of the host.

I would like to draw attention to the differences between Said's "secular criticism" and Derrida's ethics of hospitality, both discursive and political. These differences show themselves well in Said's treatment of Matthew Arnold—particularly when contrasted with his treatment of Erich Auerbach—in his *The World, the Text, and the Critic* (1983). While Arnold fairs as the instigator of a narrow, national, and hegemonic English canon and his "culture" concept as an effect of Orientalist scholarship, Auerbach is depicted as the arch-comparatist in Oriental exile and the exemplary figure of "secular criticism" that Said promotes in this book. My aim here is to examine Edward Said's harsh critique of Matthew Arnold. Said's judgment is based on Arnold's location in relation to the Orient: Arnold was "at home" within the discourse of the West that was in an imperial relation to the Muslim Orient. Once viewed from the perspective of Europe's Jewish minorities as the Semitic Orientals within,[5] Said's "mapping [of his own] affiliations" and his minority "struggle over geography" become more apparent.[6] Locating Arnold strictly on the side of Western/Anglo-Saxon orientalism—since Arnold was disparaging toward the other Semitic religion, Islam—and as the instigator of the New Critical tradition within literary criticism, allows Said to map himself strategically as a cultural materialist and as an Arab-Palestinian scholar within his own disciplinary history and discourse. His silence on the nineteenth-century Jewish emancipation movement[7]—which Arnold was supportive of—is an aspect of this strategy. Said represents Arnold's criticism as the powerful discourse of the Western host that is in a colonial relationship to the Orient, and thus, Said's thesis on Orientalism works only when the colonizer is the powerful, discursive "host" positioned in the West and the colonized is the hegemonized "guest" in the Orient as a "distant territory."[8]

Using Derrida's concept of deconstructive hospitality, I seek to show that Arnold's concept of *culture* complicates and destabilizes the positions of the host and guest in the ethical relation to the

Other. I do this by reading Arnold's dialectic of the *Hebrew* and the *Hellene* as a supportive response to the granting of rights to Britain's Jewish minorities, and by examining Arnold's appreciative reception by Lionel Trilling, Said's mentor and a Jewish literary scholar who experienced pre–World War II anti-Semitism. In looking for gestures of hospitality in Arnold's life, writings, and reception, I will keep in mind that hospitality is impossible and violent, while also suggesting that it is the only possible way of taking responsibility for minority cultures within the West. As a result, it will become apparent that Said's either/or approach to literary culture, his reluctance "to remain on the threshold,"[9] has to do with his own particular sense of responsibility he took in the face of Islam and the Arab nations.

DECONSTRUCTIVE HOSPITALITY VERSUS SECULAR CRITICISM: ARNOLD AS AN ORIENTALIST

To start addressing the idiosyncrasies in Said's critique of Orientalism, we need to complicate the relation between the host and the guest as philosophical concepts and in turn, the location of the Orient, which I propose to do through *deconstructive hospitality* as described in Jacques Derrida's writings. Derrida started writing about hospitality in the early 1990s, and did so usually in relation to Emmanuel Levinas's philosophy and following the so-called "Paul de Man affair," a change in subject matter that Simon Critchley has called Derrida's "ethical turn."[10] The first such work was *The Gift of Death* (1992), which was followed by *Politics of Friendship* (1994), *Of Hospitality* (2000), and finally the essays within the collection *Acts of Religion* (2002). The use of the neologism "Hostipitality" appears first as the title of an essay included in *Acts of Religion*. According to Derrida, genuine hospitality is impossible. He exemplifies this by the double meaning of the word *hostis* in Latin, meaning both the host and enemy. Hospitality is a contradictory term, because in order to be hospitable one must be ready to be overtaken, to be surprised; the self of the host must be open to being violated, which means that at the moment of hospitality, the host becomes obsolete and it becomes impossible to talk about hospitality. On the other hand, when the rules of hospitality are circumvented by the strict definitions of the host and the guest, or hospitality is performed as an acquired habitus, as a duty, again hospitality fails because it is not the opening of one's self to the unexpected, or in Derrida's words "let[-ting] oneself be swept by the coming of wholly other, the absolute unforeseeable stranger, the uninvited visitor, the unexpected visitation beyond any welcoming apparatuses."[11] Derridean hospitality intentionally blurs the identities of the host and the guest in a relation of hospitality, and thus invites the perpetual movement between particular identity of the guest and universal language of the host, that are in a relation of state hospitality or colonialism for instance, without a necessary closure. The ethics of hospitality suggests that admitting to undecidability but being open to the unexpected meaning in a state of hospitality can just as well be an act of responsibility. Such a philosophical perspective allows us to perceive the host and guest as strategically and temporarily assumed positions rather than unchanging roles wholly dependent on the physical locale as Said's ethical gesture implies.

To further explain how such deconstructive hospitality would apply to the mapping of intellectual history, Derrida's concept of *exemplarity* needs to be explained. *Exemplarity* in Derrida's philosophy is the condition of expressing a particularity, such as a cultural, religious, or gendered identity (in its unexpressed or inexpressible form, Derrida calls it a *singularity*) through a common language and discourse that is available to the uttering subject at a particular period in history. For example, Derrida in "Interpretations at War: Kant, the Jew, the German" (1991) reads Hermann Cohen's Kantian defense of a symbiotic German-Jewish nationalism as a product of a "German-Jewish intellectual psyche," that is, a hyphenated and unstable identity that responds to certain urgencies of Cohen's present.[12] In other words, Derrida reads Cohen's hyper-nationalism as a rhetorical strategy situated strictly in certain circumstances and discourses of the nineteenth century. Expressing and asserting a particularity—in this case of Jewish identity—by these means usually involves adapting the language or discourse of the repressive, hegemonic, and usurping Other. Cohen adapted Kant's ethical philosophy, even though the latter was mostly disparaging of the particularism of Jewish identity. By the same logic, Derrida's notion of deconstructive hospitality then is a way of reading the past by paying attention to the instabilities, contingencies and temporalities of the adapted discourses and chosen identities, and to the entanglements of one's own language with the language of the Other. Most importantly, it overcomes the crippling dilemma between trying to preserve an "authentic" identity and assimilating into a hegemonic language or culture, which may especially be the experience of minority subjects today.

Said's idiosyncratic concept of "secular criticism," on the other hand, comes out of his "affiliation" with exilic and minority intellectuals such as Erich Auerbach, to which can be added his favorable accounts of Jonathan Swift, Giambattista Vico, Joseph Conrad, and

Frantz Fanon as either minority critics or ones who sympathized with the position of a minority culture.[13] What he calls the "worldliness" of these authors is in fact the quality of Otherness they are assigned either by the laws of state hospitality or by themselves. Said in his writings makes this Otherness the condition of criticism and of the critical distance of a scholar to his or her subject, the condition of what he calls "secular criticism." As a matter of fact, Said speaks of being at home in "culture," meaning "an environment, process, and hegemony in which individuals and their works are embedded [and] overseen at the top by a superstructure and at the base by a whole series of methodological attitudes."[14] It is from here that Said moves to the negative example of Matthew Arnold's elevated sense of culture.

The chapter on "Secular Criticism" and the discussion of Ernest Renan and Louis Massignon in *The World, The Text and the Critic* reveal the paradoxes in Said's disaffiliation with Arnoldian concept of "culture." Said's response to Arnold's critical legacy proves to be very ambivalent, first, as he reads Arnold's support of a secular British state as a sign of Orientalism, and second, as he represents Arnold as the genealogical source of everything hermetic, ethnocentric, and religious in current literary criticism. Said contends that Arnoldian culture was allied with state power against anarchy and supported a "quasi-theological exterior," which was a sign of its being "at home" in religious discourse and therefore "uncritical."[15] Said's judgment against Arnold is determined, accordingly, by his conviction that "culture often has to do with an aggressive sense of nation, home, community and belonging," whereas—as we can judge from Said's positive appraisal of Auerbach—being exiled from a nation exempts one from the hegemonic premises of its culture. Thus, Arnoldian culture is a "system of discriminations and evaluations" that sides with home and national filiations; something that is decided upon by a select few as the "best that has been thought and said," which is then imposed and disseminated into society "downward from the height of power."[16] Though not directly engaged in colonial rule, Arnold is not only "at home" in it but also makes the home rules: "Distinguished intellectuals like Arnold and Renan," Said states, were active in shaping "the domestic realm" that "in turn reinforced and reinscribed [...] the imperial spheres."[17] Obviously, Said is greatly influenced by Raymond Williams's thesis in *Culture and Society* (1958) on the performative power of culture over society. As a closer analysis of Arnold's works and legacy will reveal in the next part, this is a misrepresentation of Arnold's critical support of state power. Most importantly, it shows how Said casts Arnold on the opposing side of his own affiliations without taking into consideration Arnold's own historical and political circumstances, in other words, Arnold's worldliness.

In Chapter 12 of *The World, the Text, and the Critic*, the ambivalent nature of Said's approach to Arnoldian culture becomes more apparent. This time he focuses on the "exemplary and inherently interesting figures of Renan and Massignon" and the process by which their work on Islam was produced for and within their own culture.[18] For Said the point where Renan, Massignon, and Arnold meet is the "cultural prestige" of being European/Anglo-Saxon, which "eliminate[s] the possibility of a valuable kind of radical self-criticism."[19] He starts his critique of these figures by comparing French and German New Philology to British Orientalism, which, I think, reveals his affinity for the secularizing intent of Arnold's notion of culture. He begins by discussing Arnold's yearning for French and German cultural "finish and maturity," which he convincingly links to the late introduction of "the systematic and organized advances of New Philology" in British intellectual life.[20] For Britain, where the Orient represented stylistic excess and eccentricity, the study of languages was not yet separated from the study of religion, or understood in the "secular, purely linguistic terms proposed by the New Philology."[21] Said seems to believe that Renan's philological Orientalism, with all its ethnocentric implications, entered Britain via Arnold. Curiously, Renan's philology itself is described in terms similar to those used by Said in his discussion of Giambatista Vico's humanist secularism: Renan was invested in a "philology that moved history away from the existential problems of revealed religion and toward what it was possible to study, toward those real things."[22] Elsewhere, in an appreciative mode, he sums up the philosophy of Vico (a consistently positive figure in Said's works) as the view that "what human beings can know is only what they have made, that is, the historical, social and secular."[23] Moreover, in his later writings, Said indeed comes to defend the humanistic brand of historical philology of the nineteenth century that produced comparativists like Auerbach and Curtius for its hospitality. Said comments that "philology as applied to *Weltliteratur* involved a profound humanistic spirit deployed with generosity and [...] hospitality. Thus the interpreter's mind actively makes a place in it for a foreign Other."[24] The secularizing effect of New Philology is something that Said cannot do without, yet he must criticize it for being in the wrong hands, namely those of intellectuals like Renan, Massignon, and Arnold, who are at home in their culture, which they attempt to universalize, thereby erasing, as it were, local differences abroad. That the "foreign other" could as well be minorities within Europe, particularly European-Jews who were suddenly cast as the Semitic Others and Orientals by the racial theories of the time, does not seem to catch Said's attention very much.

In short, New Philology, which Said in *Orientalism* unrelentingly critiques as the "the laboratory" of modernism and Eurocentrism, receives a more nuanced treatment in *The World*, while it continues to exempt Arnold from this secular, philological tradition.[25] Since the logic of Said's argument that leads from the Orientalism of Renan to Arnoldian culture is hazy, we might ask ourselves whether he ignores Arnold's role in Anglo-American culture in valorizing a certain "alien" intellectual class by outfitting it with the duty of cultural criticism.[26] Overall, Said avoids Arnold's critical legacy unless it is mentioned as part of New Criticism. As far as these passages in *The World* are concerned, Said reveals more ambivalence than certainty in his judgment of Arnoldian culture. I take this ambivalence as Said's oblique affirmation of Arnoldian culture, especially of the power given to the intellectuals through the function of criticism. Said proves to be very Arnoldian as he is himself authorized by his affiliation with this high culture, and the cosmopolitan possibilities it offers. However, in the end, Said prefers to settle on the moral superiority of the guest, and holds the host responsible for its actions.

Said's responsibility to draw attention to anti-Islamic Orientalism in the West prompts him to map intellectual history in such a way. But with an attitude that places the Orient strictly within the Orient, Said's criticism fails the differences within the West and thereby ignores the relation between state hospitality and colonialism. Said's severe critique of Arnold is a strategy itself that is meaningful in the context of contemporary Western politics toward Palestine and the Arab nations, and vis-à-vis Said's adopted identity as an Arab-Palestinian within the intellectual geography of literary criticism. I would like to show that Arnold and his concept of *culture* could be read as hospitality, albeit a deconstructive one, and thus through a similar gesture to Derrida's locating Cohen in a complex relation of historical circumstances. Once the contingencies embedded in certain adapted discourses are described in such transnational and temporal terms with the Jewish diaspora in mind, a new geography for literary criticism emerges. The fascinating lineage from Matthew Arnold to Said via Lionel Trilling that I will describe below aims to deterritorialize Said's notions of the Orient while revealing Said's own intellectual geography. New urgencies have emerged since Said's influential thesis in *Orientalism*, particularly pertaining to Muslim minorities within the

West, and intellectual history might need to be re-mapped with these urgencies in mind.

THE HOSPITALITY IN ARNOLD'S DIALECTIC OF HEBRAISM AND HELLENISM

Until recently, Matthew Arnold's terms of *Hebraism* and *Hellenism* have been read as abstract and dialectical symbols roughly representing the moral and the intellectual impulses respectively in culture. However, they can also be read as racial and religious categories, both markers for Jewish difference in nineteenth-century Europe. I would first of all like to re-map Matthew Arnold into this hermeneutical context, namely that of a European modernity that is in constant negotiation with its ancient other, Judaism.

What potential does reading Arnold through the lens of the nineteenth-century Jewish question offer? It shows us that taking Arnold's Hebrew as historical Judaism extracted from the figure of the living Jew and Hellene as a sign of European superiority, eventually privileged over the Hebrew, does not exhaust the complexities and responsive strategies expressed in the dialectic of Hebraism and Hellenism. There are two conditions that gave rise to the Enlightenment consideration for the Hebraism/Hellenism binary, conditions from which Arnold's terms cannot be separated: (1) the historical-philological (secular) reading of the Bible that led to Christianity's admitting its Jewish past; (2) the Jewish minority presence in Europe that complicated race- and language-based nationalisms. My analysis will show that Arnold did indeed comment negatively about the Semitic races; nevertheless, his hospitality toward the Hebrew element in culture opened up a possibility for Jewish difference in literary criticism—as the example of Lionel Trilling's reception of Arnold will exemplify.

Matthew Arnold's use of the terms Hebraism and Hellenism is radically questioned in the context of the Jewish emancipation struggle in Brian Cheyette's *Construction of the Jew in English Literature and Society* (1993), and Michael Ragussis's *The Jewish Question and English National Identity* (1995). Cheyette and Ragussis mark a different era in Arnold studies. Beyond exposing the Jewish stereotypes in English literature, they focus on the role of the Jewish figure as a point of indeterminacy and an active participant in the making of the modern, secular identity of Britain. Cheyette's study considers the Hebraism/Hellenism binary in Arnold's *Culture and Anarchy* as an expression of racial difference that can be transfigured into the higher realm of "culture" by eliminating some undesired aspects of "the Jew," which is "constructed as both an object that can be spectacularly civilized (embodying Arnold's ideal of 'culture') and, at the same time, as an unchanging Semitic 'other.'"[27] In other words, the Jew becomes the figure at the edge of Enlightenment dilemma: How much of the racial particularity of the Semite can be tolerated in an Enlightened society guided by the principle of culture? Or, to put it differently, can one still talk of Jewish difference and particularity when the Jew has become part of high culture? Ragussis contextualizes Arnold's concepts of Hebraism and Hellenism by showing how they were shaped through a dialogue with Benjamin Disraeli's Hebraic project. He argues that Arnold's ambivalence toward these terms is a strategic response to the politics of his time. Ragussis claims that since his lecture "On the Study of Celtic Literature" of 1867, Arnold employed the science of race to revise not only the status of the Celts in English society but also that of the Jews. This revision culminates in the Hebrew-and-Hellene formulations in *Culture and Anarchy* (1869).

Robert J. C. Young in *Colonial Desire: Hybridity in Theory, Culture and Race* (1995)—which also engages with Edward Said's reading of Arnold—highlights a more reciprocal relation between high culture and the figure of the Jew. Young, using Homi K. Bhabha's term "hybridity" retrospectively for nineteenth-century English culture, argues that British culture "was fissured with difference and the desire for otherness" and that it was Arnold's idea of a living racial mixture that developed "into a theory of England as multicultural."[28] While accepting that Arnold was one of the first British critics who subscribed to the discursive authority and "objectivity" of the racial science of the late nineteenth century, Young claims that Arnold's culture in *Culture and Anarchy* is defined by what it lacks and "in strictly exotic terms," and thus fails to accomplish a purist identification of English culture as Edward Said argues.[29]

As can be seen, current scholarship is gradually accepting the cosmopolitan and hybrid character of Arnold's culture concept, though doubts about its racializing and homogenizing implications are always present. The passage below, on the Indo-European versus Semitic distinction, is most commonly used to evidence Arnold's ethnographic views:

> Science has now made visible to everybody the great and pregnant elements of difference which lie in race, and in how signal a manner they make the genius and history of an Indo-European people

vary from those of a Semitic people. Hellenism is of Indo-European growth, Hebraism is of Semitic growth; and we English, a nation of Indo-European stock, seem to belong naturally to the movement of Hellenism. But nothing more strongly marks the essential unity of man than the affinities we can perceive, in this point or that, between members of one family of peoples and members of another; and no affinity of this kind is more strongly marked than that likeness in the strength and prominence of the moral fibre, which, notwithstanding immense elements of difference, knits in some special sort the genius and history of us English, and of our American descendants across the Atlantic, to the genius and history of the Hebrew people.[30]

Edward Said considers Arnold's subscription to "scientific" racial theories of the nineteenth century to be the main obstacle to his attempt to unite religious and racial differences under the transcending category of culture. Thereby, Said views Arnold's statements on the races as an evidence for exclusionist nationalism rather than a liberal cosmopolitanism. In contrast to such approaches, Donald D. Stone, for example, argues that the cosmopolitan gesture in Arnold's culture is more important than its exclusionist implications: "[Arnold] used the terms [Hebrew and Hellene] pragmatically, flexibly, to denote both a dual historical heritage and two complementary states of being (*strictness of conscience* and *spontaneity of consciousness*, respectively) that had practical bearings in a newly industrial and democratic world."[31]

Nevertheless, Arnold's emphasis on Hebrew moralism remains limited because it implies hostility toward Rabbinic tradition and Mosaic law. According to common Enlightenment belief and Protestant theology, the Rabbinic elements in Judaism continued after the correction of Christian spirituality and were incompatible with Enlightenment reason, and therefore also with Arnoldian culture. Arnold, for example, states:

> And, immense as is our debt to the Hebrew race and its genius, [...],—who, that is not manacled and hoodwinked by his Hebraism, can believe that, [...] our reason and the necessities of our humanity have their true, sufficient, and divine law expressed for them by the voice of any Oriental and polygamous nation like the Hebrews [...], a Semitic people, whose wisest king had seven hundred and three hundred concubines?[32]

Arnold was quite aware of the discussions in biblical criticism concerning the intertwined histories of Judaism and Christianity, and clearly took a stance that was in favor of the Jewish Reformation.

A proof of Arnold's awareness of this context can be found in his rejection of the claim that Christianity was a development of the Aryan race, as in his disagreement with Emile Burnouf in Chapter 5 of *Literature and Dogma*. Most of the Jewish reformers themselves subscribed to racial theories but opposed the view that the Indo-European races were superior to the Semitic ones. Like Arnold and most of his contemporaries, they also did not question the preeminence of reason. In short, though Arnold positively acknowledges the Semitic origins of Christianity, he excludes the radically different, the professing/traditional Jew and the other Semitic peoples, the Arabs, from his civilizing project.

One must also consider that Arnold's dialectic of Hebrew and Hellene only leads to the illusion of the special and unbreakable alliance of the Jewish and the Christian, with undesired aspects not only of Judaism but also of Christianity extracted. His *Literature and Dogma* (1883), for example, is a work addressed to the dogma and institutions of Christianity, not of Judaism. A reductionist and essentializing view of Christianity can clearly be observed in the following statement about Christian missionaries in the Orient facing other religions like "Mahometanism, and Brahminism, and Buddhism":

> Yet everyone allows that this strange figure [of the Christian missionary] carries something of what is called European civilisation with him, and a good part of this is due to Christianity. But even the Christianity itself that he preaches, imbedded in a false theology though it be, cannot but contain, in a greater or lesser measure as it may happen, these three things: the all-importance of *righteousness*, the *method* of Jesus, the *secret* of Jesus.... Therefore to all whom it visits, the Christianity of our missions, inadequate as may be its criticism of the Bible, brings what may do them good.[33]

Throughout *Literature and Dogma*, the Judaic background of Christianity is emphasized over and over again, while purist or science-based Christian apologetics are relentlessly criticized. In this passage it is clear that Arnold cannot deny that the Jesus of the "secret" was a Jew, yet he also implies that those other religions can never relate to this particular Judaeo-Christian "secret," which he now embeds into the heart of "European civilization." There are two ways of reading Arnold's extraction of the principles of "righteousness," "method," and "secret." First, we can read them as an affirmation of Christian onto-theology, or as Said would interpret it, a sign of Christian hermetism in literary criticism. Second, we can place Arnold in his rightful context of Romantic logocentrism, as famously refined by Samuel Taylor Coleridge in the symbol of Jesus Christ.[34] Thus, we can read the passage as a statement about the literary/secular interpretation of the Bible, which is probably how it was received upon its publication—rather than as a theologizing of literature, as we tend to interpret it today. By doing so, we might gain an understanding of those principles as relating to the "function of criticism," namely as ethical responsiveness to historical urgencies (*righteousness*), universal norms for determining the best that has been written and thought (*method*), and the indeterminacy of criticism (*secret*). One could note the similarities between such an interpretation and the secular criticism that Edward Said promotes, except that when it comes to universal method Said cannot move beyond a certain point because for him any sort of universalism means the suppression of particularity. What needs to be emphasized, I suggest, is that Arnold's literary universalism suppresses not only the particularity of the radically other religions, but also Christian identity as it has been threatened by increasing secularization of national culture in the hands of public intellectuals like Arnold. Thus, we must acknowledge that Arnold's "culture," based on the symbiosis of Judaism and Christianity, is inclusive of and violent toward *both* sides of the Judeo-Christian hyphen, resulting in a deconstructive hospitality. While such a symbiosis implies the heterogeneity of "European civilization" in the face of Jewish difference, it nevertheless works to be hegemonic and violent with respect to the radically Other religions, such as Islam. What is to be acknowledged and welcomed in Arnold's culture, I think, is an opening *toward* Jewish difference within his own intellectual context.

Another aspect of Arnold's deconstructive hospitality develops in the context of the Jewish emancipation process in Britain. Some critics have drawn attention to Arnold's support for Jewish civil rights. Even Cheyette, who is probably the harshest critic of Arnold after Said, provides evidence to this effect, and recalls that Arnold was so pro-Jewish that there were suspicions that he might have had Jewish heritage.[35] Jonathan Freedman in *The Temple of Culture* (2000) stresses the accommodation of the alien Jew within Arnold's cultural scheme: "the pattern of simultaneous incorporation and expulsion of the Jews [defines] the drama of European culture building."[36] However, in contrast to Cheyette and Ragussis, who point to the repression of the living Jew in Arnoldian culture, Freedman argues that "Arnold seizes upon and makes his own the Jew's marginalization to distance himself from his own provincial, 'Philistinish' national culture and to identify himself with a larger, European cultural project and ideal."[37] Freedman infers this from Arnold's description of criticism as a "second Moses poised in the wilderness, espying from afar the Promised Land" in *The Function of Criticism* and from his poem "Rachel," which praises the Jewish-French actress's cosmopolitan character.[38]

To conclude: Arnold's position toward minority rights in Britain was a liberal one. "The State is of the religion of all its citizens without the fanaticism of any of them," he reminds us in *Culture and Anarchy*, clearly speaking in support of the granting of full emancipation to Jewish citizens in 1858.[39] Arnold creates an opening for the historical other of Christianity, instead of essentializing culture as exclusively Protestant Christian or Indo-European. Consequently, Arnold not only defends Hebrew moralism but also supports the political rights of the living representatives of biblical Hebraism. On the other hand, Arnold's civilizing project is also violent because it excludes the other Semitic race, Arabs, and non-Caucasian races. Most importantly, it requires an assimilation of radical differences under the heading of "culture."

Rather than focusing on how the concept of culture served to suppress racial and religious difference in British society, I want to highlight the reception history of Arnold next. I believe that the cosmopolitan implications and focus on indeterminacy in Arnold's criticism created a fissure in literary criticism, which helped to make possible the careers of minority intellectuals like Lionel Trilling, the first Jewish professor of English at Columbia University.

LIONEL TRILLING'S ADMIRATION FOR MATTHEW ARNOLD

Some of the dilemmas of being a Jewish intellectual in mid-twentieth-century America are poignantly expressed in Lionel Trilling's biographical work *Matthew Arnold* (1939). Trilling reads Arnold's lecture of 1866 "On the Study of Celtic Literature" as a combination of "literary and scientific methods" toward a "right [social] feeling."[40] What Trilling means is that Arnold resorts to the authority of racial science of his day, the anthropology that assumes that the character of a nation is determined by "blood" or "race," in order to express his ethical reaction to purist, either Teutonic or Anglo-Saxon, and possibly anti-Irish, notions of Englishness. Arnold was "at pains to show that the English are an amalgam of several 'bloods'—German, Norman, Celtic."[41] Moreover, Trilling points to Arnold's use of race as a symbol for a unified national spirit consisting of varied temperaments, arguing that it serves "not to separate peoples but to draw them together."[42] As Trilling sees it, "Using the terms of 'race,' Arnold is actually speaking of reason and the complete man.[43] [...] The [race] theory, sprung from the desk of the philosopher and the philologist, had an unfailing attraction for the literary and quasi-religious mind; the conception of a mystic and constant 'blood' was a handy substitute for the soul."[44] On the grounds of Arnold's symbolic use of hybridized blood to defend "a far wider range of temperament than [England] had conceived,"[45] and the wide-spread applications of such theory in Arnold's day, Trilling both excuses Arnold's subscription to racial theories and is convinced that "some [others] used it for liberalizing purposes, as Arnold himself did."[46] Trilling's reading of Arnold, therefore, resembles Derrida's reading of Herman Cohen's German-Jewish nationalism as a strategic use of current and dominant discourses toward promoting a chosen cause, which in both cases was the granting of civil rights to Jewish minorities. Although Trilling primarily focuses on the more abstract, historical-dialectical meaning of Hebraism and Hellenism throughout the book, it is apparent from the following statement of his that the question of living Jews, and the anti-Semitism of the time when Trilling was writing this book, were looming in the back of his mind: "Today, when the anthropological doctrines which Arnold found so stirringly fruitful are supported only by political partisans or by writers whose scientific methods Arnold himself, were he now living would not accept, we must take [Arnold's] elaborate theory only as a kind of parable."[47]

Trilling begins his treatment of Arnold's career with a long prelude about the Hyde Park riots in the summer of 1866. With this, Trilling aims to show that Arnold's support for state order as opposed to working-class anarchy (the main point of critique against Arnold in both Raymond Williams and Edward Said) was rather the result of Arnold's criticism of the government for being the instigator of the riots through their weakness and indecisiveness.[48] Trilling observes that Arnold's ideal depiction of the state in the second chapter of *Culture and Anarchy* as being the representative of "our best self, or right reason," is in accordance with his reaction to the Hyde Park events and with his attempt to redefine the state in terms of "culture" as "the best that said and thought." The state for Arnold, according to Trilling, is "a way to endow reason with power."[49] Thus, in contrast to Said's interpretation of Arnold's support for the state as a sign of "being at home" in power, Trilling offers the view that Arnold with his nineteenth-century mind believed in the universality and supremacy of reason and the "Platonic myth of state," and was inviting the existing state to better itself on those principles.[50]

The most striking example for Trilling's and Said's contrasting receptions of Arnold is their sharing of quotation from *Culture and Anarchy*. Trilling, emphasizing that these were Arnold's "last words as Professor of Poetry at Oxford," quotes a long passage from *Culture and Anarchy*:

> Plenty of people will try to indoctrinate the masses with the set of ideas and judgments constituting the creed of their own profession or party. Our religious and political organizations give an example of this way of working on the masses. I condemn neither way; but culture works differently. It does not try to teach down to the level of inferior classes; it does not try to win them for this or that sect of its own, with ready-made judgments and watchwords. It seeks to do away with classes; to make the best that has been thought and known in the world current everywhere; to make all men live in an atmosphere of sweetness and light, where they may use ideas, as it uses them itself, freely—nourished and not bound by them.
>
> This is the social idea; and the men of culture are the true apostles of equality.[51]

The subsequent sentences of this passage are also used by Said in *The World, the Text, and the Critic*:

> The great men of culture are those who have had a passion for diffusing, for making prevail, for carrying from one end of society to the other, the best knowledge, the best ideas of their time; who have laboured to divest knowledge of all that was harsh, uncouth, difficult, abstract, professional, exclusive; to humanize it, to make it efficient outside the clique of the cultivated and learned, yet still remaining the best knowledge and thought of the time [...] and a true source, therefore, of sweetness and light.[52]

Trilling quotes this key passage for two purposes: First, he uses it to exemplify the romantic attitude toward the cultivation of masses as the only means to civic equality and progression toward a perfect order. Trilling defends Arnold because Arnold's idea of culture empowers the intellectuals to take on an active political role: "[Culture] is a method of historical interpretation which leads to political action"[53] For Trilling, Arnold's open-ended definition of culture signifies a promotion of historical relativity and rejection of permanent and universal systems. Said, on the other hand, reads this passage as endorsing hegemony, as elitism and as an affirmation that the universal rather than merely current form of culture is Anglo-Saxon and Christian. Said quotes this passage when he argues that it is state hegemony that determines what is "best," but Said misapplies Arnold. He could have found a dozen passages on the authoritarian role of the state from *Culture and Anarchy*. However, he chooses this passage that revealingly reflects the aim of his own project of defining the "function of criticism in the present time,"[54] namely to rid criticism "of all that was harsh, uncouth, difficult, abstract, professional, exclusive; to humanize it, to make it efficient outside the clique of the cultivated and learned."[55] Both Said and Trilling clearly see themselves as part of the high culture that was secured by Arnold's valorization of literary criticism.

However, Trilling's admiration for Arnold becomes more nuanced in his later writings. In the preface to the 1949 edition of *Matthew Arnold*, after having suffered the "assault on [his] mind of the Nazis," Trilling admits that he would not have written "quite so much as Arnold's advocate on certain particular points," clearly referring to Arnold's ethnographic writings. Nevertheless, he adds: "But I should write of him with an even enhanced sense of his standing for the intellectual virtues that are required by a complex society if it is to survive in real and not in merely simulated life."[56] Anthony Julius and Jonathan Freedman's accounts show how Trilling, as a Jewish professor in Columbia University's English Department and one who was subject to institutional anti-Semitism, clearly speaks from his Jewish subject position, both when apologizing for Arnold and when acknowledging the racialist aspects of Arnold's writings.[57] However wrought with admiration, Trilling does frequently cast doubts on Arnold's legacy, as for example when he notes, "Out of the belief that the best self, Hero or State, is in touch with the right reason, will of God, may flow chauvinism, imperialism, Governor Eyre, the white man's burden—all things which make us turn to Mill and skepticism, well-nigh willing to rest in 'anarchy'."[58]

It is possible to read this critical indebtedness to Arnold as a sign of Trilling's acknowledgement of his participation in institutional high culture, and at the same time a rejection of ethnic assimilation within this institution. Both Said and Trilling are aware of the power given to them by Arnold as classless, intellectual "aliens." Trilling admits it, as we have seen, in an act of forgiveness in his "Preface to the Second Edition." Said denies it exactly because of Arnold's ethnological ideas that are pro-Jewish in a limited sense and essentially exclude the Semitic races. Said speaks favorably about Trilling, and frequently repeats that Trilling was a mentor to him at Columbia University.[59] Although he possibly reads Arnold through Trilling, he is very antagonistic toward Arnold. If Arnold's definition of criticism as the "free play of the mind upon all subjects" made Trilling's presence in the literary institution possible (both metaphorically and literally since his doctoral dissertation was on Arnold) as a second-generation Jewish immigrant who was subject to policies of exclusion, then Trilling and his influence on the literary institution presumably also helped make possible Said's role as an Arab professor of English at Columbia University,[60] just as Said's presence in the literary academy and his legacy as a public intellectual have helped make it possible for many scholars from second and third world countries, like myself, to have a voice in English departments.

CONCLUSION

Said is quite justified in detecting a certain cultural elitism and Eurocentrism in the way Arnold assigns the guardianship of high culture to European civilization, which through the dialectic of Hebraism and Hellenism becomes primarily a Judeo-Christian symbiosis, while other cultures at best fare as anthropological cultures that need to be kept in check by this high culture. However, as we have seen, Said errs in judging Arnold's position as an uncritical closure and as religious essentialism. As the example of Trilling helps us to see, Arnold's insistence on an abstract and indeterminate "culture" could be an expression of secular historicism in the Vichian vein, since his welcoming of the Hebraic element created a new path in the history of literary criticism—and in Anglo-American culture as a whole—toward an opening for Jewish difference and therefore potentially for other kinds of difference too.

To conclude, I suggest a new way of reading Said's phrase "struggle for geography" in *Culture and Imperialism*.[61] Since Said clearly discloses his intention to solely focus on "actual contests over land and the land's people," we cannot really critique him for excluding nineteenth-century anti-Semitism and the emancipation struggle that accompanied it from his project on Orientalism. At the same time, we can draw attention—as Amir Mufti does, for example—to the "Jewish Question" as an "exemplary crisis" for European modernity in the generation of categories such as "minority" and "secular state."[62] Thus, Said's concern for "territory and possession," when viewed through Derrida's deconstructive hospitality, actually reveals that colonial and state "hostipitalities" are inseparable. In fact, we can conclude that Arnold's attempt to make the figure of the Jew part of his cosmopolitan ideal had lasting implications for the emergence of postcolonialism.

At the same time, we are invited to renew our awareness that disaffiliating with Arnold was a feature of Said's "geographical inquiry into historical [and intellectual] experience," a conscious choice going back at least to his *Beginnings: Intention and Method* (1975), in which he set out a method of objective subjectivity that derives from other theories. As far as this subjectivity is concerned, Said has always been consistent, and one of the greatest benefits we can derive from reading Said is noticing how the "struggle for geography" of minority intellectuals such as Said himself becomes an act of hospitality in which the guests and hosts are involved in more reciprocal and complex ways than we might imagine.

NOTES

1. Said, Edward W., "Nationalism, Human Rights, and Interpretation," *Raritan* 12.3 (1993), 27.
2. Edward W. Said, *Humanism and Democratic Criticism* (New York: Columbia University Press, 2004), 66.
3. Edward W. Said, *The World, the Text, and the Critic* (Cambridge, MA: Harvard University Press, 1983), 28.
4. Edward W. Said, *Orientalism: Western Conceptions of the Orient* (London: Penguin, 1978), 20.
5. For a discussion on the Orientalization of European Jewry during the nineteenth century and Said's ambivalence toward the topic, see Ivan Davidson Kalmar and Derek Jonathan Penslar, eds., *Orientalism and the Jews* (Lebanon, NH: University Press of New England, 2005).
6. Edward W. Said, *Culture and Imperialism* (New York: Vintage, 1993), 7.
7. Apart from the aside on Orientalism being the "secret sharer of Western anti-Semitism" in the introduction to *Orientalism*, 27.
8. Said, *Culture and Imperialism*, 9.
9. Jacques Derrida, "How to Avoid Speaking: Denials," in *Derrida and Negative Theology*, ed. Harold Coward and Toby Foshay (Albany: State University of New York Press, 1992), 122.
10. Simon Critchley, *The Ethics of Deconstruction: Derrida and Levinas* (Cambridge, UK: B. Blackwell, 1992).
11. Jacques Derrida, "Hostipitality," in *Acts of Religion*, ed. Gil Anidjar (New York: Routledge, 2002), 361–362.
12. Jacques Derrida, "Interpretations at War: Kant, the Jew, the German," in *Acts of Religion*, ed. Gil Anidjar (New York: Routledge, 2002), 138.
13. Said, *The World, the Text, and the Critic*, 20–23.
14. Ibid., 8.
15. Ibid., 12.
16. Ibid.

17. Said, "Nationalism, Human Rights, and Interpretation," 26.
18. Said, *The World, the Text, and the Critic*, 275.
19. Ibid., 280.
20. Ibid., 268–269.
21. Ibid., 274.
22. Ibid., 278.
23. Ibid., 290.
24. Edward Said, "Orientalism Once More," *Development and Change* 35.5 (2004), 876.
25. Said, *Orientalism*, 132.
26. Arnold famously acknowledges intellectuals as a separate class: "Therefore, when we speak of ourselves as divided into Barbarians, Philistines, and Populace, we must be understood always to imply that within each of these classes there are a certain number of aliens, if we may so call them,—persons who are mainly led, not by their class spirit, but by a general humane spirit, by the love of human perfection." *Culture and Anarchy* (Oxford, UK: Oxford University Press, 2006), 81.
27. Bryan Cheyette, *Constructions of "the Jew" in English Literature and Society: Racial Representations, 1875–1945* (Cambridge, UK: Cambridge University Press, 1993), 13.
28. Robert Young, *Colonial Desire: Hybridity in Theory, Culture, and Race* (London and New York: Routledge, 1995), 17.
29. Ibid., 57.
30. Arnold, *Culture and Anarchy*, 95.
31. Donald D. Stone, "Matthew Arnold and the Pragmatics of Hebraism and Hellenism," *Poetics Today* 19.2 (Summer 1998), 179.
32. Arnold, *Culture and Anarchy*, 134.
33. Matthew Arnold, *Literature and Dogma, an Essay towards a Better Apprehension of the Bible* (London: Smith, Elder, 1883), 134.
34. See for example, Mary Ann Perkins in *Coleridge's Philosophy: The Logos as Unifying Principle* (Oxford: Clarendon Press; New York: Oxford University Press, 1994).
35. Cheyette, *Constructions of "the Jew,"* 14.
36. Jonathan Freedman, *The Temple of Culture: Assimilation and Anti-Semitism in Literary Anglo-America* (New York: Oxford University Press, 2000), 50.
37. Ibid.
38. The last part of Arnold's poem "Rachel" is as follows:

> Ah, not the radiant spirit of Greece alone
> She had—one power, which made her breast its home!
> In her, like us, there clashed contending powers,
> Germany, France, Christ, Moses, Athens, Rome,
> The strife, the mixture, in her soul are ours,
> Her genius and her glory are her own.

39. Arnold, *Culture and Anarchy*, 10.
40. Lionel Trilling, *Matthew Arnold* (New York: Columbia University Press, 1949), 232.
41. Ibid., 233.
42. Ibid., 236.
43. Ibid., 242.
44. Ibid., 234.
45. Ibid., 242.
46. Ibid., 235.
47. Ibid., 233.
48. Ibid., 243–251.
49. Ibid., 263.
50. Ibid., 255.
51. Arnold quoted in ibid., 271–272.
52. Arnold quoted in Said, *The World, the Text, and the Critic*, 10.
53. Trilling, *Matthew Arnold*, 271.
54. Said, *The World, the Text, and the Critic*, 5.
55. Arnold, *Culture and Anarchy*, 53.
56. Trilling, *Matthew Arnold*, 3.
57. Anthony Julius, *T. S. Eliot, Anti-Semitism and Literary Form* (Cambridge and New York: Cambridge University Press, 1995), 53; Freedman, *The Temple of Culture*, 192–195.
58. Trilling, *Matthew Arnold*, 277.
59. Said, *The World, the Text, and the Critic*, 142, 164–165.
60. Freedman mentions Trilling's influence on Harold Bloom while providing a context for second- and third-generation Jewish immigrants and their history in the literary academy; Freedman, *The Temple of Culture*, 213–215.
61. Said, *Culture and Imperialism*, 7.
62. Aamir R. Mufti, *Enlightenment in the Colony: The Jewish Question and the Crisis of Postcolonial Culture* (Princeton, NJ: Princeton University Press, 2007), 39.

CHAPTER 3

EDWARD W. SAID, THE SPHERE OF HUMANISM, AND THE NEOLIBERAL UNIVERSITY

Jeffrey Hole

Is there space beyond the reach of the market? A site not yet annexed by the domain of finance? A sphere, perhaps, in which orders of life are not reducible to relations of exchange, consumption, and valuation? Reflecting on the transformations of the recent past and, likewise, attempting to imagine a future some two, five, or more decades from our present, one wonders—of the human and its creations (its institutions, its knowledges, its arts)—what will survive or perish, extirpated in the name of austerity? What have we lost already? Not tangential to the topic of legacy, these questions arise out of a set of concerns for the fate of the university, historically and materially, in fostering the conditions necessary for humanistic education and the production of knowledge under now-prevalent doctrines positing that "market exchange captures an essential and basic truth about human nature" and that, moreover, the market serves as the arbiter of social relations within all realms and forms of heterogeneous human experience.[1] A meditation on humanism in a moment of danger, this essay focuses on Edward Said's intellectual life and thinking—a life and thinking coincident (but not aligned) with particular global economic experiments and the reshaping of a political consensus that took root during the late 1970s and 1980s. From his earliest articulations on the topic of humanism, Said further anticipated and vociferously challenged the

barbarisms that have accompanied the cultural-political doxa and economic policies ushered into being under the names of "Reaganism"
or "Thatcherism," "neocolonialism" or "*la pensée unique*,"[2] and that
have since intensified into a "broad and multifaceted social movement with widespread implications for all aspects of politics, society
and culture."[3]

For those whose intellectual formations have also coincided with
(or are now occurring within) an academic milieu saturated by the
influences and forces of neoliberalism, and there is hardly anyone
alive today for whom this is not the case, Said's thinking provides
important lessons and advantages, materials for the survival of the
humanities—teaching us to reflect on what it means to engage in
an order of knowledge and intellectual work whose legitimacy or
"value" (a more ominous but now ubiquitous category) has been
called into question. Said referred to this form of reflection by making use of Antonio Gramsci's notion of "inventory," and it serves our
purposes here as well: "The starting-point of critical elaboration," as
Said quotes Gramsci in the opening of *Orientalism* (1978), "is the
consciousness of what one really is, and is 'knowing thyself' as a product of the historical processes to date, which has deposited in you an
infinity of traces, without leaving an inventory." As Said further notes,
"The only available English translation inexplicably leaves Gramsci's
comment at that, whereas in fact Gramsci's Italian text concludes by
adding, 'therefore it is imperative at the outset to compile such an
inventory.' "[4] What follows is an attempt at such an inventory, an
essay to give thought to the "infinity of traces" and the "historical
processes" that have shaped our present.

Although "neoliberalism" is a placeholder, a term that stands in
for a complex set of material and political transformations, we have
at hand the means to define it, the capacity to trace out its effects
historically, and to anticipate its future devastations.[5] Among these we
might include the increasing disparity of resources between workers of
all variety and an elite *rentier* class;[6] the erosion of civil liberties (often
in the name of security or, ironically, liberty); the financialization and
privatization of public institutions and infrastructures (schools, universities, prisons, and hospitals);[7] the dismantling of the welfare state and
its metamorphosis into a highly militarized, imperial "deep state";[8]
as well as the growth of managerialism and the further valuation of
information over humanistic knowledge.

Preeminent among the characteristics of neoliberal doctrines,
moreover, is the notion of inevitability. In the 1980s then prime
minister Margaret Thatcher succinctly and rather ominously apotheo-
sized "market realities" when, referring to the ostensibly necessary

neoliberal reforms that her administration had been implementing, she announced, "There is no other choice."[9] Thatcher's words have reverberated and amplified over the last several decades and function presently as a form of common sense. "Inevitability" serves as a lens for the neoliberal imaginary, the event horizon for imagination itself, envisioning world-historical processes as governed by a grotesque version of Adam Smith's "Invisible Hand." "What is most discouraging," Said had remarked in 2000, just as the presidential election was shaping up between George W. Bush and Al Gore, "is the sense that most people have that not only is there no other alternative, but that this is the best system ever imagined, the triumph of the middle-class ideal, a liberal and humane democracy—or, as Francis Fukuyama called it, the end of history."[10] Said was referring not to the "various issues that divide[d]" the candidates and the respective Republican and Democratic parties, but how both proved "mirror images of each other," how both were aligned in a "passionate" and "unquestioning [belief] in the corporate free market system" and the end of "'big' government."[11]

I invoke in my title Said's lecture-turned-chapter "Humanism's Sphere" from one of his final and posthumously published books, *Humanism and Democratic Criticism* (2004), a work I will refer to often, oscillating between it and other texts by Said from the past four decades, in order to draw attention to the necessity of creating, intentionally and unremittingly, a set of conditions and spaces for humanism. Referring to the "sphere" of humanism, we recognize, too, Said's spatial categories, his "geographical inquir[ies] into [human] historical experience," his elaborations on territory in the broadest sense, and the specific idea that "none of us is completely free from the struggle over geography."[12] And yet one should take care not to confuse the creation or struggle for space with the sense of being "at home" in it.[13] A sphere of humanism does not relinquish the humanist intellectual from the conditions of exile; one cannot simply take "refuge inside a profession or nationality."[14] For Said, quoting Theodor Adorno, "It is part of morality not to be at home in one's home."[15]

While Said had recognized that humanism in the academy has not been innocent of forming complicit relations with state and corporate power, orders now intent on undermining the conditions for humanistic study, he maintained that humanism still enables various practices and styles of thinking that stand in opposition to neoliberalism:

> For if, as I believe, there is now taking place in our society an assault on thought itself, to say nothing of democracy, equality, and the environment, by the dehumanizing forces of globalization, neoliberal values,

economic greed (euphemistically called the free market), as well as imperialist ambition, the humanist must offer alternatives now silenced or unavailable through the channels of communication controlled by a tiny number of news organizations.[16]

Humanism and "the intellectual humanist's work" specifically can act as a counterforce to a project that has, in the words of Said, "swallowed up the world in its clutches, with grave consequences for democracy and the physical environment that can be neither underestimated nor dismissed."[17] Furthermore, we can learn from Said and discover in his writing the possibilities for thinking and imagining that stand in contradistinction to and challenge neoliberalism's doctrine of inevitability. A recollection of his life's work, culminating in *Humanism and Democratic Criticism*, reveals that we must act on the imperative to sustain (1) historical memory over the propensity toward willful amnesia; (2) curiosity over the anxieties induced by the psychology of an inhuman and whimsical market; (3) careful, attentive reading over the arrogance associated with the "cult of expertise";[18] and (4) the precision of language over the professional jargon, the empty neologisms or clichés of corporateez, and the idioms of finance now shaping worldviews. For Said, "the process of reading and philological reception" are the tools central to humanism, and as such—"*ijtihab*, close reading, hermeneutic induction"—serve as the "irreducible core" for acts of "resistance."[19]

In the context of the transformations shaping higher education, it is no accident that Edward Said in a 1999 lecture in Cairo and on other occasions strategically referred to the university as a utopia.[20] He had elaborated on this idea up until the final moments of his life, suggesting, "It is still very fortunately the case, however, that the American university remains the one public space available to real alternative intellectual practices: no other institution like it on such a scale exists anywhere else in the world today."[21] Said was not expressing a form of blind optimism, nor was he naïve to the material conditions affecting adjunct knowledge workers or the rising cost of tuition and the accumulation of more and more debt by students, to name just a few of the problems facing the university.[22] Eliciting Thomas More's sixteenth-century imaginative wordplay, the term utopia denotes for Said the site "where freedom of inquiry and thought occur and are protected"—a good place (*eu topos*)—yet also signals simultaneously and etymologically its negation—a non-space, a displacement (*ou topos*).[23] The full force of meaning bears as much on Said's conviction that education "is a special province within society" as it does his recognition of the tenuousness of human institutions broadly and historical humanism specifically.[24]

By using the word "utopia" as a means for characterizing the university, Said had not precluded but actually opened up an important analysis of what he called "overlapping terrains,"[25] the contradictions within the university: "The university is a terribly contradictory place. There's no doubt that, within the university," he stated, "there is an extremely powerful and entrenched hierarchization of functions, authority, style of work." He continues,

> And the connection between the university and the corporation in America is rarely looked at with the kind of rigor that it ought to receive; nor is the connection between the university and the state. One of the reasons is, of course, that everybody's too busy to do those kinds of things, and after a while you take for granted the existence of contradictions as part of the environment.[26]

From this 1986 interview, Said's brief deliberations on the growing contradictions within the university, its affiliations with corporate and state power, and the conditions that produce a type of myopic intellectual work by the professionals or specialists within it, mark the economic and political pressures, the tectonic shifts restructuring the terrain of higher education at that moment. His critique then was one among many he would make, and had made previously, in attempting to characterize the humanist's role in the wake of neoliberal reforms and to disentangle the relationship between humanism and the forces that had given rise to what he and others would call "the Age of Ronald Reagan."[27]

During the inaugural years of Reagan's presidency, in a work titled "Opponents, Audiences, Constituencies, and Community" (1982), for instance, Said had styled an account of the pressing issues confronting humanism. Preeminent among these concerns was the "tacit compliance" forming between humanists and the "antidemocratic view[s]" manifest within the broader political climate. Criticism and the "traditional academic humanities," Said further argued, "[had] gone through a series of developments over time whose beneficiary and culmination [was] Reaganism."[28] Indeed, the "Reagan era" had constituted a "context and setting" in which the work of literary scholarship and the humanities in general, wittingly and unwittingly, had aligned with the Cold War political and cultural scene, a scene in which the persona of Reagan had adeptly performed its role and which criticism had all-too-often corroborated. But there was more to

Said's essay than what has now become an important, though familiar, story about the role of criticism and Cold War ideology. Tarrying with questions that focused on the conditions of knowledge production, the "circumstances" of literary interpretation, and the practices of the humanist—a term for which he then held "contradictory feelings of affection and revulsion" and which would remain, throughout the rest of his life, a central object of critical reflection and interrogation— Said's essay had figured importantly in a constellation of works addressing the consequences of what he described then as the "brutal Darwinian picture of self-help and self-promotion" taking shape.

Anticipating the conditions of our present occasion, Said's essay from 1982 has served as an important reference—a point of departure—for much of the critical scholarship addressing the institutional history and plight of the humanities in the wake of neoliberal restructuring of the university. For instance, we can trace its influence on Rey Chow's theorization of informationalization,[29] which, in turn, had allowed Bill Readings in the *The University in Ruins* (1996) to examine further the managerial or administrative cooptation of interdisciplinarity. As a means for increasing "excellence" and "flexibility" among the university's curriculum and ostensibly entrenched faculty, Readings remarked all too accurately how "the time is not far off when [interdisciplinary departments or programs] will be installed in order to replace clusters of disciplines."[30] These works along with Said's continued writing on the topic of humanism and the university have further impacted Henry Giroux's efforts, including his recent *Neoliberalism's War on Higher Education* (2014), as well as Chris Newfield's *Unmaking the Public University* (2008) and Steven Ward's *Neoliberalism and the Restructuring of Knowledge and Education* (2012), to name just a few.

Said's reflections on the university and the role of humanism drew upon a number of figures, a constellation of traditional and oppositional intellectuals, from Erich Auerbach to R. P. Blackmur, John Henry Newman to R. S. Crane, and Antonio Gramsci whom I have mentioned already, among others. By far the most influential of these had been the Neapolitan philosopher, rhetorician, and teacher Giambattista Vico in whose elucidation of human institutions Said found a way to elaborate on the importance of secular knowledge or *sapienza poetica*, "historical knowledge based on the human being's capacity to make knowledge, as opposed to absorbing it passively, reactively, and dully."[31] "The core of humanism," invoking Vico, "is the secular notion that the historical world is made by men and women, and not by God, and that [...] we can really know only what we make or, to put it differently, we can know things according to the way they are made."[32] At once, Vico's *verum/factum* principle, humans can know only what they make, brilliantly expresses a dialogical tension: humans can know, but human knowledge is subject to its own tenuousness, the possibilities and limitations of human-historical memory. It was Vico, after all, whose philological insight in *The New Science* noted that the word human "comes first and properly from *humando*" or "burying."[33] Humanism, like the utopian possibilities of the university and other institutions, contains the elements of its own demise.[34]

Humanistic criticism, therefore, is a "consciously intentional, productive activity [...] whose circumstances include" and proceed from "a sense of loss," a topic that Said had expounded upon in *Beginnings*, a work that evinces the traces of political events and economic transformations occurring between the late 1960s to its publication in 1975—including the 1967 war and the student revolutions of 1968.[35] Loss, burial, and negation recur as leitmotifs throughout Said's writing, often in contrapuntal arrangement with his elaborations on intention, memory, and invention—a term he had drawn on from the fields of rhetoric, philology, and music. As opposed to the technocratic language of innovation, or the romanticized idea of creating something "from scratch," invention (from the Latin *inventio*) emphasizes human discovery and making—more precisely, "finding again," drawing on the materials of history, "reassembling from past performances."[36] "As a discovery of what the past keeps hidden," Vico scholar Giuseppe Mazzotta emphasizes, "invention finds and brings to light what is always already there."[37]

Not only does "invention" recall important affinities to Gramsci's political and philosophical notion of "inventory," it also allows us to see Said's complex views of the relation between tradition and imagination. We cannot begin to read Said without noticing immediately, his deep formation in the traditional humanities—the rigorous philological training, mastery of rhetorical eloquence and style, the references and allusions to literature, art, music, history, politics, and critical theory. He made clear, however, that a blind obedience to tradition for the sake of tradition has produced "the dry-as-dust academic humanities that had for years represented an unpolitical, unworldly, and oblivious (sometimes even manipulative) attitude to the present, all the while extolling the virtues of the past, the untouchability of the canon, and the superiority of 'how we used to do it.' "[38] Such a mummification of the humanities into an inert institution produces forms of uncritical "veneration and repression."[39] Stated paradoxically or dialectically in one of his final articulations on the subject, "It is possible [even necessary] to be critical of humanism in the name of humanism."[40] Criticism requires deep historical memory and strong imagination, and Said's insistence on Vichian "invention" recalls the capacity of the critic to "hypothesize a better situation from the known historical and social facts."[41] Invention, therefore, "enables intellectual performances on many fronts, in many places, many styles that keep in play both the sense of opposition and sense of engaged participation."[42] A decade after Edward Said's death, we discover in his legacy a sustained, protracted attention to the interrelations between human *poiesis* and invention, on the one hand, and the potential for loss, the lapse of memory, that leads to forms of doxa, on the other.

Following Vico, Said has insisted that "there is always something radically incomplete, insufficient, provisional, disputable, and arguable about humanistic knowledge," which gives "the whole idea of humanism a tragic law." Against the "dry-as-dust," ossified forms of humanism that have all-too-often aligned with imperial and hegemonic powers, Said has maintained that this "flaw can be remedied and mitigated by the disciplines of philological learning and philosophic understanding [...] but it can never be superseded."[43] That this flaw, this vulnerability or tenuousness of humanism, as I have referred to it, cannot be "superseded" requires that the critic unremittingly attend to the risks to which humanist knowledge can fall prey. And so humanists must be conscious of and resist "idées recue" and offer "opposition to every kind of cliché and unthinking language" that arise in and benefit academic trends, market rationalities, and state violence.[44]

Said's elaborations on invention and his critique of rarefied language, moreover, allow us to understand better why he maintained an exilic relationship to both traditional "dry-as-dust" humanism as well as to movements in theory that tended toward antihumanist thought. Indeed, Said's 1982 polemic, "Opponents, Audiences, Constituencies, and Community," to return to this important work again, assessing the cozy alliances between humanism and Reaganism and other forms of US economic and military power, still held: "What I argue is that a particular situation within the field we call 'criticism' is not merely related to but is an integral part of the currents of thought and practice that play a role within the Reagan era. Moreover, I think, 'criticism' and the traditional academic humanities have gone through a series of developments over time whose beneficiary and culmination is Reaganism."[45] However much Said had engaged with, read, learned, or borrowed from antihumanist theory—and he did significantly—he thought it necessary to challenge its broader implications.[46] "It must be remembered," he writes, "that antihumanism took hold on the United States intellectual scene partly because of widespread revulsion of the Vietnam War." But while he expressed the same "revulsion" to the practices of racism, sexism, and imperialism with which traditional humanism had been complicit, he insisted, "attacking the abuses of something is not the same thing as dismissing or entirely destroying that thing."[47]

Said's formulation here requires further emphasis and exploration. By characterizing antihumanism's propensity toward the *dismissal* and *destruction* of humanism and the things humans have created, Said made explicit a set of historical linkages between antihumanist critique from within the academy and those external forces that have been shaping the role of the university under emerging neoliberal programs. This is not to say that Said thought antihumanists were neoliberals. Far from it. Antihumanist theory was at the forefront of defining and confronting neoclassical economics and neocolonial practices. What Said was trying to articulate in *Humanism and Democratic Criticism* was the danger of dismissing humanism and with it the human capacity for secular criticism and invention, in the Vichian sense of knowing what humans create, "the ability to see human history as something made by the unfolding capacity of the working human mind."[48] To give further context, I quote the passage that proceeds from his line of argument:

> So, in my opinion, it has been the abuse of humanism that discredits some of humanism's practitioners without discrediting humanism itself. Yet in the past four or five years, an enormous outpouring of books and articles has, in a vast overreaction to this purported or attempted antihumanism—which in most cases was an often idealistic critique of humanism's misuses in politics and public policy, many of which were in regard to non-European people and immigrants—gone on to diagnose such lugubrious improbabilities as the death of literature or the failure of humanism to respond robustly enough to the new challenges.[49]

While antihumanist theory may have put forth an "idealist critique" of "humanism's misuses" and inadequacies to address "new challenges," Said aptly sensed that the disavowal of humanism altogether, the call for the "death of literature," would serve only tragic ends for criticism itself. "Look at the whole history of humanism and criticism—the two are invariably associated."[50] Invoking Vico again, Said argued, "Humanism is not about withdrawal and exclusion. Quite the reverse: its purpose is to make more things available to critical scrutiny as the product of human labor."[51] What then would "destroying" humanism bring? What would rise in its wake? And what would it mean to ignore the human capacity for criticism? If Said challenged antihumanism for its propensity toward "destruction"—a force too closely aligned with Schumpeterian economic theories that then served as a precursor to and architectonic for neoliberal processes—he also recognized how the demise of humanism (and the humanities) unwittingly coincided with and would ultimately benefit other more nefarious efforts by those whose interests and vision of the world were antithetical to both humanists and antihumanists alike.

As a literary critic of the last half of the twentieth-century, Said had witnessed and pointedly examined the forces acting on and influencing the institution that shaped humanistic knowledge.[52] As economic and cultural transformations signaled a "crisis" in the humanities,[53] specific disciplines such as English and comparative literature—the disciplines in which Said committed his life's work—bore the obligation of responding to those forces that challenged both the financial viability and the cultural *raison d'être* for humanistic studies. Without dismissing humanism fully and thus risk losing what historical humanism made possible as a practice of criticism, Said alternatively articulated the necessity for an order of humanism that could contest the Reagan culture warriors—the "irate traditionalists" and "callow polemicists" such as Irving Kristol, Lynne Cheney, Dinesh D'Souza, and Roger Kimball, among others—who saw the growing multicultural interests, the further radicalization of students, and the general democratization of the university after the Vietnam War as a threat to the conservative and Arnoldian vision of the humanities.[54]

Imbricated in the contest over culture and knowledge production, however, were conservative or neoliberal preoccupations with privatization, economic liberalization, and finance. While pundits strategically painted cultural and economic issues as separate and distinct topics, both their "economic goals" and concerns about "cultural values," however, had been tightly "intertwined," one serving to validate the other.[55] For instance, as conservatives gave more attention to the topic of "political correctness," a phrase they used to vituperate and delegitimize a progressive politics within the university that had sought to raise awareness about racial injustice, white privilege, imperialism, among other social, economic, and historical inequalities, the conservative culture warriors characterized the university's curricular reforms and institutional accommodations for a multicultural student population as antithetical to the "free market." For conservatives and their neoliberal ilk, Steven Ward reminds us, "Knowledge [...] had over the course of the twentieth century also become 'over-socialized' and much too public."⁵⁶ "As the historical center of most knowledge production for the last century and a half," he continues, universities "were much too isolated from market forces and the direct productive and workforce needs of corporations and the economy as a whole to serve as [...] engines of innovation and economic growth."⁵⁷ The politics of "equality" endorsed by the university, in other words, had become "the enemy of economic competitiveness" and, therefore, a "synonym for mediocrity, failed government programs, and coddled incompetence."⁵⁸ As proponents of neoliberalism pushed for reforms throughout all public sectors, the university had become a principal target for a "major retooling, reorganization and intensification much like other lagging industries or unresponsive state bureaucracies."⁵⁹

To complicate this history further, 1990s "New Democrat" political strategies under Bill Clinton simultaneously advocated for transnational, global free trade agreements and neoliberal policies, "promoting it as a means to reinvigorate the antisexism and antiracism of Cold War liberalism."⁶⁰ That is, like other instantiations of neoliberal discourse, Clintonian multiculturalism and identity politics invoked the ostensible equalizing effects of the market as a primary force for social change. The conflation between political representation and civil rights, on the one hand, and market participation and economic rights, on the other, marked how neoliberalism had absorbed the radical elements of an early "grassroots" civil-rights movement and transformed it into a mechanism for organizing or further managing the relations between "economy" and "biological and social life."⁶¹ As Jodi Melamed correctly shows, "neoliberal multiculturalism [...] sutures official anti-racism to state policy in a manner that hinders the calling into question of global capitalism."⁶² Neoliberal multiculturalism, moreover, "produces new privileged and stigmatized forms of humanity, and it deploys a normative cultural model of race (which now sometimes displaces conventional racial reference altogether) as a discourse to justify inequality for some as fair and natural."⁶³ By claiming multiculturalism and antiracism as central tenets of neoliberalism, neoliberal practices nevertheless re-instantiated and insidiously codified racialist logics on a grander, transnational scale. To be clear, the development or mutation of multiculturalism from the late 1970s through the early 2000s had played a specific role in the context of the university. While initially an object of ridicule by conservative Reagan culture warriors, multiculturalism's democratic and antiracist potential for providing higher education to a greater and more diverse number of students, staff, and faculty populations had become further weakened in its appropriation by neoliberal efforts to align the university with market logics and global capital.

Throughout the 1980s, 1990s, and 2000s under neoliberal pressures, the university became subject to forms of scrutiny and coercion in order to make it comply with the "inevitable" conditions that the market demanded—to recall Thatcher's terminology again. Reconceived as less "a public right or direct governmental responsibility [...] and more as a private investment in 'human capital' made by knowledge consumers in order to better their position in the marketplace,"[64] the university's relationship with finance not only became more entangled, but its forms of governance gave way to new styles and structures of management within it. Much of this historical and economic transformation requires more space than I have in this essay to develop. Fortunately, there are at present important studies that have addressed the topic in significant depth, some of which I have mentioned already. What I want to emphasize, however, is that the university and the education system broadly had been placed in a "paradoxical and contradictory position," one in which it was subject to "competitive market forces"—the ideological manifestation of neoliberal fantasies about *laissez-faire* capitalism—as well as to a "more rigorous monitoring, auditing and evaluation" by both state and market pressures.[65] This contradiction gets at the heart of neoliberal economic conditions of our present: As neoliberal discourse and rhetoric had called for "less government," it simultaneously had obfuscated the degrees to which neoliberal policy had required (even demanded) state power to intervene in and coerce institutions that had been reluctant or incapable of aligning with market exchanges to do so. The principal example of this form of coercion emerged in the 1970s with a "series of legal and policy changes" directed at the privatization of knowledge of production.[66] The outcome was the passage of the Bayh–Dole Act in 1980, "the same year the U.S. Supreme Court recognized the patenting of life forms."[67] While the Bayh–Dole Act had been praised by neoliberalists for having produced thousands of new patents and billions of dollars in a new economic environment that opened up the knowledge, information, and technology links between universities and businesses, critics claimed that "many of these patents were awarded for basic research that used to be shared freely and widely disseminated but was now horded and private" and that it further "undermined the basic purpose of the modern university," which was "to produce knowledge independent of commercial or political interests."[68]

By the time Said's *Humanism and Democratic Criticism* had been published, "the Bayh–Dole Act had so penetrated academia," Steven Ward further notes, "that it had begun to alter the internal standards and procedures" of university life, culture, and governance.[69] Said had recognized and lamented how the university had been further "annexed by defense, medical, biotechnical, and corporate interests, who are much more concerned about funding projects in the natural sciences than they are in the humanities."[70] While the natural sciences were able (even required) to participate in a market nexus that brought together private enterprise, scientific research, technological and informational innovation, and intellectual property (i.e., patents and trademarks), the humanities had little in the way of capital under these new conditions and forms of valuation. For those of us whose work and thinking resides in humanistic disciplines, this is a story we know all too well. Said continues, however, by remarking that these changes had placed the university within the "province of the corporate manager."[71]

What Said alluded to—and what others since have attempted to make clear—was that the forms of faculty governance, intellectual autonomy, critical inquiry and exploration that had once been central to university structures had come under the domain of new methods and doctrines for reorganizing and realigning the university and the production of knowledge around "new business principles,"[72] including rendering a costly and inflexible full-time, tenured faculty into a more nimble, less expensive labor pool of adjuncts.[73] With the increased corporatization of the university, there emerged various manifestations of managerialism, which borrowed from and put into practice the techniques of organizing labor, information, production, and valuation found in the corporate business world: "new public management (NPM)," "knowledge management (KM)," "innovation management," and, the counterpart to corporate "total quality management (TQM), 'responsibility-centered management' (RCM)," to name just a few. By the 1990s with the loss of "confidence in the stability of both state and federal funding,"[74] universities had become more entangled in the various machinations of finance capital—designing "new financial strategies toward its education mission,"[75] engaging in capital campaigns for amassing historically unprecedented endowments,[76] venturing into new and potentially profitable fields for research and teaching that approximate market trends. All of these endeavors ostensibly required an increase in a new specialized managerial class that spoke and encouraged the "language of finance."[77]

The neoliberal transformation of the university did not merely legit-imize and increase the presence of a professional managerial class (PMC), Steven Ward again explains; it was, importantly, about the degree to which managerialism, as a "regime of truth" or "belief in the universal application of management principles in whatever form," coopted the mission of the university as well as all orders of public enterprise. As "a new civil religion," according to Martin Peter,[78] managerialism's core tenet was that management "is not only desirable for efficiency purposes but [is] also part of an inevitable his-torical progression toward better, more effective structures."[79] That neoliberalism imbues the market with such quasi-theological and tele-ological power, and its managers with sacerdotal reign, as if the market presented a new metaphysics, should remind us of Said's secular caveat: "gods always fail."[80] Neoliberalism is certainly about economic, political, and legal policies and practices, but it is also about a form of human acquiescence to the institutions that humans have made but have ignored or refused to *know*—in the most sec-ular, Vichian sense of *sapienza poetica*, "historical knowledge based on the human being's capacity to make knowledge, as opposed to absorbing it passively, reactively, and dully."[81] Managerialism is theo-logical and sacerdotal because it practices a "hermetic, self-referential" discourse, rendering it "completely resistant to all criticism."[82] The notion of "inevitability" inaugurated by Margaret Thatcher's remark, "There is no other choice," functioning as if it were a self-fulfilling prophecy, haunts (as a form of colonization) the present and the future.[83]

Said's reference to the university as having come into the "province of the corporate manager" recalls, again, the importance of spatial metaphors, spaces of struggle, as well as his strong argument for sec-ular humanist historical criticism. As the university becomes further "colonized" by managerialism and finance, cultures of assessment and administrative alignment, careerism and rankings, we should recog-nize that neoliberalism projects onto our futures an indeterminate set of possibilities but within a determined matrix of market real-ities. This can only manifest insecurity, anxiety, and crisis. These are neoliberalism's corollary—tautologically legitimizing the necessity and value of a managerial class. Secular humanist criticism stands as a counterforce to the sense that the future is foreclosed. Coinciden-tally, and as a matter of necessity, Said argues for the role of human will and agency as central to Vichian principles of making, discovering, and knowing—*invention*. In the words of one of his last doctoral stu-dents, Andrew Rubin, Said's "writings, and even his presence, always seemed to express and embody a kind of will."[84] As Said eloquently states, "Humanism is the achievement of form by human will and agency; it is neither system nor impersonal force like the market."[85] Following Edward Said, I see criticism (secular and inventive) as the only way out of our present condition. While we may try to convince our students and ourselves that studying the humanities provides marketable and fungible skills—and I believe it does to some degree—we should be skeptical of totally appropriating the language of the market, the idiom of finance or entrepreneurialism, and the system of valuation that neoliberalism has provided.[86] This is a difficult but not a cynical endeavor. To be clear, neoliberalism is a politics of cynicism. Critical humanism may "proceed from a sense of loss," in the words of Said, but it is also "the means, perhaps the consciousness we have for providing that kind of finally antinomian or oppositional analysis" in "the search for knowledge and justice, and then perhaps also for liberation."[87]

NOTES

1. Steven Ward, *Neoliberalism and the Restructuring of Knowledge* (New York: Routledge, 2012), 1.
2. See Chris Newfield on the various names for neoliberalism. Christopher Newfield, *Unmaking the Public University: The Forty-Year Assault on the Middle Class* (Cambridge and London: Harvard University Press, 2008), 23.
3. Ward, *Neoliberalism and the Restructuring of Knowledge*, 10.
4. Edward W. Said, *Orientalism* (New York: Vintage, 1978), 25.
5. Thomas Piketty's *Capital in the Twenty-First Century* (Cambridge and London: Harvard University Press, 2014) offers one of the most recent empirical studies gaining important recognition, although Said among other humanists had long been writing about these issues using different methodologies.
6. See Jim Puzzanghera, "Oxfam Report Highlights Widening Income Gap between Rich, Poor," *The Los Angeles Times* (January 20, 2014). Electronic. http://www.latimes.com/business/la-fi–income–inequality–20140121,0,3481555.story#axzz30omRJlAp.
7. See David Harvey, *A Brief History of Neoliberalism* (Oxford: Oxford University Press, 2005), which addresses at length what he calls the "financialization of everything" (33).
8. http://billmoyers.com/2014/02/21/anatomy-of-the-deep-state/.
9. Ward, *Neoliberalism and the Restructuring of Knowledge*, 3. Ward cites David Felix, "Why International Capital Mobility Should Be Curbed and How it Could Be Done," in *Financialization and the World Economy*, ed. G. Epstein (Northampton: Edward Elgar, 2005), 407.

10. Said, "Problems of Neoliberalism," *Al–Ahram.* 498 (September 7–13, 2000). Electronic.

11. Ibid.

12. I have in mind Robert Tally's important observation regarding Said's concepts of space and geography. See, especially, Robert T. Tally Jr., *Spatiality* (The New Critical Idiom) (New York: Routledge, 2013), 92.

13. Said, *Representations of the Intellectual* (New York: Vintage, 1996), 53.

14. Ibid., 98.

15. Ibid., 57.

16. Said, *Humanism and Democratic Criticism* (New York: Columbia University Press, 2004), 71.

17. Ibid., 71. See also Said, "Problems of Neoliberalism."

18. Said, *Humanism and Democratic Criticism,* 123.

19. Ibid., 70–71.

20. Edward Said, "On the University," in *Edward Said and Critical Decolonization,* ed. Ferial J. Ghazoul (Cairo and New York: The American University in Cairo Press, 2007), 26–36. See his earlier 1991 interview with Bonnie Marranca, Marc Robinson and Una Chaudhuri, "Criticism, Culture, and Performance," in *Power, Politics, and Culture: Interviews with Edward W. Said,* ed. Gauri Viswanathan (New York: Vintage Books, 2001), 94–117, 113. In this same collection, see also Said's 1993 interview titled "Culture and Imperialism" (183–207, 190) with Paul A. Bové and Joseph A. Buttigieg, originally published in *boundary 2.*

21. Said, *Humanism and Democratic Criticism,* 71.

22. Ibid., 13–14.

23. Said, "On the University," 28.

24. Ibid.

25. Said, "Overlapping Territories: The World, The Text, and the Critic," in *Power, Politics, and Culture: Interviews with Edward W. Said,* ed. Gauri Viswanathan (New York: Vintage Books, 2001), 53–68, 58.

26. Ibid., 66.

27. Said, "Opponents, Audiences, Constituencies, and Community," *Critical Inquiry* 9.1 (September 1982), 1–26.

28. Ibid., 1–2.

29. See Rey Chow, "The Politics of Pedagogy of Asian Literatures in American Universities," *differences* 2.3 (1990), 30–51.

30. Bill Readings, *The University in Ruins* (Cambridge and London: Harvard University Press, 1996), 39.

31. Said, *Humanism and Democratic Criticism,* 11.

32. Ibid., 11.

33. Giambattista Vico, *The New Science,* trans. Thomas Goddard Bergin and Max Harold Fisch (Ithaca and London: Cornell University Press, 1984), 8.

34. Said, *Beginnings: Intention and Method* (New York: Columbia University Press, 1975), 373.

35. Ibid., 372. In an interview entitled "Wild Orchids and Trotsky," Said had recollected how the war of 1967 and the student revolutions of 1968 weighed heavily on his intellectual development and, therefore, on his thinking while writing the book. See Said, "Wild Orchids and Trotsky," in *Power, Politics, and Culture*, 164.

36. Said, *Humanism and Democratic Criticism*, 140.

37. Giuseppe Mazzotta, *The New Map of the World: The Poetic Philosophy of Giambattista Vico* (Princeton: Princeton University Press, 1999), 60.

38. Said, *Humanism and Democratic Criticism*, 13.

39. Ibid., 32.

40. Ibid., 11.

41. Ibid., 140.

42. Ibid.

43. Ibid., 12.

44. Ibid., 43.

45. Said, "Opponents, Audiences, Constituencies, and Community," 1.

46. Although here I borrow Said's use of the terms humanism and antihumanism from *Humanism and Democratic Criticism*, it is important to note that Said was never simply against "theory," as Stathis Gourgouris reminds us: "Nor were the so–called post–structuralist theorists simply 'anti–humanist' " (40). While Said spoke against the further commodification or even the "fetishism" of theory, readers of his work will understand how important theory was to his thinking. See Gourgouris, "The Late Style of Edward Said," in *Edward Said and Critical Decolonization*, ed. Ferial J. Ghazoul (Cairo and New York: The American University in Cairo Press, 2007), 37–45.

47. Said, *Humanism and Democratic Criticism*, 13

48. Said, *On Late Style: Music and Literature Against the Grain* (New York: Pantheon, 2006), 128.

49. Said, *Humanism and Democratic Criticism*, 13.

50. Ibid., 23.

51. Ibid., 22.

52. For a detailed, informative overview of what now has become called the "golden era" in higher education and middle-class inclusion, see Christopher Newfield's *Unmaking the Public University*, specifically his introductory chapter.

53. Again, see Newfield's deliberations on what were really three entangled crises, one of which was the "decline" of the humanities "in the public eye." The sentiment arose out of the notion that the humanities produced "no useful knowledge, only complications, ambiguities, multiple interpretations, and attacks on current social arrangements that arose from an irrational grudge against capitalist success"; see Newfield, *Unmaking the Public University*, 25.

54. Said, *Humanism and Democratic Criticism*, 13.

55. Newfield, *Unmaking the Public University*, 269–270.
56. Ward, *Neoliberalism and the Restructuring of Knowledge*, 4.
57. Ibid., 4.
58. Newfield, *Unmaking the Public University*, 66–67.
59. Ward, *Neoliberalism and the Restructuring of Knowledge*, 4.
60. Jodi Melamed, "The Spirit of Neoliberalism: From Racial Liberalism to Neoliberal Multiculturalism," *Social Text* 24.4 (Winter 2006), 14.
61. Ibid., 15.
62. Ibid., 14.
63. Ibid., 14. Similarly, see the opening of David Harvey's *A Brief History of Neoliberalism* in which he outlines the links between Bush administration's imperial efforts and military conquest of Iraq in order to bring Iraqi populations into compliance with market forces, using the power of the "neoliberal state" to eliminate those populations who might inhibit the "conditions for profitable capital accumulation." (7).
64. Ward, *Neoliberalism and the Restructuring of Knowledge*, 5.
65. Ibid., 6–7.
66. Ibid., 91.
67. Ibid., 92.
68. Ibid., 93.
69. Ibid.
70. Said, *Humanism and Democratic Criticism*, 14.
71. Ibid., 14.
72. Newfield, *Unmaking the Public University*, 129.
73. See Frank Donoghue, *The Last Professors: The Corporate University and the Fate of the Humanities* (New York: Fordham University Press, 2009).
74. Newfield, *Unmaking the Public University*, 163.
75. Ibid., 165
76. Again, on endowments, see Newfield, *Unmaking the Public University*, 162.
77. Newfield, *Unmaking the Public University*, 169.
78. Quoted in Ward, *Neoliberalism and the Restructuring of Knowledge*, 49.
79. Ibid., 48–49.
80. Said, *Representations of the Intellectual*, 103–121.
81. Said, *Humanism and Democratic Criticism*, 11.
82. Chris Lorenz, "If You're So Smart, Why Are You under Surveillance? Universities, Neoliberalism, and New Public Management," *Critical Inquiry* 38.3 (Spring 2012), 599–629, 602. Lorenz also correctly observes, "Remarkably the case has never been properly made for why the professional autonomy of academics should be mistrusted and bureaucratic formalism preferred. It is a crucial presupposition that is built into [new public management] discourse and is therefore not open to debate and criticism" (607). I am also reminded of

a lecture given by Paul A. Bové, entitled "Priests and Financiers," in Pittsburgh, Emory, and Montreal ca. 1998 that bears much on this reading.

83. I follow Chris Lorenz in his use of "colonization" to describe the effects of managerial power on the university. (609). See also the Introduction to *Questioning the New Public Management*, ed. Mike Dent, John Chandler and Jim Barry (London: Ashgate, 2004).

84. Andrew Rubin, "Edward," in *Edward Said and Critical Decolonization*, ed. Ghazoul (Cairo and New York: The American University in Cairo Press, 2007), 15–17.

85. Said, *Humanism and Democratic Criticism*, 15. We can imagine why Said took exception to Michele Foucault's analysis of power—a topic too complex to rehearse here but which offers further insight into Said's critique of those forms of thought that gave rise to the notion of inevitability, of the idea that it is impossible for human intelligence, imagination, and knowledge to grasp or understand the things the human has made.

86. A recent survey conducted by the Kettering Foundation and the National Issues Forum suggests that policy makers are misrepresenting the public's actual views of education and have instead directed colleges to focus "more on short–term job outcomes, and on science and technology disciplines over other fields." Importantly, the study actually supported the following: "But an even larger majority—89 percent—agreed that 'college should be where students learn the ability to think critically by studying a rich curriculum that includes history, art and literature, government, economics and philosophy.'" See Doug Lederman, "Politician-Public Divide," *Inside Higher Education* (February 10, 2014). Electronic. http://www.insidehighered.com/news/2014/02/10/survey-suggests-politicians-overstate-publics-desire-vocational-view-higher-ed.

87. Said, *Humanism and Democratic Criticism*, 83.

CHAPTER 4

BACK TO *BEGINNINGS*: READING
BETWEEN AESTHETICS AND
POLITICS

Daniel Rosenberg Nutters

Beginning an essay on Edward Said with George Eliot's use of the word "worldliness" is quite anachronistic. But despite the difference between Said's more specialized theoretical vocabulary and Eliot's mundane signifier for cosmopolitan, cultivated, or urbane, a brief exchange at the beginning of *Middlemarch*'s second book entitled "Old and Young" is uncanny nonetheless. The scene in question comes as we are just being introduced to the novel's supporting cast; learning their values, character, and seeing how their existence in the first half of the nineteenth century anticipates Eliot's, and by extension our own, modern world. It is in this respect that I begin with an exchange between Mr. Vincy and Mr. Bulstrode concerning the upbringing of the former's son, Fred, and his profligate lifestyle. Both are businessmen, but Bulstrode believes that Vincy's faith in a "father's duty to give his sons a fine chance," that is a college education, engendered bad habits under the auspices of some idea of "worldliness."[1] The conversation goes as follows:

> "I don't wish to act otherwise than as your best friend, Vincy, when I say that what you have been uttering just now is one mass of worldliness and inconsistent folly."

> "Very well," said Mr. Vincy, kicking in spite of resolutions, "I never professed to be anything but worldly; and, what's more, I don't see

anybody else who is not worldly. I suppose you don't conduct business on what you call unworldly principles. The only difference I see is that one worldliness is a little bit honester than another."[2]

Vincy's retort that one doesn't "conduct business on what you call unworldly principles" is quite timely considering that earlier in this chapter, and later on in the novel, we witness Bulstrode's unscrupulous use of money and power. Yet as the word "worldliness" hangs in the balance between Vincy's paternal "duty" and Bulstrode's questionable ethics, and as the novel develops its interest and critique of the increasing exigency for "professional enthusiasm" and its relationship with the kind of "liberal education" that might allow one "free [time] to read the inclement passages in the school classics," we can see how Eliot proleptically discloses the role of literature in the twenty-first century global university.[3]

More to the point, the overt concern of this chapter is the consequences that theoretical jeremiads have upon critical legacies. In other words, there is currently an attempt by academics to resuscitate intellectual life by lamenting the impotency of critique and searching for alternative methodologies that might herald the new and save the humanities that seems to pit the progress-oriented thinking of a Bulstrode against older methods of literary critical "duty." If the tension between real-world institutional pressure and a lack of an organizing rationale for particular genres of scholarship makes self-critique, perpetual revisionism, mandated generational conflict, and the rhetoric of crisis the most publically visible game in town, then this chapter will hope to demonstrate how Edward W. Said's work represents an attempt to place the humanities and criticism on stable ground without allowing that ground to imprison and restrict critical practice.

In this regard, I am working under the assumption that Said was acutely aware of the debilitating effects of scholarly fashions and hope that, in titling my essay "Back to *Beginnings*," we can channel Said's investments in literature to ameliorate our contemporary moment. But alas, this chapter is not the occasion to offer a jeremiad of my own. My narrower topic will be to demonstrate how Said enables a mode of close reading that remains consistent throughout his career and obviates the pitfalls of totalizing positions.[4] In this sense, my essay is an appreciation of a career that models how the scholar can simultaneously remain committed to literature and its worldly implications, without rendering such a belief susceptible to that inimical trend in the humanities of scholarly innovation for innovation's sake. By turning to *Beginnings*, I will argue how Said theorizes a style of reading that shapes his more well known scholarship, and which resurfaces again in *Humanism and Democratic Criticism*, his posthumously published overt discussion of the role and place of the humanities and criticism in the twenty-first century. Linking Said's early and late work can help demonstrate how his critical practice resists instrumentalizing tendencies and maintains a particular fidelity to the creative imagination that, following Vico, accounts for the production of human history. This essay is thus an attempt to understand how Said's secular humanist project can stymie potential critical entropy if we consider the fecund possibilities latent in the critic's engagement with a text.

Beginnings: Intention and Method appeared in 1975 before the full English translations of many of Jacques Derrida's most significant works and exactly contemporaneous with Michel Foucault's yet to be translated *Surveiller et punir*.[5] Along with the works by these famous French theorists, it would be appropriate to describe *Beginnings* as a literary-critical event of equal measure. It not only won the inaugural Lionel Trilling Book Award, something of a symbolic passing of the torch at Columbia as Trilling died in 1975, but the book also immediately demanded the attention of all serious students of literature. The innovative journal *diacritics* devoted an entire issue to *Beginnings* that included reviews by such significant scholars as J. Hillis Miller, Eugenio Donato, Joseph Riddel, and Hayden White, as well as a lengthy interview with Said.[6] Yet, as Michael Wood explains, "there is a temptation, given the directions and importance of Edward Said's later work, and missing as we now do the sanity and passion of his thinking about the Middle East, to treat his literary work as subordinate to his political essays and to see his early work as a mere prelude to what was to come."[7] The "later work" that more ostensibly dominates the discussion of Said's legacy is, of course, *Orientalism*.[8] Regardless of such overshadowing, what makes *Beginnings* a courageous book is its original attempt to position itself within the burgeoning field of theoretical discourse and, simultaneously, its unique ability to anticipate the potential limitations of that field. Such limitations will become clearer in *The World, the Text, and the Critic*, a work that seems, at times, to resemble a manifesto outlining Said's unique vocabulary and its relation to currents in critical thought. But, at the same time, in its engagement with the debates concerning the rise of theory, *The World, the Text, and the Critic* is liable to obscure Said's indebtedness to such innovations.[9] *Beginnings* not only anticipates this later text by clarifying and elucidating Said's methodical theorization of the crucial issues surrounding theory, it also lays the foundation for a malleable notion of critical and human agency that authorizes the vocabulary that will emerge in the years to come.[10]

In the second chapter, "A Meditation on Beginnings," Said eloquently summarizes some of the questions animating both poststructuralist discourse and *Beginnings* as a whole:

> I am really circling around a very acute problem faced by any researcher whose primary evidence is textual. The problem can now be put in the following ways: To what extent is a text not something passively attributable, as effect is to cause, to a person? To what extent is a text so discontinuous a series of subtexts or pre-texts or paratexts or surtexts as to beggar the idea of an author as simple producer? If the text as unitary document is more properly judged as a transindividual field of dispersion, and if [...] this field stands as the *locus princeps* of research, where does it begin if not in a "creative" or "producing" individuality?[11]

Although this passage puts into focus the theme of intertextuality that haunts poststructuralist thought, Said hints at the same question articulated in the preface to Harold Bloom's *A Map of Misreading*, a book published in the same year as *Beginnings*. For Bloom, "The ultimate issue that became clear in extensive conversations with Paul de Man was: how does meaning get started anyway?"[12] Said, of course, would use his word "beginning" to supplant Bloom's phrase "get started anyway," but it is important to keep both Bloom and de Man in mind since the question that comprises their dialogue also pervades Said's book.[13] That relationship notwithstanding, the series of questions that Said raises in the passage cited above, questions that appear 58 pages into this mammoth work, seem to approach the heart of its polemic. Opposing Bloom's theological romantic understanding of the origins of meaning, or Derrida's notion of the event, Said emphasizes the role of an "individuality" in the act of producing meaning. By placing this emphasis on human agency, Said begins to position himself against the totalizing tendencies of theoretical discourses that would reduce and impede such agency. This difference becomes ostensible in his famous essay "Secular Criticism," where he takes to task criticism that "privately set[s] loose the unrestrained interpretation of a universe defined in advance as endless misreading of a misinterpretation," and, in turn, "risk[s] becoming wall-to-wall discourses, blithely predetermining what they discuss, heedlessly converting everything into evidence for the efficacy of the method, carelessly ignoring the circumstances out of which all theory, system, and method ultimately derive."[14]

If Said is to become the socially and politically conscious critic we recognize him as today, he will need to not only escape the textual traps and theoretical abysses emanating from his contemporaries and their progeny, but he will also need to forge a link between his role as a "literary scholar, critic, and teacher" and his "political involvements."[15] How, in other words, can Said "assess the role or place of writing [or creative, intellectual activity] in 'the world'" or how can he "engage with the larger world, and do things there that [his] peculiar, not to say eccentric, capacities and training suit [him] for[?]"[16] *Beginnings* not only responds to and anticipates the havoc wreaked by the poststructuralist critique of the subject, it also, by emphasizing the agency involved in the production of meaning, erects out of that havoc a style of reading that will, as we will see in greater detail when I turn to *Humanism and Democratic Criticism*, allow Said and others to write "criticism [that] think[s] of itself as life-enhancing and constitutively opposed to every form of tyranny, domination, and abuse; its social goals are noncoercive knowledge produced in the interests of human freedom."[17]

Such a style of reading is grounded in the relationship between the authorial or individual will and the role a text plays in representing the world. "No one can doubt," Said writes, "that there is an original [. . .] if not a beginning connection between text and individual author, yet to readers, even to a writing author, a text is not whole, but distorted" (*B* 58–59). After Barthes's "Death of the Author," first translated in 1967, and Foucault's vision of the author function from a few years later, not to mention the New Critical intentional fallacy, Said seeks to recover that "beginning connection" between the author and his work insofar as such a connection will allow him to investigate the influence that texts exert in the world. If the author is merely a text himself, shaped by the discursive forces of his or her time, what hope might he have of engendering real-world change through his scholarship and writing? Of course Said recognizes that one cannot wholly attribute a text to an author, which would risk simplified, finite, meaning and fatuous hero-worship, so he discusses this relationship as a "beginning connection" to imply a dependent relationship between the authorial will and the process by which a text becomes "distorted." This relationship emerges in the act of writing which, for Said, "is not coterminous with nature, and therefore deforms its subjects...more than forms them. Reading and writing have this in common: they are particular distortions of general realties.

There is a violence in texts, which is answered by the reconstructions of the examining critic" (*B* 59). Though I have commented on this passage elsewhere with respect to how Henry James theorizes and enacts a similar link between the author's mind and the world at large, I would like to elaborate on how this central passage seeks to give the "examining critic" the leverage to demonstrate how his "answer" can play an ethical, political, and experiential role in shaping the world.[18] To this end, Said seems to be revising and updating Lionel Trilling's remarkable analysis of the dialectical ebb and flow between reality and the creative imagination for the poststructuralist moment.[19]

The "violence in texts" passage cited above, which governs Said's thinking on the role of reading, writing, and representation, is followed by a citation from Freud's *Moses and Monotheism*. Here the psychoanalyst invokes the "double-meaning" of *Enstellung* to suggest that textual representations, or representation in general, are deceptive and, in that deception, disavow particular meanings. Though he cites this passage without providing any commentary, it allows Said to assert: "To begin to apprehend a text is to begin to find intention and method in it—not, in other words, to reduce a text to a continuous stream of words emanating from a disembodied voice, but rather to construct the field of its play, its dispersion, its distortion" (*B* 59). V. L. Parrington, whom Trilling castigates, is a version of this reductionist position that does not construct a "field of play" but sees the writer as statically mirroring in his writing the reality he observes. Said's more direct version of the reductionist critic, the one who reduces a text to a "disembodied voice" where agency always lies somewhere other than a concocting consciousness, is a critic who transforms a text into an ideological vessel that merely mirrors back, via repressed discursive traces, lost cultural contexts.

This does not mean that the text can be solely attributed to an *embodied* voice, an autonomous individual who might stand outside of time, but, rather, that the "dispersion" of the textual representation begins with the adversarial relationship between such a consciousness and both the world it exists in and the world it seeks to represent. In order to recreate this relationship the critic must "construct the field of [a text's] play," that is, to discover how a non-authorial agency manipulates the authorial intention. This process of manipulation—the textual violence—engenders the "field of play" or the array of representations that become transfigured as a text remains, forever, in its beginning inchoate state.

In the remainder of the second chapter of *Beginnings*, Said attempts to account for a text's inability to accurately represent in terms that take into account the writer's beginning intentions. For example, the discussion that follows the passage I've just cited describes the irrational representational method of language as a series of displacements in terms of what Said labels dynastic and adjacent relationships. For readers of Derrida and de Man, Said's insights will not seem entirely original, but I should emphasize that his handling of the problematic nature of language anticipates the limitations of these other critics, which will become manifest in *The World, the Text, and the Critic*. For Said, literature that attempts to "imitate nature" or language that assumes a stable "center" or "*cogito*" or simply some kind of prior "authority" creates a "dynastic" filial relationship between the object represented and the mode of representation and, moreover, such a relationship is one "bound to sources and origins" (*B* 66). On the other hand, writing that calls into question such an origin, writing that realizes itself as merely a displacement or deems itself inadequate to fully represent is a form of literature characterized by "adjacency [where] instead of a source we have the intentional beginning, instead of a story [as in the dynastic use of language] a construction" (*B* 66). These contrasting uses of language coincide with the assumptions of the status of writing in different historical periods; we might compare the dynastic and adjacent relationships to the mirror and the lamp or, more aptly, Schiller's distinction between naïve and sentimental poets. In other words, Said is elaborating his own history of the Romantic-Modern Tradition where for the "modern writer" "the methods of the old Muse are insufficient [since] he is no muse-inspired seer" (*B* 67).

The "painful knowledge" that there is no prior authority either to one's self, or one's attempt at representation, allows Said to describe two kinds of beginnings: transitive and intransitive.[20] The former is the writer's "point of departure," where he actually begins, which, in the act of beginning, includes an "anticipated end, or at least [an] expected continuity," but the latter beginning, the intransitive, is what attempts to clarify, authorize, and inaugurate that beginning moment, to locate its existence and authority: "the transitive mode is always hungering" for something, Said writes, "while the intransitive beginning merely hungers for itself, constantly drawing attention to itself as that which hungers" (*B* 72–73). It is in this double-bind that the tension between authorial intention and the results of that intention come into conflict. The transitive beginning has an aim, a *telos*, or a representational goal while the intransitive beginning acts as the voice of self-doubt, questioning the ability to fulfill such a goal. Rather than describe this relationship in the language of semiology, or as the yearning for a pure presence, symbolic wholeness, or even in terms of the anxiety of influence and one author's attempt to subsume a prior author, Said discloses this predicament in terms that allow the writer to attempt beginnings that do not fall within the confines of these other more limiting theories.

Part of Said's critical acumen lies in his ability to avoid the absolutist language of his peers. Having described the representational nature of language in terms of dynastic/adjacent relationships or transitive/intransitive beginnings, he describes the same conflict, in his discussion of the history of the novel, in terms of "authority and molestation" (B 83). While the novel preoccupies itself with characters searching for their origins, this feature mimics the novelist who, like the modern poet, seeks to establish for himself some kind of absolute authority over a particular terrain such as the sincerity of his poetic expression. But just as the writer yearns for that authority, he will inevitably encounter "restraint[s] upon his inventiveness" (B 83). These "restraints" fall under the broad term "molestation" by which Said means the forces that impede and stymie a writer's claim to authority. On the one hand, it is important to think of the "molestation" of a text not in purely theoretical terms. An obvious example of worldliness would be the troubles of editorial decisions involving word limits or even censorship. Such problems account for the molestation of an intention just as much as the innate qualities of language. It is this kind of theoretical openness, or a theorizing that allows for the possibility of various kinds of molestation, that Said's work can accommodate. Not only does he account for a range of factors that engender textual transfiguration, but he also preserves the creative "individuality." Despite the limitations of language, molestation, paradoxical beginnings, or the analogous logic of words (their non-dynastic representational status), Said opens up a space for the author that allows the critic leverage to reconstruct that author's vision by attempting to examine its conflicting relationship with any number of impediments. A text, in this regard, might be an ideological vessel carrying with it traces of particular historical discourses, but the text also has an aim and a purpose, its author also sought to intervene in the culture. Said's understanding of beginnings allows for a plethora of critical methodologies that enable criticism to emphasize the cultural dynamics of literature and, at the same time, he discloses the importance of demonstrating a particular fidelity to aesthetic vision.

If *Beginnings*, with the benefit of hindsight, seems to work out Said's understanding of such fecund topics as writing, reading, textuality, authority, and representation, amid the backdrop of what we now consider high theory, his later writings attempt to develop a critical praxis for fulfilling the potential left latent in this important work. *The World, the Text, and the Critic* would seem like the logical text to consider in this regard since many of its essays emerged out of the same context as *Beginnings* and, more importantly, it is in this volume that Said expounds upon the critical vocabulary that will come to define his unique style. However, I turn to his posthumously published work *Humanism and Democratic Criticism* because it not only returns us to our contemporary environment, an environment that witnesses weekly articles discussing the decline of the humanities, but it also illustrates how the main ideas I am trying to extract from *Beginnings* come into sharper focus when situated against this dramatically alerted academic landscape.[21] In other words, Said rearticulates how the critic "constructs the field of [a text's] play" by linking it with a form of critical humanism that might help bolster "the humanities [which have] as a whole lost their eminence in the university."[22]

The two opening essays of *Humanism and Democratic Criticism*, "Humanism's Sphere" and "The Changing Basis of Humanistic Study," outline a rough sketch of how Said understands the humanist tradition in terms of its continuously evolving function in the world. While a full discussion of humanism is well beyond the scope of this essay, in these two essays Said simultaneously seeks to understand the tradition's legacy, from Arnold through the poststructuralist critique, opening of the canon, culture wars, and the emergence of cultural studies, while arguing in favor of the tradition's still unfulfilled democratic potential.[23] My more direct concern is with the volume's third essay, "The Return to Philology," and I want to demonstrate how in it Said revises, or modifies, the kind of scholarly practice theorized in *Beginnings*. If "humanism is [or involves] the exertion of one's faculties in language in order to understand, reinterpret, and grapple with the products of language in history" (*HDC* 28), then the significance of my reading of *Beginnings*, specifically how Said navigates the problems encountered by any "researcher whose primary evidence is textual" (*B* 58), will make itself obvious.

"The Return to Philology" echoes a short essay by Paul de Man of the same name in which de Man defends literary theory by describing its philological roots, showing its generational continuity, and emphasizing how it merely asks students "to begin reading texts

closely as texts and not to move at once into the general context
of human experience as history."[24] Such reading, for de Man, forces
strict attention on rhetoric and the way language produces meaning
and prevents students from "hid[ing] their non-understanding [of lan-
guage] behind the screen of received ideas that often passes, in literary
instruction, for humanistic knowledge."[25] Though Said places equal
emphasis on language's ability to construct meaning as we've seen,
unlike de Man his version of "The Return to Philology" examines
the links between "reading texts closely" and the "general context
of human experience as history" that emerges from such reading. For
Said, "words [are] bearers of reality, a reality hidden, misleading, resistant, and difficult" (*HDC* 58) and "a true philological reading [. . .]
involves getting inside the process of language already going on in
words and making it disclose what may be hidden or incomplete or
masked or distorted in any text we may have before us" (*HDC* 59).
As should be clear, the idea of a "misleading, resistant, and difficult"
reality returns us to the "violence in texts," but unlike *Beginnings*,
which seems only to explore the sources of such violence, "The Return
to Philology" draws upon the former book's findings to argue that
the "patient scrutiny of and lifelong attentiveness to the words and
rhetorics by which language is used by human beings who exist in
history" (*HDC* 61) is "paramount for humanistic knowledge" (*HDC*
58) and has significant worldly implications. Even though the books
that stand between *Beginnings* and *Humanism and Democratic Criticism* demonstrate how the study of language leads to such knowledge,
when Said turns to two contrasting modes of reading, what he calls
reading as reception and as resistance, we see a return of intention or
"individuality" as categories that can help prevent criticism from over-
looking the role that the aesthetic (reception) plays in achieving a kind
of socially responsible, politically informed, criticism (resistance).

"Reception," Said writes, is the process of "[s]ubmitting oneself
knowledgably to texts and treating them provisionally at first as discrete objects [. . .] moving then, by dint of expanding and elucidating
the often obscure or invisible frameworks in which they exist, to their
historical situations and the way in which certain structures of attitude, feeling, and rhetoric get entangled with some currents, some
historical and social formations of their context" (*HDC* 61). At first
glance this passage seems to suggest that the task of reading involves
simply recovering the manifold ways in which a text becomes, to borrow Said's language from *Beginnings*, molested. Making lucid the
"obscure or invisible frameworks" seems to amount to the recovery
of repressed discourses that are either lost in the act of creation or

that are subtly transmitted with the text, that is *within* the text, as it makes its way through history. It is important to recognize, however, that any critical endeavor that expands and elucidates such frameworks cannot subordinate the writer's inventiveness to the "historical and social formations of [his or her] context." The crucial word in this passage is neither *submit, expand,* nor *elucidate,* all of which refer to the critic, but rather *entangled.* This latter verb describes the relationship between the text, as the creation of the writer's "individuality," and the particular "currents" mentioned. Simply reconstructing such an entanglement has the potential deleterious consequence of demonstrating the overwhelming power of such "currents," allowing us to neglect to understand how the author remains the artificer of the work in question, for, as Said reminds us, a chief goal of "the act of reading is the act therefore of first putting oneself in the position of the author, for whom writing is a series of decisions and choices expressed in words" (*HDC* 62).

Such an "act" of "putting oneself" in an author's position clearly recalls the phenomenological component of criticism that permeates *Joseph Conrad and the Fiction of Autobiography.* While Said is not attempting to revitalize a lost criticism of consciousness, his remarks suggest a central continuity amongst criticism from a bygone era: namely, the belief in the experiential dimension of the aesthetic. Despite Said's charge that for Northrop Frye "the notion that there was a genre called 'women's' or 'minority' writing never entered [his] system" (*HDC* 39), Said tacitly shows a debt to the Blakean who remarks, in the beginning of his preface to the second edition of *Fearful Symmetry,* that "the critic must know his poet's text to the point of possession."[26] We could debate the difference between Said's "putting oneself" and Frye's "possession," but this is beside the point. One of the chief merits of *Humanism and Democratic Criticism* is its ability to not forsake the past merely because of its more limited sense of a critic's vocation or its idea of democratic criticism. Nowadays, despite his fervent concern for democracy, a writer like F. O. Matthiessen is condemned for both constructing an elitist exclusionary canon that not only reifies an exceptionalist ideology, but helps such an ideology authorize and legitimize a Cold War national consensus.[27] Said, by contrast, would recognize how his own work is not merely a repudiation or supplanting of someone like Matthiessen, but continuity, despite many differences, between how each critic understands the role of close reading, especially when Matthiessen is the author of the following sentence: "Aesthetic criticism, if carried far enough, inevitably becomes social criticism, since the act of perception [Said's 'putting oneself' or Frye's 'possession'] extends through the work of art to its milieu."[28]

Said's own work exemplifies what it means to "carry far enough" because he describes how reading is the attempt to balance the "act of perception," which is always aesthetic, with the ability to see "through the work of art to its milieu." His concern, however, is not with questions of value or defining a "work of art" but demonstrating how its "entanglement" with different contexts lays a blueprint for the task of criticism.[29] He writes, drawing on Adorno, "there is a fundamental irreconcilability between the aesthetic and the nonaesthetic that we must sustain as a necessary condition to our work as humanists. Art is not simply there: it exists intensely in a state of unreconciled opposition to the depredations of daily life" (*HDC* 63). In order to make the jump from "literature" to "politics," a problem that, as we saw in the *diacritics* interview, fascinated him during the writing of *Beginnings*, Said conscientiously preserves the status of art, the role of the aesthetic, as a necessary medium that mediates our access to any knowledge of life's "depredations." If *Beginnings* theorizes the problematics inherent in making such a jump, *Humanism and Democratic Criticism* provides Said the occasion to demonstrably assert the kind of knowledge that that earlier book allowed him to fathom. Jane Austen's novels, he writes, "can never be reduced only to social, political, historical, and economic forces but rather, are, antithetically, in an unresolvable dialectical relationship with them, in a position that obviously depends on history but is not reducible to it" (*HDC* 64). Roughly 30 years later the "disembodied voices" become "social, political, historical, and economics forces" but Said attempts to stave off such reductionism and keep whatever we deem to be a source of authority in an *unresolvable* relationship with work of art. Such "unresolvability" is what authorizes and justifies the humanities and humanistic scholarship; it prevents any formal closure, provides a buttress against instrumental reason and utilitarian values, and because it is "deeply subjective," preserves Said's emphasis on the individual; such is, moreover, the "enlightening" (*HDC* 65) and "emancipatory purposes of close-reading" (*HDC* 67).

The other side of reading, however, is resistance, which allows Said to cross the gap between a solitary experience with a text and the political commitments of the critic. Resistance at once builds upon the enthusiasm of "Secular Criticism" while situating the central animus of that project within the contexts discussed above. We see Said, for example, re-characterize the exilic requirements of oppositional criticism when he remarks that "the task of the humanist is not just to occupy a position or place, nor simply to belong somewhere, but rather to be both insider and outsider to the circulating ideas and values that are at issue in our society or someone else's society or the society of the other" (*HDC* 76), and, in order to occupy such a position, we must sharpen our "ability to differentiate between what is directly given [in a text] and what may be withheld" (*HDC* 75–76). The elucidation of a text's "obscure or invisible frameworks" from the vantage point of an "insider and outsider" and, moreover, the ability to "differentiate" and make judgments about those "frameworks" based upon the "issues in our society" that such texts raise, is, ultimately, the link between reading as reception and reading as resistance.

But if one considers that criticism as a resistance is merely another form of literary violence, that is, that the critic's act of apprehending a text leads to the same problems that the original author encountered while representing an intention and, moreover, that our own attempts at representation will create necessary distortions, then the task of criticism must always suffer the same fate as the original works of art studied. Criticism produced in language, in other words, is impeded by the same constraints that impeded the original production of the texts under critical scrutiny. Simply put, the work our criticism performs in the world correlates to the work texts in general perform and *Beginnings* theorizes a necessary requirement for preventing the gap between reading as resistance and reading as reception from closing up. It discloses the limitations of linguistic acts of resistance and staves off quixotic critical idealism. Merely moving from reception to resistance is a form of closure that subordinates the always distorted, unfinished, inchoate, Sisyphean act of reception, and thus renders acts of resistance impotent. That is, the leap from reception to resistance can potentially disavow the conditions that make such a leap imaginable and, as a result, beguile socially minded critics.

There is clear evidence of this kind of beguilement today when we consider the neglect of the theoretical linguistic turn for what appears to be more egalitarian forms of criticism that speak to our exigent political concerns. The proliferation of titles lamenting the loss of theory or the self-congratulatory belief in the accomplished work of theory—unearthing repressed discourses and decentering loci of power in order to emancipate previously marginalized voices—leads some critics to write that in "the demand for 'close' and 'careful' reading there is also a profoundly conservative impulse to keep us focused on familiar texts recognized as 'difficult' and 'serious.'"[30] This call for "close and careful reading" that this critic whimsically dismisses is the simultaneous call to recognize, as Said does in *Beginnings*, that the objects of reception are produced by individuals and that they are not static and sterile when placed in their specific contexts. The status of the individual authorial vision, like our own critical vision, in other words, precludes an easy bridge between reception and resistance. It forces us to acknowledge that such a bridge is always inadequate to connect these two poles of reading. Consider the following passage, which I will quote at length in anticipation of a conclusion:

> It is necessary to realize that close reading has to originate [or begin?] in critical receptivity as well as in a conviction that even though great aesthetic work ultimately resists total understanding, there is a possibility of a critical understanding that may never be completed but can certainly be provisionally affirmed. It is a truism that all readings are of course subject to later re-readings, but it is also good to remember that there can be heroic first readings that enable many others after them. Who can forget the rush of enrichment [while experiencing great art] and [. . .] the sense of change in oneself [that] result[ed]? It takes a kind of heroism to undertake great artistic efforts, to experience the shattering disorientation of [their] "making" [. . .]. This is proper [. . .] to the humanistic enterprise, the sense of authorial heroism as something to emulate, admire, aspire to for readers, [and artists]. It is not only anxiety that drives [them to surpass their predecessors]. There is competitiveness of course, but also admiration and enthusiasm for the job to be done that won't be satisfied until one's own road is taken after a great predecessor has first carved out a path. Much of the same can and must be said about humanistic heroism of allowing oneself to experience the work with something of its primary drive and informing power. We are not scribblers or humble scribes but minds whose actions become a part of the collective human history being made all around us.
>
> (*HDC* 67–68)

The key word in this passage, as I read it, is *enable*. Criticism should seek to embody all that Said characterizes as resistance, but such amelioratory aspirations derive from, or begin, in the enabling powers of subjective reading. While we must acknowledge our unstable relation to the text, the text's anxieties about its own authority, and the necessary limitations inherent in the production of knowledge derived from language, we still retain an "enthusiasm for [our] job" because such acknowledgment ensures that the task of criticism is always ongoing. This does not mean that the creation of new knowledge and societal improvement is impossible, rather, it assumes that critical work is part of the same "collective human history" that the "great artistic efforts" we study continue to partake in. To this end, criticism might also be characterized by Said's notion of late style with its "nonharmonious, nonserene tension, and above all, a sort of deliberately unproductive productiveness going *against*."[31] Such a trait is intimately bound up in the act of reception and resistance. Late style involves "the power to render disenchantment [that is the recovery of the hidden frameworks within a text] and pleasure [our active of subjective reception] without resolving the contradiction between them."[32] In terms of reading and writing, it allows the "unproductive" nature of our productive scholarship to prevent a text from ossifying, prevent us from turning it into mere armature for critical battles, and, most importantly, prevent our criticism from only yielding diminishing returns. Or, as George Eliot puts it at the conclusion of *Middlemarch*, "Every limit is a beginning as well as an ending."[33]

NOTES

1. George Eliot, *Middlemarch*, ed. Bert G. Hornback (New York: W. W. Norton and Company, 1977), 87.
2. Ibid., 87.
3. Ibid., 99, 98.
4. My use of the phrase "close reading" will become clearer as this essay progresses. I should note now, however, that while a close reading clearly invokes the New Critics and their poststructuralist avatars, I want to help extend the scope of its usage. On these issues, see Jane Gallop, "The Historicization of Literary Studies and the Fate of Close Reading," *Profession* (2007), 181–186; and Jane Gallop, "Close Reading in 2009," *ADE Bulletin* 149 (2010), 15–19.
5. *Speech and Phenomena and Other Essays on Husserl's Theory of Signs* was translated into English translation in 1973 while *Of Grammatology* appeared in 1976 and *Writing and Difference* in 1978. Moreover, *Surveiller et punir* was published in 1975 and translated as *Discipline and Punish* in 1977.
6. See *diacritics* 6.3 (Fall 1976).
7. Michael Wood, "Beginnings Again," in *Edward Said: A Legacy of Emancipation and Representation*, ed. Adel Iskandar and Hakem Rustom (Berkeley: University of California Press, 2010), 60. I should also emphasize that Wood's eloquent essay further contextualizes *Beginnings* in relation to the theory moment.
8. We would be lucky if students being introduced to Said for the first time have even heard of *Beginnings*, let alone understand its significance not just for literary studies, but also in the context of Said's career. The following three introductory books exemplify how the critical community represents his legacy or, at the very least, how such a legacy is taught to subsequent generations. Valerie Kennedy's

Edward Said: A Critical Introduction (Cambridge: Polity Press, 2000) begins her introduction with *Orientalism* and devotes one paragraph to *Beginnings*. Bill Ashcroft and Pal Ahluwalia's *Edward Said* (London: Routledge, 2009), part of the Routledge Critical Thinkers series, uses *The World, the Text, and the Critic* as its theoretical master text and builds upon Kennedy's work by discussing *Beginnings* in two paragraphs. Conor McCarthy's *The Cambridge Introduction to Edward Said* (Cambridge: Cambridge University Press, 2010) ameliorates the major defects of the previous introductions, but McCarthy, in the final chapter discussing Said's reception and lasting influence, discusses only *Orientalism*.

9. William Spanos provides a definitive account of Said's relationship to poststructuralism and corroborates much of the context I've provided here: "Said was [...] an antihumanist humanist or at any rate was engaged in thinking a humanism that was in its errancy more truly humanist than the traditional humanism [of, for example, Arnold or Trilling] [...] that became hegemonic in the West in the wake of the apotheosis of Man—the anthropo-logos—in the Renaissance and especially after the Enlightenment. Indeed, he was, despite an increasing negativity toward poststructuralism, thinking a humanism that was consistent with the posthumanism (i.e., 'antihumanist humanism') that was the unsaid assumption of the so-called poststructuralists from Heidegger, through Derrida [and company]." Through superb readings of *Orientalism*, *Culture and Imperialism*, and *Humanism and Democratic Criticism*, Spanos demonstrates Said's continuously fraught relationship with theory. However, in his focus on the still untapped revolutionary potential in Said's thought, Spanos only provides a brief discussion of *Beginnings*. I hope that the present essay can bolster Spanos's emphasis on the political stakes of critical theory by thinking through the more pedestrian concept of how Said understands the role of the critic's engagement with literature. See William V. Spanos, *The Legacy of Edward Said* (Urbana: University of Illinois Press, 2009), 5.

10. For concise essays on Said's use of different terminology, see R. Radhakrishnan, *A Said Dictionary* (Oxford: Wiley-Blackwell, 2012).

11. Edward W. Said, *Beginnings: Intention and Method* (New York: Columbia University Press, 1975), 58; hereafter cited in text as *B*.

12. Harold Bloom, *A Map of Misreading* (New York: Oxford University Press, 1975), xiv. I should note that the preface to Bloom's *Map* appears in the second edition published in 2003.

13. Bloom's essay "Poetic Crossing," which powerfully contrasts his position with that of Derrida and de Man, also demonstrates the correlation between his work and Said's. The essay's opening makes this perfectly clear: "A poem *begins* because there is an absence. An image

must be given, *for a beginning*, and so that absence ironically is called a presence. Or, a poem *begins* because there is too strong a presence, which needs to be imaged as an absence, if there is to be any imaging at all" (emphasis mine). Harold Bloom, "Poetic Crossing," *Wallace Stevens: The Poems of Our Climate* (Ithaca: Cornell University Press, 1976), 375. Such a passage, coupled with Bloom's emphasis on the Vichian imagination, albeit in its romantic, un-secularized form, suggests that of all the major theorists of the 1970s, his work is closest to that of Said's. This similarity might account for the huge emphasis placed on Bloom by both Said and his interlocutor in the interview that appeared in the special issue of *diacritics*. See Edward W. Said, "Interview: Edward W. Said," *diacritics* 6.3 (1976), 30–47.

14. Edward Said, "Secular Criticism," *The World, the Text, and the Critic* (Cambridge, MA: Harvard University Press, 1983), 25–26.
15. Said, "Interview: Edward W. Said," 35.
16. Ibid., 40.
17. Said, "Secular Criticism," 29.
18. See Daniel Rosenberg Nutters, "Between the Romance and the Real: Experiencing Jamesian Reading," *Henry James Review* 35.1 (Winter 2014), 12–22.
19. See Lionel Trilling, "Reality in America," in *The Moral Obligation to be Intelligent*, ed. Leon Wieseltier (Evanston: Northwestern University Press, 2008).
20. Paul de Man, "The Rhetoric of Temporality," in *Blindness and Insight: Essays in the Rhetoric of Contemporary Criticism* (Minneapolis: University of Minnesota Press, 1971), 207.
21. Spanos argues that *Humanism and Democratic Criticism* is a "deeply problematic book" because it obscures its relationship to poststructuralist theory. While Spanos's careful readings attempt simultaneously to recuperate what he sees as this lost relationship and demonstrate how Said's humanist project attempts to fulfill the unfulfilled potential of the theory revolution, my more narrow focus will be to illustrate a continuity between early and late Said simply in terms of his reading practice. See Spanos, *The Legacy of Edward Said*, 151–186.
22. Edward W. Said, *Humanism and Democratic Criticism* (New York: Columbia University Press, 2004), 14; hereafter cited in text as *HDC*.
23. A special issue of *Cultural Critique* entitled "Edward Said and After: Toward a New Humanism" provides an excellent discussion of the place of *Humanism and Democratic Criticism* within his corpus and its potential impact for future scholarship. In particular, R. Radakrishnan's essay "Edward Said's Literary Humanism" looks at the role that literature and art play in realizing Said's democratic vision. Moreover, Abdirahman A. Hussein's "A New 'Copernican' Revolution: Said's Critique of Metaphysics and Theology" focuses on the Vichian contexts of *Beginnings* to argue how Said's philosophical

thought anticipates many of the concerns of *Humanism and Democratic Criticism*. See *Cultural Critique* 67 (Autumn 2007).

24. Paul de Man, *The Resistance to Theory* (Minneapolis: University of Minnesota Press, 1986), 23.

25. Ibid., 23.

26. Northrop Frye, *Fearful Symmetry: A Study of William Blake* (Princeton: Princeton University Press, 1969), no pag.

27. See the editors' introduction to *American Literature's Aesthetic Dimensions*, ed. Cindy Weinstein and Christopher Looby (New York: Columbia University Press, 2012).

28. F. O. Matthiessen, *Henry James: The Major Phase* (New York: Oxford University Press, 1944), xiv.

29. While Said tacitly implies a distinction between, to put it baldly, good and bad literature, he cautions one to stay away from such overdetermined and discussed qualifications. Nonetheless, the following dictum might suggest how he would approach the question of value: "Texts that are inertly of their time stay there: those which brush up unstintingly against historical constraints are the ones we keep with us, generation after generation." See Said, *Freud and the Non-European* (London: Verso, 2003), 26–27.

30. John Carlos Rowe, "The Resistance to Cultural Studies," in *Aesthetics in a Multicultural Age*, ed. Emory Elliott, Louis Freitas Caton and Jeffrey Rhyne (Oxford: Oxford University Press, 2002), 112.

31. Said, *On Late Style: Music and Literature against the Grain* (New York: Vintage Books, 2007), 7.

32. Ibid., 148.

33. George Eliot, *Middlemarch*, 573.

CHAPTER 5

REVISITING SAID'S "SECULAR CRITICISM": ANARCHISM, ENABLING ETHICS, AND OPPOSITIONAL ETHICS

Darwin H. Tsen and Charlie Wesley

A decade after his departure, Edward Said still surprises us with his affiliative reach, and situating his complex body of work continues to pose a great challenge to scholars. Given the breadth and variability of his writings, critics have put him in a variety of camps: humanist, public intellectual, secular critic, Palestinian activist. In the words of Neil Lazarus, there has "always been an academic and intellectual struggle" over Said's significance, directed toward "the bearing of his work" and its "ideological, epistemological, and methodological commitments."[1] A recent example of this ever-changing contest in situating Said's *oeuvre* is William V. Spanos's fascinating but overwrought argument that Said's work can be read concomitantly with poststructuralism.[2] Despite such attempts to redefine Said, his work has resisted fitting snugly into any particular intellectual tradition. Recognizing this, Benita Parry notes that writings from the "middle period" of Said's career are "erudite, innovative, nonconformist and mutable."[3] It is our intention to chart yet a few more relatively unexplored zones of Said's complex intellectual map, yet we do so in the spirit of contributing to a complex whole, not to reduce Said to a set of easily identifiable characteristics. We acknowledge that Said's work and ideas changed over the course of his career, so we trace the dual axes of his method and ethics from *The World, the Text and the Critic* and *Orientalism* up to *Culture and Imperialism.*

While Said's work strongly gravitates toward Marxism, as noted by critics like Stephen Howe and E. San Juan Jr.,[4] we argue that this influence is only one strain of his dynamic and contextually situated *critical approach* and that "Secular Criticism" in particular, as well as a number of his other works, demonstrates an *oppositional ethics* that drives his criticism, alongside an *enabling ethics* that endeavors to realize potentiality. To Said, a method—be it poststructuralist, Marxist, or Anarchist—becomes an identity conflated with the force that drives one's intellectual/political projects, and therefore it must be avoided rigorously. Instead, what guides an intellectual enterprise and leads the critic to embrace various methods is a broad, underlying body of principles that comprise what could be called an ethical core.

Through elaborating how this ethics is embodied in Said's work, and taking seriously Aamir Mufti's suggestion that one must approach Said's work through the interlocking triad of the *secular*, the *exilic*, and the *critical*,[5] we want to suggest that Said can be reconsidered as a critic affiliated with the ethical concerns of the anarchist tradition. Said once stated in a 1992 interview, "I find myself to a certain degree in sympathy with Chomsky's position, a kind of anarcho-syndicalist position, which has great romantic appeal."[6] Anarchism, in the vein represented by figures like Noam Chomsky, is strongly concerned with how institutional structures limit, govern, create, or enable possibilities for its members. Finally, Said's ethics, in turns oppositional and enabling, helps us to better understand his complex and changing stances on the Palestinian issue.[7] What is at stake here is how Said's critique of institutionality exists alongside his various attitudes toward the state in its nationalist forms, including his advocacy for Palestinian self-determination.

We start by untangling the intertwining of methodology and ethics in an early milestone in Said's career, his influential essay "Secular Criticism." This essay, which opens *The World, the Text, and the Critic*, is a dense elaboration of his critical position, ethics, and methods alongside the contradictions of affiliation.[8] Critical of institutional politics and the conventions, orthodoxy, and dogma it tends to promote, Said's critical orientation in "Secular Criticism" posits the critical individual consciousness simultaneously within and against culture. "Secular Criticism" foregrounds an individual critic contending with cultural forces, an individual agent standing for its potentiality who also plays the gatekeeper of other possibilities. The latter term of the essay's title carries tremendous weight. "Criticism" is what Said calls "the individual consciousness placed at a sensitive nodal point"[9] between culture and system, between filiation and affiliation, central concepts he elaborates throughout *The World, The Text, and the Critic*.

The spatial metaphor at play in these terms demarcates the way Said links a critical and exilic position. "Secular criticism" is positioned as "an isolated voice out of place but very much of that place, standing consciously against the prevailing orthodoxy and very much for a professedly universal or humane set of values" (15). For Said, the space between what is already in the world and what the critic has the capacity to demarcate constitutes the very essence of criticism. This critic is not infallible; the possibility of this individual's cooptation is a major concern for Said, which is why his work evokes the *trahison des clercs*, warning against the danger of the "specialist" who promotes orthodoxy and clichés and who catalyzes the ossification of ideas. Said's critique of Matthew Arnold in the piece develops along these lines, stating that Arnold too formally established a hierarchy between culture, society, and the State, a structure Said dubs the "quasi-theological exterior order of the State" (11). The implicit role of the critic, then, is to elucidate these silences and recover excluded narratives—to "speak truth to power" in the famous formulation— and therefore to open up a space where new possibilities can be expressed. In other words, "Secular Criticism" outlines a rich collection of orientations that advocate the possibility of opposition while avoiding a programmatic or clearly defined methodology.

Reading Arnold critically, Said clarifies his own relationship to the concepts of culture and society, and points out the tendency of the former to rule over the latter. Said explains that Arnold designates "culture" as a hierarchical force that should be identified with the state, "insofar as culture is man's best self and the State its realization in material reality" (10). Noting that the Arnoldian concept of culture is not only "a system of discriminations and evaluations," but also "a system of exclusions" (11), Said's reading of Arnold understands culture as "combative" and represents "the assertively achieved and won hegemony of an identifiable set of ideas" (10). This is to say, Arnold views culture's opposite, "anarchy," as a potential alternative that did not become dominant, suffering from marginalization at the hands of its antagonist. Anarchy, for Arnold, is what culture's "stability" seeks to avoid. If anarchy stands for all that has been excluded and excised from the sphere of "culture," it thus occupies a position analogous to the "other," whose interactions, circumventions, and resistances against the pressures of Eurocentric "culture" all take center stage in

Said's subsequent work. It is in Said's later concerns that "anarchy" can be retroactively understood as a realm of possibility that the critic is ethically obliged to engage and disclose against the veil of power.

Returning to the context of "Secular Criticism," Said's evocation of Arnold at the beginning extends beyond the purview of merely an opportunity to define culture and anarchy as such. In fact, Said's reading of Arnold helps to problematize the question of culture's influence on the individual, what he calls "a system of values *saturating* downward almost everything within its purview" (9). Simultaneously, culture is not "available" to us, by which Said means it is hegemonically "invisible" in a way we consider it to be normal or given (9). Abdul JanMohamed reads this culture/anarchy dichotomy spatially, in that culture in this construction is "home," producing a "necessary sense of belonging" in contrast with Arnold's notion of "anarchy," which JanMohamed identifies as "defined negatively" with "homelessness" and therefore is (quoting Said) "the culturally disenfranchised, those elements opposed to culture and state."[10] From the position of geocriticism, Said's visual schemata posits an individual simultaneously enmeshed within a culture and a system and at the same time resistant to its orthodoxies and assumptions, creating the possibility of what he calls "distance" between the critic and his filiative and affiliative influences (15).

Here one can see how Said's formulation of culture against anarchy, as well as what JanMohamed calls the "enabling concept" of homelessness connected to "Raymond Williams's rearticulation of Gramsci," speaks to an exilic (individual) critical position that is resistant to institutional norms and the conformity it produces.[11] This does not mean, however, that Said advocates an absolute rejection of these influences. As his example of Auerbach makes clear in "Secular Criticism," Said points out that a latent and necessary filiation and affiliation are present in the great philologist's work, and were *productive* forces in forming his critical consciousness. Therefore, we read Said's understanding of filiation and affiliation as neither a rejection nor an all-encompassing embrace of culture or system. In this way Said begins to shape his complex relationship to institutional structures, communities of belief, and potentialities of resistance.

In the underappreciated essay "Criticism Between Culture and System," which builds on the productive tension between filiation and affiliation outlined in "Secular Criticism," Said states that "no one makes statements about a body of texts on an empty field" (181). Note again the spatial metaphor that Said relies on: he advocates unveiling the "inscribed terrain" on which criticism relies (181).

Critiquing the "assumed consensus" inherent to a field of discourse, Said advocates an individual position that seeks to highlight and critique this consensus while seeing oneself as inexplicably immersed within it, as opposed to sitting above or outside it, and he codes this self-critical position as a component of his critical approach (180).[12] The inscribed space of criticism thus acts as the methodological hinge that gives way to a critical awareness; what is produced by the spatial metaphor is a clearer vision of the ethical grounding that should undergird one's inquiries, precisely because, not in spite of, one's worldliness. Here one senses resonances with the resistance to methodology and systematization palpable in Said's "Secular Criticism."

Yet the spatial position of the margin, linked as it is with the position that one must maintain an "exilic" attitude in contrast to the mainstream, can itself become a rigid critical attitude. Said suggests in *Representations of the Intellectual* that even an attitude of nonalignment can become a comfortable affiliation. He writes, "that state of in-betweenness can itself become a rigid ideological position, a sort of dwelling whose falseness is covered over in time, and to which one can all too easily become accustomed."[13] Said's work suggests a critical attitude toward oneself, what Abdul JanMohamed identifies as the "self-reflexivity" of criticism,[14] while at the same time affirming the possibility of working within or in conjunction with filiative or affiliative positions. Said finds further confirmation of this textual attitude in Theodore Adorno's *Minima Moralia*, which he describes as "dodging both the old and the new with equal dexterity" in terms of structure as well as content.[15]

Given the centrality of "Secular Criticism" as a text establishing the major motifs orienting Said's critical work, we now turn to examine a problem of his critical position. More precisely, we want to outline the tension between a critical individual consciousness and the possibility of collective action, the latter being the foundation of historical change.[16] This is a question so severe in its urgency that Said perceives it to be the major lacuna in Michel Foucault's work, resulting in a serious inability to "deal with, or provide an account of, historical change" (188).[17] Said attempts to work through this issue by foregrounding the individual as a figure aware of the "collective whole" and larger contexts, who then utilizes criticism as the opportunity to register not merely a filiative or affiliative validation of what already is, but also elucidate a different, perhaps even new, way of seeing (15). This very complex set of distinctions open up some unresolved questions about Said's work, in particular the way in which he shifts quickly at times between the individual and the collective: for example, should individual criticism, then, always be conducted before solidarity with the group? And does Said's continual shifting between individual and collective in "Secular Criticism" chart a complex relationship between the two, or even attempt to blur such a distinction?

Given the relationship between action and knowledge, Giambattista Vico is a key interloper in this issue. Said relies on Vico's ideas to present his conception of secular knowledge, which states that since the world is made by human beings, it is knowable, and therefore what human beings make can be grasped by the human intellect. The identity of the subject who endeavors and enacts such "grasping" is not at all clear, teetering between the individual and the collective. A passage from "Traveling Theory" helps us to demonstrate this dilemma:

> When instead of inexplicable shortage of bread you can imagine the human work and, subsequently, the human beings who produced the bread but are no longer doing so because there is a bakers' strike, you are well on your way to knowing that crisis is comprehensible because process is comprehensible; and if process is comprehensible, so too is *some sense* of the social world created by human labor.
>
> (232, our emphasis)

The use of "some sense" demarcates the limits of Said's idealized vision of human beings as agents who can know what they make, tempering the teleological drive that humans are fully in control of the history they shape. More uncertainty is present. Human work, taking form in the hidden social relationships that produce the bread, is "imagined," not ascertained; the apprehender of this phenomenon is "well on the way," but not exactly on track to knowing. The larger implication of our critique of Said's work is that it is unclear whether the actor who knows or produces a "critical consciousness" is individualistic or collective.

The critical consciousness promoted by Said seems to be embodied by a group who have taken collective action (the bakers), rather than a specific critic or individual. And yet the figure that Said has been describing in "Secular Criticism" has been primarily an individual, or rather, a critical consciousness that attempts to distance itself from collective formations that too easily coagulate. The second-person pronoun "you," addressed to the singular reader twice in the passage above, strengthens the notion that the individual is where the critical consciousness begins. Because the "individual mind registers and is very much aware of the collective whole" and is not "naturally and easily a mere child of the culture, but a historical and social actor in it," the individual acts in a semiautonomous fashion, while also constrained by its being-in-the-world (15). For Said this works as a flawed, but fundamental, standpoint; you cannot think about the collective without beginning by acknowledging your own place within it. And that place is knee deep in the bogs of history, confined by the prison of one's consciousness.

This makes for an interesting problem when thinking about Said's work: namely, at what moments does individual consciousness inform collective action, and how are collective movements possible when they involve a certain amount of acquiescence and orthodoxy that Said's position is critical of? In other words, in what ways does one cultivate a critical consciousness and participate in collective action while being sure that one does not subsume or cannibalize the other? How can criticism *synergize* with solidarity, instead of coming into conflict with it? These questions are left open by Said himself, and they form sites upon which his critics and supporters quickly converge.[18] E. San Juan Jr, who (we think, wrongly) accuses Said of being the herald of a "neoliberal" humanism, believes that Said's inability to think through the dynamics between individuals and groups in history stems from his neglect of "the category of a differentiated and dynamic totality that underlies historical development, the principle of a Marxist critique of imperialism."[19] In contrast to San Juan's identitarian claims, Neil Lazarus approaches the question more fruitfully by noting that it appears "strange that [Said] seems not even to entertain the idea that criticism and solidarity might coexist." Lazarus observes that in many places of Said's writing, the distance between loyalty and unquestioning solidarity "seems so narrow as to disappear altogether, and with it the possibility of solidaristic critical practice."[20] Where does this tendency stem from?

Said's severe disagreements with the Palestinian Liberation Organization's Yasser Arafat, documented in *The Question of Palestine*, reveal why, especially in the face of collective crisis and displacement, the urgency of an individual's criticism cannot be discounted, and perhaps partially explains Said's qualms regarding "solidarity."[21] The imperative for exiles to place solidarity before criticism can also be inferred from "The Mind of Winter," a 1984 essay he penned for *Harper's Magazine* (and later rewritten as "Reflections on Exile" in the collection of the same name), when he laments that the exile is pressured to join "parties, national movements, the state. The exile is offered a new set of affiliations and develops new loyalties. But there is also a loss—of critical perspective, of intellectual reserve, of moral courage."[22] In accordance with Lazarus's criticism that the line between loyalty and servility for Said is too thin, we see the language quickly shift from the exile's "new set of affiliations" and "new loyalties" to the forfeiture of "critical perspective," "intellectual reserve," and more severely "moral courage." Thus, in the mind of Said the activist-intellectual, subsumption and cannibalization always seem to come from the side of the collective, the majority encroaching upon the individual.

As a way of addressing this problem, the first thing we can say is that Said's ideas about human understanding does not claim unmediated access to the world and its complexity, and therefore abstraction becomes a necessary component of knowledge. "Classes are not real the way trees and houses are real," Said writes in *The World, the Text, and the Critic*; "they are imputable by consciousness, using its powers to posit ideal types in which with other beings it finds itself" (233). In his reading of Lukács, another one of Said's key interlocutors when considering these issues, "consciousness [had the capacity to claim] its theoretical right to posit a better world outside the world of simple objects" (234). Said says that for Lukács, this better world is not "attainable without the transformation of passive, contemplative consciousness into active, critical consciousness" (232). It seems undeniable now that the individual has always been the starting point of critical work for Said. The individual is cognizant of his/her collective situation, but it is from that awareness that critical consciousness begins, and it is in this methodical manner that Said's work fits perfectly with Marxism. Agreeing with Lukács's view that the critical individual is a necessary precondition for positive collective action, Said suggests that "class consciousness therefore begins in critical consciousness" (233). Said's notion that potentially revolutionary collective knowledge gets its start in a critical (independent, individual) position suggests affiliation between "secular criticism" and the Marxist project, even while Said continued to reject "doing Marxism" or calling himself a "Marxist."[23] Nor does Said embody the abstract nature of Lukács's theorization of this relationship (233). As we have already suggested, it is tempting to affiliate Said with Marxism as both a political ideology and a theoretical apparatus, but he is ever resistant to totalizing labels and systems, stressing instead the oppositional ethos of secular criticism.

So far we've examined Said's oppositional positioning against Arnold in "Secular Criticism," his reliance on spatial metaphors to outline a critical position and the ethical charge embodied within them, and the unresolved dynamic between the critical individual and solidaristic collective. With each case it becomes a little clearer how the influence of Gramsci, Lukács, and Adorno helps Said find the methodological language to articulate his overall ethical thrust. As Stathis Gourgouris exclaims, these three are the "twentieth-century figures with whom Said remains consistently in dialogue [. . .] but they are distinct insofar as they preside over the *methodological* coordinates of the task of secular criticism, which Said's work conducts in such uncompromising fashion."[24] Out of the three, it is perhaps Gramsci who leaves the most visible mark on Said.

In an interview entitled "Overlapping Territories," Said discusses how Gramsci's conception of history maintains a critical distance from a linear teleology that typifies modernity's "traditional" conceptions of historical agency. At the same time, Said sees in these formations the possibility of human potential—in collective formations—to shape history. He states,

> the Gramscian conception of history, which is essentially geographical and territorial, a history made up of several overlapping terrains, so that society is viewed as a territory in which a number of movements are occurring. The vision of overlapping and contested terrains is to me a more interesting view of history than the [early Marxist] one going back to a *fons et origo*—a miraculous, originating point. Given that, it becomes possible to see engagement in the historical process as in fact a collective struggle—not a struggle to be won by an individual subject trying to grasp the whole of history in all of its complexity, as Dilthey tried to do, but a collective struggle in which various interests interact over particular sites of intensity and contested domains.[25]

Despite the tendency of some critics to identify Said's emphasis on collective struggle with Marxist traditions, Said's focus on a "number of movements" demonstrates a concern with heterogeneous ("various interests and contested domains"), and therefore *horizontal*, forms of struggle. Said's conception of the secular—and secular criticism—is far more than a theoretical application or a naive notion that a single human being can alter the world. Collective movements often face the all-too-real possibility of failure. The Marxist strain that exists in Said's critical project, while it does help us to clarify the potentialities of structural affiliation with regard to collective resistance, not to mention the productive possibilities of certain institutional movements, fails to fully accommodate the complexities of Said's critical project that we began with, namely a position between "culture and system," critical of both filiation and affiliation but not necessarily opposed to it.

We have mapped Said's intellectual terrain with a number of ideas, such as culture, criticism, space, and the dynamics between the individual and the collective. The relationships among these terms gain a newfound clarity if we observe them from the viewpoints of the methodological and the ethical, two major axes in Said's work. It helps to imagine that on the one hand, the ideas of the various thinkers Said engages with and employs in his work construct a methodological framework, while on the other, the ethical functions as fuel, catalyzing the resistant, anti-systematic energy burning within secular criticism. In this formulation filiation and affiliation collide, converge, and exist in a dialectical relationship that exists in continual tension, never arriving at a comfortable synthesis.

Said showed us that Arnold's formulation of "culture" stood for an orthodox system of dominant intellectual practices and methods, which he refused to be identified with and instead showed an ethics that sides with the marginal and the oppressed. Regarding the centrality of space in his work, Said adopts Gramsci's eye for the uneven development of cultural and political economies, as well as his insistence on how locale and geography makes an intellectual. Expanding these analytical frameworks to discuss how European imperialism exerted itself on cultures globally, Said nonetheless does not share Gramsci's belief that the organic quality of the intellectual is primarily expressed through class affiliations. Similarly, unlike Lukács, with whom Said finds an affirmation of the need for a critical individual consciousness, Said does not endorse the notion that such individuals should group together and become the vanguard of a social movement, one that will revolutionize society and place these intellectuals at its forefront. His reading of Adorno extends this critique, emphasizing a ruthlessly self-critical stance. Considering Adorno's *Minima Moralia* as the essential exilic text, Said's reading emphasizes the self-conscious individual who avoids the "slackening of rigor in self-analysis."[26] This movement from collective to individual and back again is indicative of Said's shifting geographical and political affiliations, always contextual, intuitive, and urgent in their immediacy.

Said places the utmost importance on one's capacity to recognize the substantial difference between intellectual and political projects. This is why he declares in an interview after the publication of *Beginnings*, that the "doing of Marxist literary analysis alone cannot constitute the basis of a political program in the great world [...] to turn a literary or intellectual project immediately into a political one is to try to do something quite undialectical."[27] From here we can see why Said's affiliation with the methodological arsenal of these figures stops just short of embracing their political conclusions.[28] Against the confining choices of culture or system, Said's solution in "Secular Criticism" consists of configuring criticism along an ethical line, whose oppositional character is "reducible neither to a doctrine nor a political position [. . .] and if it is to be in the world and self-aware simultaneously, then its identity is its difference from other cultural activities and from systems of thought or of method" (29). As a practice that is defined by being against authority, Said's secular criticism is primarily characterized and driven by its ethics, not its methods. This is precisely what we mean by an *oppositional ethics*: the underlying ethos of his criticism is suffused with a "self-aware" attitude that is characterized by its "difference" with "doctrine" and its nonconformity to "political positions."[29] Gourgouris comes closest to our articulation of such an ethics, as he expresses that the "meaning of *secular* in the term *secular criticism* does not designate an ensemble of properties—to be therefore enacted in the critical practice—but characterizes the substance of the critical act itself."[30] The practice of criticism is modified by the secular attitude, which draws from multiple methodological sources to accomplish its goals, as long as it continues to be ethically oppositional. The other face, its critical force, is an *enabling ethics* working to create potential and enlarge horizons; construction must begin with a thorough dismantling. Thus for Said, ethics, which forms the core of one's politics, should not be easily conflated with the political orientation of one's methodological referents, taken and transplanted from another time and place with their own specific concerns. Doing so would risk vacating history, and distort the shape of one's own worldliness.

To illuminate how the ethical dimension of Said's criticism connects him to the anarchist tradition, as well as the role it plays in his approach to the Israel–Palestine issue, we must turn to his relationship with the institution known as the state, and in extension, nationalism. Throughout his work, Said never treated literature and culture as something embodying, in the words of Pheng Cheah, "humanity's freedom from the given."[31] Said posits that every cultural artifact is situated within a historical context, and fully acknowledges the social, political, and epistemological constraints placed upon them. For Said the term "worldly" precisely functions as a multivalent concept signifying the inextricable quality of texts from the messy entanglements of history. The nation-state, as the most powerful modern institution governing sovereignty and belonging, is one such "given" that exerts tremendous pressure upon texts and its authors. In *Orientalism*, Said shows us how even Louis Massignon, an eclectic scholar highly sympathetic to the East, could not "resist the pressures on him of his nation or of the scholarly tradition in which he works."[32] By the twentieth century, the weight of the Orientalist system, coupled with the imperatives of the nation-state, has become so immense that "[t]o write about the Arab Oriental world [...] is to write with the authority of the nation [...] with the unquestioning certainty of absolute truth backed by absolute force."[33] The nation-state is the exceptional sovereign, possessing, exercising, and embodying unquestionable authority over the production of intellectual discourse; from *Orientalism* onwards, Said never loses focus on the state and its hegemony. In "The Mind of Winter," Said critiques the "worship" of the state grounded in a longing for rootedness, writing that "statism" is "one of the most insidious" because it "tends to supplant all other human bonds."[34] Not only does the spatial politics of Said's "exilic" position return here, but this idea links up with his secular concern about unthinking adherence to a collective group whose beneficent facade masks an oppressive exclusion that severs meaningful connections with other human beings.

In the examples above, the nation-state is primarily depicted by Said as a hegemonic power. While the subject of these sentences obviously comprised *imperialist* nation-states, Said does not give significant leeway to Palestinian nationalism either. In the afterword written 16 years after the publication of *Orientalism*, Said declares that he "expressed all sorts of reservations about the insouciant nativism and militant militarism of the nationalist consensus."[35] Unambiguously, he compares unmitigated nationalist fervor to the urge for "domination and control also to be found in imperialism."[36] His critiques of nationalism, of course, has drawn many critics of its own. In a now familiar polemic on Said's work, Aijaz Ahmad criticizes Said's statements as inconsistent: "the most sweeping statements about 'nation' and 'state' as 'coercive identities' are frequently delivered alongside resounding affirmations of national liberation, of the Palestinian *intifada* in particular."[37] Surely one could say that "inconsistency" is at the center of Ahmad's critique of Said. Ahmad sees the juxtaposition of Julien Benda with Antonio Gramsci and the paradoxical cohabitation of Auerbachean high humanism with Foucauldian genealogy as examples of Said's sloppiness, betraying an inability to respect the austere borders of historical specificity. Such criticisms are easily met with their reverse arguments. Nadia Abu El-Haj counters that we need not see such features as inconsistency, but as a sign of Said's intellectual maturity, who "drew on different theorists to do very specific intellectual and political work."[38] Rather than judging Said's textual attitudes according to the criterion of consistency, we think that his various and sometimes contradictory positions can be better understood through the ethics informing his work, and that again, one important tenet of secular criticism is precisely its eschewal of methodological "consistency" in favor of continuously challenging, engaging, and revising supposedly dominant values.

Part of the confusion over Said's consistency comes from our conventional image of him. Most of us know what Said is up against as an intellectual, but we're not quite sure what alternatives he supports. Exploring Said's work through his ethics provides the distinct advantage of seeing that the very institutions, orthodoxies, and ideas he critiques were at times historical actors that should have, in their supposed intentions enabled more possibilities, but instead foreclosed them. This is why Said's outlooks on nationalism and the nation-state vary in their contexts: he recognizes that nationalism, especially the anticolonial type that emerged in the twentieth century, has the potential to be a productive, liberating force, but pulls no punches when criticizing other versions of nationalism, namely the various separatist ethnonationalisms, fundamentalist Islam, and ideologies espoused by corrupt postcolonial regimes. This divergent attitude corresponds to the two faces of Said's ethics: one oppositional, the other enabling. As we have attempted to show, the oppositional aspect fights against anything that aims to minimize human agency, pleasure, and possibilities. Now we turn to examining what we call an enabling ethics.

The enabling face of Said's ethics is an important component of his humanism. As Rokus de Groot observes, this ethics is in support of "alternatives, always with room for dissent, ultimately geared to further human (rational) enlightenment and liberty."[39] Modifiers such as "room" and verbs like "further" emphasize the desire to expand and deepen enlightenment and democracy, to draw out and realize such potential. Such ethics favoring the enlargement of horizons is evident in *Culture and Imperialism*, where Said shows support for the unfinished project of enlightenment modernity by saying that "narratives of emancipation and enlightenment in their strongest form were also narratives of *integration* not separation."[40] The two nouns "integration" and "separation," both abstract conditions, indicate that what is emphasized here are the ends of cultural politics, not the specific procedures or forms it occurs through. For Said, it doesn't matter whether the processes happen under the nation-state or the commune, as long as it enables its participants to do more than they could before.

To be in favor of human potentiality, one must know the actually existing constraints set upon them. Said sees such historical shackles embodied in the negative forms of what we call "institutionality." Gauri Viswanathan's comments in her introduction to *Power, Politics, and Culture* are helpful in explaining it: "Said's driving interest is in how systems and institutions come into being, how they acquire the force they do, and what new forms of thought and representation they stabilize through their discursive power."[41] So in addition to his investment in humanism, the secular, and the relationship between literary form and politics, Said, as Viswanathan describes, is an examiner of institutionality. An analogue to what we call "institutionality" here, in Said's own word, would be "system." What Said's oppositional and enabling ethics sets itself up against are institutions that cripple human potential, that amplify and reproduce the worst in humanity. This critique does not pertain to any and every institution, but the shifting, contextual *qualities* of the institutions that perpetuate such tendencies. Institutionality can thus be seen as a set of practices originating from an institution that are replicated, transplanted, or implemented in other institutions or sectors of society; these techniques have a self-sustaining and self-reproducing tendency that does not preclude internal change or the possibility of collapse; institutionality also encompasses the resistances and reactions to such practices by individuals and collectives. These practices are akin to what Michel de Certeau calls "tactics," subterranean navigations invented to subvert everyday life; institutionality operates much like hegemony, it exercises power upon and seeks consent from those involved in the process.[42] What Said's enabling ethics would open to us, in the face of institutionality, is a choice to refuse "the wish to dominate, the capacity to damn," and to vitalize the "energy to comprehend and engage with other societies, traditions, histories."[43]

Said's refusal to let institutional parameters drown out human development aligns his position with some core tenets of anarchism, which can be found in the term's roots. Consider what is meant by "an-arch": a fundamental ambiguity resides in anarchism's very lack of an *arkhē* (in English, *arche* refers to a commencement of things, or and organizing principle).[44] If there can be no *arkhē*, what sort of positive structure shall take the place of the institutionality removed by the negative work of anarchism? This is the question of anarchism approached on a purely philosophical level; the political tradition of anarchism certainly shows otherwise as it is active in creating new, horizontal institutions in practice.[45] That is to say within anarchism there coexists, in a tense but productive manner, a perpetual desire to dismantle existing institutions and a drive to build new ones in their place. Viewed this way, Said's relentless critique of institutions and his aim to open and expand possibilities of knowledge closely resembles the anarchic impulse we've defined here.

But what kind of anarchism does Said's thought resonate the most with? It is with Noam Chomsky, the anarcho-syndicalist, that Said's oppositional and enabling ethics find their closest affiliation. Anarcho-syndicalism's goals, as Chomsky explains in the collection of essays titled *Chomsky on Anarchism*, are geared towards the practical goal of forming "free associations of free producers" under capitalism, and ultimately to "take over the organization of production on a democratic basis."[46] Its emphasis is therefore not on individual freedom—the focus of other anarchist strains—but the possibility of incubating new organizations and institutions that function more democratically than those of the past.

This approach toward institutionality is deeply attractive to Said, who does not conceal his admiration for Chomsky. During a 1987 interview with Imre Salusinszky, Said praises Chomsky for his "intellectual commitment," "relentless erudition," and most of all, "his capacity for not being put off by professionalism of any sort [...] have really encouraged me and a lot of other people not to be defused and put off by disciplinary barriers."[47] For Chomsky the sentiments are mutual. In an interview with Chomsky by Adel Iskandar after Said's passing, Iskander mentioned to Chomsky how Said once expressed sympathy with this anarcho-syndicalist position. Chomsky, unsurprised by this statement but not seeing a direct connection, ultimately cannot "recall anything specific in his writings that would point in that direction." This is not a testimony to Chomsky's unfamiliarity with Said's work. Nor would it have mattered if Chomsky knew that in 1973, Said wrote an article titled "United States Policy and the Conflict of Powers in the Middle East," a piece of political criticism quite similar to his own in terms of style, argument, and target audience. To be fair, Chomsky does identify their projects as affiliated along the lines of a "sense of justice and fairness that permeated [Said's] approach to human affairs."[48] This exchange again hints at the dense, multiple layers over which Said envelopes his influences and affiliations within his thought.

Those layers are not so easily peeled back. While Said does not consider himself an anarchist or engage canonical anarchist thinkers like Mikhail Bakunin, Peter Kropotkin, Joseph-Pierre Proudhon, or Emma Goldman—such absences elicit Chomsky's doubts about the possibility of Said's own anarchism—Said's emphasis on humanism, pleasure, and inclusion all directly or indirectly echo anarchist concerns with the proliferation of potentiality within and without institutional parameters. In an article titled "The Relevance of Anarcho-Syndicalism," Chomsky further details the enabling work that anarcho-syndicalism sets out to do: "its purpose is to create institutions which will contribute to that transformation in the nature of work, the nature of creative activity, simply in social bonds among people, and through this interaction of creating institutions which permit new aspects of human nature to flourish."[49] It is through the willed creation of new institutions that mediate human relationships, work, and creativity differently from the authoritarian, capitalist, and plutocratic present, that unseen potential within us may blossom. Such idealistic yet practical goals are one way to articulate the potential Said's enabling ethics anticipates. And Said's unwavering stance as a "humanist" throughout the years of poststructuralist and postmodern theoretical dominance in the humanities finds an ally in Chomsky, who turns out to be a fellow radical humanist. Unambiguously, Chomsky writes in "Notes on Anarchism" that "it is libertarian socialism [or anarchism] that has preserved and extended the radical humanist message of the Enlightenment and the classical liberal ideals that were perverted into an ideology to sustain the emerging social order."[50] One is unmistakably reminded of Said's insistence, through the enabling ethics of his humanism, on realizing the philosophical goals of the Enlightenment, despite its political catastrophes; again we see the deep affiliations between socialisms (of both Marxist and anarchist varieties) and humanism.

Not only does the enabling face of Said's ethics dovetail with Chomsky's anarchic concerns, secular criticism's oppositional ethics is also highly compatible. Recalling our earlier discussion of Matthew Arnold in "Secular Criticism," it is obvious that Said's and Arnold's sympathies sit at two extremes: there is on the one hand Arnold, who celebrates the high "culture" of the state, and on the other Said, who aligns himself with the expunged others/"anarchy." What secular criticism—with its basic assumption that worldly, historical structures are constructed hence understandable by humans—allows Said to do here is make Arnold's "culture" reveal itself as not *natural*, but as something that can only be established by, in the words of Aamir Mufti, "rendering *certain* cultural practices, *certain* institutions, *certain* ethical positions representative of 'the people' as such."[51] The secular is therefore an attitude that compels the filiative, the natural, and the hallowed to acknowledge their concretely *historical* character. Relating this back to anarchism: secular criticism's charge against "culture" and/or authority is thus identical to Chomsky's conviction that "the burden of proof has to be placed on authority, and that it should be dismantled if that burden cannot be met," a guideline succinctly defined as the core of his anarchist principles.[52]

The thorny term "principles" introduces a new question: that of belief. As a political ideology, to what degree do the beliefs and conventional goals of anarchism (and anarcho-syndicalism) affect its ethics and praxis? Recalling the dialectical tug-of-war between method and ethic and between political convictions and historical immediacy in Said's work, Chomsky exhibits an ethics strikingly similar to Said. Addressing the issue of the state, the "outer limits" of anarchism in the key essay "Goals and Visions," Chomsky confirms his agreement that "the anarchist vision, in almost every variety, has looked forward to the dismantling of state power," although it also "runs directly counter to [his] goals."[53] These goals involve "[defending] and even [strengthening] elements of state authority which, though illegitimate in fundamental ways, are critically necessary right now to impede the dedicated efforts to 'roll back' the progress that has been achieved in extending democracy and human rights."[54] The elements of state authority Chomsky opts to fortify are clearly welfare systems, basic labor rights, and institutions that have the capacity to enlarge and extend rights to all. This fascinating passage reveals a key tension between goals and visions in Chomsky's anarchism: goals, constituted by the more pressing, historical avenues of struggle, should *not* conform to the convictions of yet-to-be realized visions. Noting once again Said's insistence that "narratives of emancipation and enlightenment in their strongest form were also narratives of *integration* not separation,"[55] for Chomsky, the eight-hour working day, socialized medicine, and other fragile welfare systems are exactly the result of an *integrative* process that incorporated the historical struggles of workers, women, and other oppressed minorities. Agreeing to the dismantling of such forms of state authority as a mark of fidelity to anti-statism, in Arnoldian parlance, is to identify with the orthodox "culture" of anarchism that impels one to place its long-term vision ahead of defending actually existing, enabling institutions.[56] In short, Chomsky's anarchism does not subscribe to a politics of belief, one that demands faith against historical needs; its willingness to embrace goals that contradict its ideological convictions reveals an ethics not unlike the oppositional and enabling ethics of Said.

Alert toward systematic methods and the beliefs they endorse, Said and Chomsky share an ethical orientation that is both critical and positive. Their intellectual tasks, besides critically unmasking the historical quality of authority, aim to discern (and, at times, to promote and create) the enabling qualities within institutions. Returning to the context of literary studies and the Palestinian issue, Said once wrote in *Orientalism* that "perhaps the most important task of all would be to undertake studies in contemporary alternatives to Orientalism, to ask how one can study either cultures and peoples from a libertarian, or a non-repressive and nonmanipulative perspective."[57] In this regard, the idea of national literatures presupposes for Said an organization, canonization, and manipulation by the nation-state, hence not quite forming an alternative to the ruthless institutionality of orientalism.[58] For Said, unchecked nationalism can be nothing more than a fetish and idol of the tribe, enclosed within a cave. And yet nationalism was one means by which Said envisioned Palestinian liberation, as many anticolonial movements throughout history have been explicitly nationalist in their formation and goals. This returns us to Said's complex views on the question of Palestine throughout his career and his life. If we view Said's multiple attitude shifts on the issue of Palestinian statehood through his enabling ethics, the seeming inconsistencies between his critical attitude toward nationalism and his endorsement of a Palestinian state can be dismantled; more concretely, we can see Said's shift from a two-state solution in the 1980s to a one-state solution in the late 1990s not as a break, but as the continual development of his understanding of the situation.

In a telling 1992 interview with Jennifer Wicke and Michael Sprinker published in *Edward Said: A Critical Reader*, taking cues from Frantz Fanon, Said draws a difference between the idea of liberation and the goal of independence for Palestinians.[59] He questions how much of the goals of "liberation" will be abandoned by the nationalist consensus' decision to make "independence" the main goal of the Palestinian struggle. This distinction is closely related to Said's caution toward the question of representation in identity politics. In an earlier conversation with Bruce Robbins in 1988, Robbins asked Said what he thought about employing "strategic essentialisms" in social struggles. Said answered that while the right to self-representation is important, but "unless they are linked, on the other hand, to a wider practice which I would call liberation, beyond national independence—liberation that would include attacking the question of the relationships between classes, between other 'tribes' if you like—then I'm totally against it."[60] Differing qualitatively from independence, liberation hints at changing the relationship between one party and others on many fundamental levels. By liberation, Said concretely refers to the wholesale transformation of the Palestinian–Jewish relationship not only within Israel but also abroad, in the Palestinian diasporas of other Middle Eastern countries. Independence and the establishment of a nation-state for Palestinians is but a means to that end. This refusal to confine the Palestinian struggle within the boundaries of Israel precisely pinpoints the dimensions of Said's thought that Lazarus neatly characterizes as "nationalitarian."[61]. Such tendencies are evinced earlier in an adversarial interview conducted in 1986, when a reporter questioned whether the object of Said's desire was two independent states: "Independent or connected; not hermetically sealed, I wouldn't have thought."[62] Palestinian liberation must be premised on the ground of connectivity and dialogue with the Israeli Jews, with inclusive rather than exclusionary conditions. Two independent states being in constant war does not solve the problem in Said's eyes.

This is why, ultimately, in another interview in 1999, Said boldly comes out in support of a one-state solution. Referring to the further penetration into Gaza and the West Bank by Israeli settlers, Said says: "[b]y their own aggressive zeal, the settler movement and the Israeli government have in fact involved themselves so deeply in Palestinian life that in my opinion there is no separation between them [. . .] the only conclusion to be drawn from this is to devise a means where the two peoples can live together in one nation as equals—not as master and slave, which is the current situation."[63] These historical developments, despite their violence, oppression, and horror, have nonetheless brought two peoples into closer contact with one another. As Gourgouris comments, we cannot avert our eyes to the fact that the "coexistence of the two peoples has become historically insurmountable" both "politically and theoretically": to insist on separation now would be to recuperate the logic of partition, that poisonous legacy left by the British empire.[64] To Said, the path of liberation is the one that can bring both Palestinians and Jews a more auspicious future, one brimming with potential, as well as with untold challenges. The coexistence, the compulsion of living face-to-face as equals in a one-state solution, is thus entirely consistent with Said's ethics. It is an act of secular criticism *par excellence*: Said calls out the logic of partition slithering within the two-state solution at a time when it is almost accepted as natural, authoritative, and perhaps sacred, by many.

Perceived from his anarchist affiliations and ethics of enablement, Said's "inconsistencies" toward the nation-state and the Palestinian struggle are revealed as illusions, mere appearances. What these affiliations concretely show is that Said's goal was to understand the functioning of institutionality and to combat it with an enabling ethos that valued unseen human potential. A particular task of Saidian criticism, here, is to cultivate and make apparent the underlying intelligence of any institutional formation through an oppositional ethos, followed by imagining what further intellectual, educational, and pleasurable valences may be generated by breaking down its barriers. The way we see it, this task and its ethics contains an unmistakably anarchic, transformational thrust that, despite the pessimism of the present moment, nevertheless dedicates itself to enlarging the possibilities for an uncharted future.

It should be clear by now that we do not think that Said's entanglements with nationalism, the nation-state, and the Palestinian cause, are best examined through its relationship to particular bodies of thought (e.g., Marxism, poststructuralism). Nor is it enough to evaluate Said's own intellectual terminology and legacy on that basis. By laying such entanglements along the axes of methodology and ethics, we see with heightened clarity that Said's political, methodological, and intellectual practices are primarily motivated by his ethics, which is by turns oppositional and enabling. Secular criticism, fueled by these ethics, settles with no methodology; it is an ever-evolving practice.

The Anarchist and Marxist affiliations that surround Said's body of writing hint at new possibilities and as-yet-unexplored avenues of thought within Said studies. The resonance between Said's ethics and Chomsky's anarcho-syndicalism that we have identified suggests the new and multifaceted ways analyses of Said can continue to develop. While the motifs of exile, marginality, orientalism, and contrapuntal critique will remain central to appraisals of Said's work, perhaps it is time for studies of Said to move beyond these canonized and ossified constructions, and instead seek, in the spirit of his critique, fresh directions that can complicate and expand the geographical terrain of his work. In particular, the geocritical modes of inquiry that maintain Said's insistence on the importance of space in the shaping of history and subjectivity may provide exciting new mappings of literary, political, and cultural landscapes we once thought familiar.

NOTES

1. Neil Lazarus, "Representations of the Intellectual in 'Representations of the Intellectual,'" *Research in African Literatures* 36.3 (2005), 112–113.
2. See William V. Spanos, *The Legacy of Edward W. Said* (Urbana and Chicago: University of Illinois Press, 2009).

3. Benita Parry, "Countercurrent and Tensions in Said's Critical Practice," in *Edward Said: A Legacy of Emancipation and Representation*, ed. Adel Iskandar and Hakem Rustom (Berkeley: University of California Press, 2010), 499.

4. See Stephen Howe, "Said and Marxism Anxieties of Influence," *Cultural Critique* 67 (2007), 50–87; see also E. San Juan Jr., "Edward Said's Affiliations," *Atlantic Studies* 3.1. (2006), 43–61.

5. Aamir R. Mufti, "Why I Am Not a Postsecularist," *boundary 2* 40.1 (2013), 18.

6. Edward W. Said, *Power, Politics, and Culture: Interviews With Edward W. Said* (New York: Vintage, 2001), 161.

7. Noam Chomsky stated that Said was in favor of the two-state solution and then embraced the one-state solution "a couple of years after the collapse of Oslo." See Chomsky, "The Incalculable Loss," in *Edward Said: A Legacy of Emancipation and Representation*, ed. Adel Iskandar and Hakem Rustom (Berkeley: University of California Press, 2010), 384.

8. Historicizing Said's position in the American academy, critics like Timothy Brennan have suggested reading *The World, the Text, and the Critic* as a text that "localized *Orientalism*'s themes, although now in the form of a collection of essays on problems of literary theory, the politics of the university, and the 'treason' of the intellectuals working in the United States." See Brennan, *Wars of Position: The Cultural Politics of the Left and Right* (New York: Columbia Press, 2006), 95.

9. Said, "Secular Criticism," *The World, the Text, and the Critic* (Cambridge, MA: Harvard University Press, 1983), 15. Reference to this essay and others in *The World, the Text, and the Critic* hereinafter cited by page number in the text.

10. Abdul R. JanMohamed, "Worldliness-Without-World, Homelessness-as-Home: Toward a Definition of the Specular Border Intellectual," in *Edward Said: A Critical Reader*, ed. Michael Sprinker (Cambridge: Blackwell Publishers, 1992), 110.

11. Ibid.

12. One notes Said's own filiation in this formulation, and he states in his memoir *Out of Place* that he grew up "living in colonial Cairo as members of a Christian minority within a large pond of minorities." Here Said's *critical* position that is "secular" in its nonalignment is filiative with his geographic sense of positionality (in Cairo) as well as his social experience as part of a Christian religious minority. See Said, *Out of Place: A Memoir* (New York: Vintage, 2000), 19.

13. Said, *Representations of the Intellectual* (New York: Vintage, 1994), 58.

14. JanMohamed,   "Worldliness-Without-World,   Homelessness-as-Home," 111.

15. Said, *Representations of the Intellectual*, 56.

16. This tension can also be detected within the themes of Said's later work such as *Orientalism*, as it manifests itself between individual authors and the larger Orientalist system they form. Nadia Abu El-Haj notes that Said "has differential respect for different Orientalist scholars and writers, recognizing the particular 'creativity' of specific figures over others, the more sympathetic engagement with the East by some Orientalists than by others." The pressures exerted upon these more "sympathetic" and "engaging" individuals by the collective discourse of Orientalism nevertheless keeps them from truly breaking free of the mold. See El-Haj, "Edward Said and the Political Present," *American Ethnologist* 32.4 (2005), 543.

17. For a succinct account of Said's entanglements with Foucault, see Yumna Siddiqi, "Edward Said, Humanism, and Secular Criticism," *Alif: Journal of Comparative Poetics* 25 (2005), 74–76. Stephen Howe notes that Said's turning away from Foucault is ultimately a "turn to history, both in the sense that narratives of historical change can [...] carry messages of progress and emancipation" (see Howe, "Said and Marxism: Anxieties of Influence," 78). Howe argues that in this aspect Said comes very close to the concerns of "classical" Marxism in its kinship with Enlightenment thought.

18. Roughly a decade after the publication of "Secular Criticism," Said's allusion to Deleuze and Guattari's conception of the "war machine" near the end of *Culture and Imperialism* continues to work through these questions. Said writes, "A great deal of this immensely rich book is not easily accessible, but I have found it mysteriously suggestive. [...] The war machine, Deleuze and Guattari say, can be assimilated to the military powers of the state—but, since it is fundamentally a separate entity, need not be, any more than the spirit's nomadic wanderings need always but put at the service of institutions." See Said, *Culture and Imperialism* (New York: Vintage, 1993), 332. The idea of the war machine and "spirit," rendered for Said in their ambivalent relationship to the state and official institutions, is a relation he is still working through in this later book. Intrigued by the fresh ways of conceptualizing and perhaps surpassing the individual and the collective in *A Thousand Plateaus*, Said's interest in this issue remains continually vexed.

19. San Juan, "Edward Said's Affiliations," 53.

20. Lazarus, "Representations of the Intellectual in 'Representations of the Intellectual,'" 119.

21. We refer specifically to the content of chapters 3 and 4 in *The Question of Palestine* (New York: Vintage, 1992), respectively titled "Toward Palestinian Self-Determination" and "The Palestinian Question After Camp David," where Said's positions on Yasser Arafat and the PLO undergo significant modification.

22. Said, "The Mind of Winter," *Harper's Magazine* (September 1984), 54.

23. See Said, *Power, Politics, and Culture*, 160–161.

24. Stathis Gourgouris, "Transformation, Not Transcendence," *boundary 2* 31.2 (2004), 64.

25. Said, *Power, Politics, and Culture*, 58.

26. Said, *Representations of the Intellectual*, 58.

27. Said, *Power, Politics, and Culture*, 21.

28. This is not to say that Said's ethical concerns were entirely uninfluenced by these thinkers, as Adorno's and Gramsci's thought helped Said formulate his stances regarding exile, intellectualism, and music enormously. For texts that clearly demonstrate their influence, see *Representations of the Intellectual* and *On Late Style: Music and Literature Against the Grain* (New York: Vintage, 2007).

29. The oppositional component of his ethics is a driving force within Said's vision of secular criticism, which Aamir R. Mufti views as not merely a "sociological" drive to explanation, but a practice whose priority is in "ethical engagement rather than historical explanation"; see Mufti, "Why I Am Not a Postsecularist," 111.

30. Gourgouris, "Transformation, Not Transcendence," 66.

31. Pheng Cheah, "Given Culture: Rethinking Cosmopolitical Freedom in Transnationalism," in *Cosmopolitics: Thinking and Feeling Beyond the Nation*, ed. Bruce Robbins and Pheng Cheah (Minneapolis: University of Minnesota Press, 1998), 291–292.

32. Said, *Orientalism* (New York: Vintage, 1978), 271.

33. Ibid., 307.

34. Said, "The Mind of Winter," 54.

35. Said, *Orientalism*, 338.

36. Ibid.

37. Aijiz Ahmad, *In Theory* (New York: Verso, 1992), 201. To Ahmad's urging of Said to come out of the Marxist closet, Said might reply that "Marxism has nonetheless always struck me as more limiting than enabling in the current intellectual, cultural, political conjuncture"; see Said, *Power, Politics, and Culture*, 158.

38. El-Haj, "Edward Said and the Political Present," 548.

39. Rokus de Groot, "Perspectives of Polyphony in Edward Said's Writings," *Alif: Journal of Comparative Poetics* 25 (2005), 231.

40. Said, *Culture and Imperialism*, xxvi.

41. Gauri Viswanathan, "Introduction," in *Power, Politics, and Culture*, ed. Said, xiv.

42. See Michel de Certeau, *The Practice of Everyday Life*, trans. Steven Rendall (Berkeley: University of California Press, 1984).

43. Said, *Culture and Imperialism*, xx.

44. For a detailed exploration of the etymology of the term *arkhē* and its relationship with archives as well as organizational principles, see

Derrida's *Archive Fever: A Freudian Impression,* trans. Eric Prenowitz (Chicago: University of Chicago Press, 1996).

45. For what we mean by a purely philosophical discussion of anarchism, see Simon Critchley's *Infinitely Demanding: Ethics of Commitment, Politics of Resistance* (New York: Verso, 2007). The most recent and significant manifestations of political anarchism's projects, in the tradition of social anarchism, would be the organizational assumptions underlying the Occupy Wall Street movement (see David Graeber, "Occupy Wall Street's Anarchist Roots," *Al-Jazeera America* November 20, 2011 [accessed September 19, 2013]), as well as the actions taken by anarchists in Greece's anti-austerity movement (see Maloney, "Greek Anarchists on Anarchist Movement in Greece," *Libcom.org* January 17, 2013 [accessed September 19, 2013]).

46. Chomsky, *Chomsky on Anarchism* (Oakland: AK Press, 2005), 124.

47. Said, *Power, Politics, and Culture,* 76. Of course, for Said there cannot merely be solidarity. Said notes two differences he has with Chomsky that he claims to be "not very interesting or important" (77). In the same interview, he implicitly raises such differences onto the level of a critique: the first difference is that Chomsky "writes out of some sense of solidarity with oppressed people, but his direct involvement in the ongoing political activity of a group of people or a community—partly because of his many interests and the demands on his time—has been different than [Said's]" (77). The next and more crucial difference is methodological, that Chomsky is "not really interested in theorizing whatever it is that he does," whereas Said heavily emphasizes such theorizing (77).

48. Chomsky, "The Incalculable Loss," 373.

49. Chomsky, *Chomsky on Anarchism,* 147.

50. Ibid., 122.

51. Mufti, "Auerbach in Istanbul: Edward Said, Secular Criticism, and the Question of Minority Culture," *Critical Inquiry* 25.1 (1998), 107.

52. Chomsky, *Chomsky on Anarchism,* 178.

53. Ibid., 192–193.

54. Ibid., 193.

55. Said, *Culture and Imperialism,* xxvi.

56. This point is expressed by Chomsky with a note of his signature dryness in "Anarchism, Intellectuals and the State": "As a result of centuries of extensive popular struggle there is a minimal welfare system that provides support for poor mothers and children. That's under attack in an effort to minimize the state [...] anarchists can't seem to understand that they are to support that. So they join with the ultra-right in saying 'Yes, we've got to minimize the state'" (*Chomsky on Anarchism,* 213). Both compelled by a politics of belief, the far right and doctrinaire anarchists become odd bedfellows, joined

together in a fetishistic dream, despite the fatal misidentification over the signifieds of "statelessness."

57. Said, *Orientalism*, 24.

58. While many might view *Humanism and Democratic Criticism* (New York: Columbia University Press, 2004) as the culmination point of Said's desire to search for an alternative, we think that this project remains fundamentally and radically open in his work.

59. See Michael Sprinker, ed., *Edward Said: A Critical Reader* (Cambridge: Blackwell Publishers, 1992), 221–264. Said's discussion on Fanon's differentiation between independence and liberation can be found in *Culture and Imperialism*, 274.

60. Bruce Robbins, "American Intellectuals and Middle East Politics: An Interview with Edward Said," *Social Text* 19/20.4 (1988), 52.

61. Lazarus, "Representations of the Intellectual in 'Representations of the Intellectual,'" 114. Lazarus derives the term from the work of Anouar Abdel-Malek, who defines nationalitarian as the following: "[The] nationalitarian phenomenon [...] has as its object, beyond the clearing of the national territory, the *independence* and sovereignty of the national state, uprooting in depth the positions of the ex-colonial power—the reconquest of the power of decision in all domains of national life. [...] Historically, fundamentally, the struggle is for national *liberation*, the instrument of that reconquest of identity which [...] lies at the heart of everything" (see Lazarus, "Representations of the Intellectual in 'Representations of the Intellectual,'" 121, footnote 3, emphasis ours). Abdel-Malek's understanding of national liberation as a project beyond independence can thus also be understood as a form of deep decolonization, one that acknowledges what must be combated is the haunting neocolonial grasp that continues to exert power on the formerly colonized.

62. Said, *Power, Politics and Culture*, 289.

63. Ibid., 434.

64. Gourgouris, "Transformation, Not Transcendence," 74.

CHAPTER 6

TRANSNATIONAL IDENTITY IN CRISIS: RE-READING EDWARD W. SAID'S *OUT OF PLACE*

Sobia Khan

In his memoir *Out of Place*,[1] Edward W. Said chronicles the multiple homes he has occupied in his life, everywhere from Jerusalem and Cairo to Lebanon and the United States. The memoir, written in 1994 during his treatment for leukemia, represents his attempt to reconstruct his identity creation over time, examining the experiences that connect his life in 1994 to its beginnings in 1935. Writing as a displaced and a homeless subject, Said uses his work to ground himself in a specific place. I am interested in how Said understands and classifies his nomadic life all over the globe, and I would argue that this memoir helps to illuminate bigger questions of identity for transplanted, displaced, dislocated, and relocated individuals, including those whom I label *transnational.*

From the very beginning of his memoir Said questions his identity as a Palestinian, as a non-Muslim Arab, and as an American. Through his writings, he assesses the situation of his existence as rootless. His memoir not only becomes a chronicle of his transnational existence, but also becomes the space through which he tries to find a "place" to belong. In this chapter, I read Said's life as shaped by a transnational identity, that is, as one who never quite settled in the geographical spaces he occupied, which resulted in his always remaining a sort of outcast, one who was never at-home. Furthermore, I argue that this being out-of-place is equivalent to being a transnational and that the condition is detrimental to a sense of identity. In my re-reading of Said, his work is not that of an exilic writer, but that of a transnational writer stuck in the depths of despair because of his displaced or dislocated life. For Said, the multiple acts of displacement—of departures, arrivals, farewells, exile, nostalgia, homesickness, belonging, and travel—constitute a disaster. *Out of Place* demonstrates how Said's self-writing exemplifies the enactment of a transnational identity in crisis.

DISPLACEMENT AS CRISIS

My reading of Said's *Out of Place* as the chronicle of a displaced and transnational subject is reinforced by Said's biography and his writings in the memoir. And it is also reiterated in what Said left unsaid. His struggle to pin down an identity for himself is revealing.

Said's sense of crisis began from a very early stage in his life. In his memoir, *Out of Place*, he traces back to when he was given a name, the first marker of identity imposed on him. He is named Edward, after the Prince of Wales who was very popular in the 1930s. His last name Said is not shared by anyone else in his family. He is not named after any grandparents or according to a family tradition. It is as if in pairing two seemingly disconnected names, one English, the other Arab, Said's identity was constructed from birth so that he would suffer a sense of being not quite in sync with the world—of always being in a state of "*trans*." Growing up speaking Arabic and English, Said could not discern which language he spoke first or which truly was "his" language. In his memoir he terms this confusion an "instability," a harsh word to describe his relation with these two powerful languages. As he goes on to trace his ascription of identity, he labels the stories that contribute to his name construction and his engagement with languages as "meanderings" and "interruptions" (5). Said's word choices here are indicative of his conflict and struggle with the most perfunctory and basic tropes of identity formation as any individual and as a member of a community. But his identity markers leave him bewildered and lost. He always had a sense of being out of place in his environment. He equates this sense of being out of place with having a deep flaw. He writes, "I have retained this unsettled sense of many identities—mostly in conflict with each other—all my life, together with an acute memory of the despairing feeling that I wish we could have been all-Arab, or all-European and American, or all-Orthodox Christian, or all-Muslim, or all-Egyptian, and so on" (5). This identity crisis is not limited to how he perceives himself alone; it extends to others in similar displaced and uprooted conditions. Throughout his life, Said was asked questions such as: "What are you?"; "You're American without an American name, and you've never been to America"; "You don't look American?"; and "How come you were born in Jerusalem and you live here?" Said does not remember ever answering these questions with a satisfactory or a memorable answer. In his attempt to identify himself, he hearkens back to his past. His memoir, then, becomes not only a chronicle of his journeys as he crosses multiple national boundaries that complicate his sense of identity at each border crossing, but also an attempt at answering that pregnant question: "What are you?"

Said was offered American citizenship in his youth because of his father's military service to the United States during World War II. This American citizenship was in addition to his Egyptian citizenship, both of which never compensated for the lack of an official Palestinian citizenship for Said. He was born a Palestinian, but would never spend his life in Palestine except for short vacations. So, while Said laments his lack of Palestinian attachment, for most of his life he and his family lived outside Palestine. Later, Said bemoans the loss of Palestine and champions the cause of a Palestinian state as he forever remains an outsider to Palestine, living first as a child in Egypt and then as an adult in America.

Said writes of this sense of an uprooted displacement in *Out of Place*: "how an extraordinarily increasing number of departures have unsettled my life from its earliest beginnings. To me, nothing more painful and paradoxically sought after characterizes my life than the many displacements from countries, cities, abodes, languages, environments that have kept me in motion all these years" (217). What emerges from this text is the fact that Said identifies dislocation as integral to his sense of identity, but he does not characterize himself as a foreigner in every new land he resides. It is as if Said harbors the hope of returning to his place of original departure whatever that may be at each departure. He had an "eradicable fear of not returning" (217) at every departure. He envied those who did not have to travel and stayed behind in the comforts of their home and routine, saying "their faces [are] unshadowed by dislocation" (218). He goes on to elaborate that his departures are permeated with "the great fear is that departure is the state of being abandoned, even though it is you who leave" (218). This acute sensitivity to leaving and never returning permeates every page of his memoir making his own departures at different stages of his life more poignant. It is the fear of an impossibility of a return home that destabilizes Said.

While I read Said's memoir as that of a transnational subject, Assad Al-Saleh, in his essay "Displaced Autobiography in Edward Said's *Out of Place* and Fawad Turki's *The Disinherited*," claims that Said's memoir is a self-narrative that reasserts Said's relationship to his homeland in which Palestine plays the central role as the place where Said's identity was formed and where he still belongs.[2] I reference Al-Saleh to not only rethink what Said's undeclared intentions were in writing his memoir, but to discuss how Al-Saleh distinguishes Said's memoir as that of a "displaced Palestinian" rather than that of an "exile." He uses John Thieme's *Post-colonial Studies* glossary to define displacement. He writes, "displacement is defined as the enforced movement of Africans during slavery or other non-voluntary movements over borders due to religious or political persecution, leaving issues of identity and culture wide open for discussion and consideration."[3] This definition excludes dislocated persons like Said and his family. Their dislocation was originally due to economic mobility and later in the pursuit of higher education and opportunities. Later, the family could not return to Jerusalem because of the hostile political climate between the Palestinians and the Israelis. Literally, they could have returned to Jerusalem to their native homeland, but chose to stay out of the area because of the political turmoil. Al-Saleh goes on to quote Angelika Bammer in *Displacements: Cultural Identities in Question*, which more expansively defines displacement as "the separation of people from their native cultures either through physical dislocation (as refugees, immigrants, exiles, or expatriates) or the *colonizing imposition of a foreign culture*."[4] With Bammer's definition, Al-Saleh is closer to how I want to read displacement and dislocation. This definition more accurately depicts what displacement is for Said. Al-Saleh's attention to the term displacement highlights the need for us to read Said as a displaced subject rather than as an exile.

However, Al-Saleh's astute reading of Said as being a displaced subject loses credibility when he claims that "Said's autobiography might not show displacement in its full, painful weight and psychological effects."[5] Al-Saleh understands "displacement" very differently, especially as he is constantly comparing and drawing parallels to Fawaz Turki's *The Disinherited* to Said's *Out of Place*. Turki's autobiography is that of a Palestinian exile who was denied entry to Palestine and who openly laments the loss of Palestine as the cause of his anguish. The term *exile* has a definite sense of expulsion, of deportation, of being thrown out of a place one calls home. This negative and forceful connotation is well established by Turki's account of his life in his book. In comparison, Al-Saleh finds Said's writing to be self-indulgent. Al-Saleh labels Said's displacement as a "smooth displacement" when compared to the anguish suffered by Turki. He sees tension, loss, and humiliation as an essential part of Turki's writings but not necessarily of Said's. I propose that we read Said's memoir, as Al-Saleh suggests, as that of a displaced subject, but that we view his displacement as being parallel to Turki's exile, since Said too suffers tension, loss, and humiliation as a consequence of his displacement. Al-Saleh's "smooth displacement" is an inadequate term to talk about the anguish Said suffers. Later in his essay, Al-Saleh softens his assertion of Said's "smooth displacement" when he writes that "Said's narration of his and his family's displacement also testifies to the loss of place and the consequence of such loss. [...] Linked with the loss of his homeland, this *change of culture* vastly *complicates his displacement.*"[6] It would have been interesting to read how and what Al-Saleh terms as the consequences of a loss of place, or what he views are the "complications" associated with displacement, but his essay does not explore these questions. It is the loss and complications that Said suffers that are the focus of my investigation here.

I hope to illustrate in my rereading of Said's memoir that "displacements" intensely complicate identity. It is not only change of culture, but change in a subject's physical location even when it is within a similar culture that can have devastating effects on their sense of belonging. Al-Saleh is helpful in thinking through Said's memoir as more than just about displacement, and furthers my thinking that his memoir is more than only writing about the loss of Palestine.

SAID AND EXILE

Said viewed himself as an exile, living an exilic life outside Palestine, his country of origin and birthplace. Before examining how Said viewed the condition of being an exile, it is important to consider why he came to define himself as an exile. He was born in West Jerusalem to a wealthy family in 1935. Although he was born in Palestine, his family moved to Cairo, Egypt, where his father had run a successful business since 1929.[7] Said spent most of his life in Cairo until the time he moved to the United States for further education. In Cairo, the Saids lived without their extended family and instead developed a strong network of friends. As he was growing up, his family took long vacations in Jerusalem and Lebanon. Their vacations to a remote village in Dhour, Lebanon, were also spent apart from their relatives in Palestine. But when Said's family visited Palestine, they spent time in their ancestral home and were surrounded by both sides of the family.

In 1947, Said's family lived most of the year in Jerusalem where Said was enrolled in his father's school. They left Jerusalem in December 1947 because of continuous political upheaval and unrest, and, with the rest of their extended family, they were forced to leave Palestine in 1948. So, while Said and his family did live that last year in Palestine, their place of business and their other home and life were already well established in Cairo.

Said writes in the introduction to *Out of Place*, "I left Palestine in December 1947" due to Israeli atrocities; when he writes, "For by the early spring of 1948 my entire family had been swept out of place, and has ever since remained in exile ever since" (x), his words and his attestation to exile since 1947 are highly symbolic. Said views himself as a part of the larger Palestinian family, and shows solidarity with the plight of those Palestinians, both family and strangers, who were forced to leave Palestine in 1948 after the Israeli invasion. Later in his memoir Said writes that since his family's departure in 1947 he did not return to Palestine until 1992, which is when he visited West Jerusalem, Nazareth, and other cities where his relatives had once lived. He uses the pronoun "our" to talk about his family's departure from Palestine, clearly exhibiting his solidarity with all those who were forced to leave Palestine. It is also important to note that Said was not banned from visiting Palestine until he joined Palestine National Council (PNC) in 1977. Moustafa Bayoumi and Andrew Rubin write that "Exile was an existential reality for Said who, as a member of PNC, was prohibited from visiting Israel."[8] Again, not to diminish the sincerity of Said's solidarity with the people of Palestine, but it is important to note that he already had a life outside Palestine at the time of the Israeli invasion. What is worth dwelling on, however, is the idea that he could only "visit" Palestine, now renamed Israel. Living in Jerusalem or reestablishing familial roots in Palestine was now out of the question for Said and for the rest of his clan. There was no longer a possibility of a return home or a homecoming to Palestine after 1948. That is when his metaphorical exile from Palestine and his personal crisis began.

The question then arises: why did Said consider himself primarily a scholar of exile, writing in exile about exile? In his seminal essay "Reflections on Exile," Said works through the idea of what it is like to live outside a "true home." Said defines exile as the "unhealable rift forced between a human being and a native place, between the self and its true home," and he states, "true exile is a condition of terminal loss."[9] Attention needs to be paid to Said's use of the adjective "true" in "true homes" and in "true exile." He identifies as his "true home"

Jerusalem, Palestine, as his country of origin, the place of his birth, and his ancestral residence. The loss of his true home had made him a true exile. From the beginning of his essay on exile, Said believes his condition to be of a true exile. He claims that modern Western culture is inundated with, and composed largely of, works of exiles, émigrés, and refugees. George Steiner, Said writes, thinks "that a whole genre of twentieth-century Western literature is 'extraterritorial,' a literature by and about exiles, symbolizing the age of refugee."[10] These are strong and emotional words that strike a chord with Said and his readers. Following this strong claim of refugees' impact on the Western literary canon, Said conceded that this is not a condition unique to his time and age. In his essay, Said further illustrates the scale and magnitude of exile in twentieth century, calling exile a condition "that is produced by human beings for other human beings; and that like death but without death's ultimate mercy, it has torn millions of people from the nourishment of tradition, family and geography."[11] Said is accurate in outlining the suffering caused by exile. While Said sees these characteristics as the result of exile, I want to show that the absence of tradition, family, and geography is equivalent to the crisis caused by "exile" even in the absence of a true exilic condition.

While Said suffers the symptoms and anxieties of a true exile, he himself is not a true exile. Said has described himself as an exile, whereas I claim that his is in fact a transnational identity, which is distinct from that of an exile. This is not to contest the reason why he cannot be literally called an exile, but rather to explain that his particular circumstances and experiences reveal his situation to be that of a transnational subject. To show how *Out of Place* is the writing of a displaced person and not that of an exile, I want to read "exile" in its literal sense and show how it differs from displacement and dislocation. Exile is the result of forced and terminal displacement from a person's home. The prevalent connotation of the word "exile" is negative—someone who is forced, coerced into moving from their place of origin to another place. The word comes from a Latin term suggestive of "banishment." The Oxford English Dictionary defines it as "(1) expulsion from one's native land by authoritative decree, (2) the fact or state of expulsion, (3) a person banished from his or her native land, (4) or a prolonged separation from one's own country by force of circumstance," and, as a last possibility, exile could be voluntary by "force of circumstances." In contrast to *exile*, Steven Vertovec defines *transnationalism* as social morphology, a type of consciousness, a mode of cultural reproduction, avenue of capital, a site of political engagement, and (re)construction of place or locality.[12]

Among the many ways Vertovec defines transnationalism, the above definition is most useful in relation to Said, as I redefine Said's work as that of a transnational subject rather than that of an exile.

In "Reflections on Exile," Said examines those subjectivities who voluntarily relocate from a place of origin with a broad brush stroke, lumping together forced exile and voluntary exile in his understanding of exile. His definition of exile focuses on the displaced subject's ability to return to their homelands. He writes, "anyone prevented from returning home is an exile, some distinctions can be made between exiles, refugees, expatriates and émigrés." Said continues to say that exile originates in the practice of banishment. He writes, " 'exile' carries with it, I think, a touch of solitude and spirituality."[13] Said also relies on Georg Lukács's work *Theory of the Novel* to argue that "the novel is *the* form of 'transcendental homelessness.' " For Said, "exiles are eccentrics who *feel* their difference."[14] It is clear from this brief discussion of Said's essay on exile that Said uses the term "exile" in a very specific and yet contradictory manner. While he understands the typical definition of exile, he also propagates a different way of examining the condition of the exile as those who are unable to return to their homeland. His definition is idealistic, highly theoretical, and problematic in defining his own situation as that of an exile.

It becomes clear from reading Said's essay that he is operating under an illusion of an exile. John D. Barbour's examination of Said's use of the term "exile" furthers how I also want to rethink Said's relationship to exile. Barbour writes, "Said frequently used exile as a metaphor to describe his vision of the modern intellectual, who needs a critical, detached perspective from which to examine his culture."[15] I call attention to Said's romantic notion of an exile to show how he willed exile to be the condition and space in which he preferred to work. Said is clear in claiming that exile is not a site of privilege or a matter of choice when he writes, "I speak of exile not as a privilege, but as an alternative to the mass institutions that dominate modern life. Exile is not, after all, a matter of choice: you are born into it, or it happens to you."[16] However, based on his writings, Said comes across as a writer who views the label of being an exile as a place of privilege rather than that of despair. The contradictory stance that Said takes on the position of the exile reveals Said's ambivalent relationship with the identity of an exile. The theoretical idea of an exilic identity opens up a new space of exploration for Said, whereas the literal idea of a physical displacement experienced by his own "exile" leaves him distraught and homeless. In *Out of Place*, his exilic identity is a result of his transnational experiences. In my view, Said occupies a space in

between these two ways of understanding exile. It is as if Said is neither here nor there even in the position he takes as an exile. Rereading
Said as having a transnational identity rather than an exilic one is necessary precisely because he is neither here nor there; this is a symptom
of Said's transnational life not because of his self-imposed status of
an exile. An exilic sense of identity is a symptom of a transnational
identity in crisis, not the other way around.

Said concludes "Reflections of Exile" on the pleasures of exile. It is,
again, worth noting the discrepancies in his writing about an exile.
Earlier he has stated that exile is not a privilege, but in talking about
exile as pleasure he reaffirms the idea of exile as a privileged space.
His reference to the pleasures of exile is how he prefers to imagine
the space of exile for himself in the role of an academic. He writes
that one of the privileges is to be able to see the entire world as
a foreign land that enables an originality of vision. Another advantage, he claims, is that exiles are aware of more than one culture and
one home; that is, they are aware of simultaneous dimensions that
are "contrapuntal."[17] Moreover, he attests, "There is a unique pleasure in this sort of apprehension, especially if the exile is conscious of
other contrapuntal juxtapositions that diminish orthodox judgment
and elevate appreciative sympathy. There is also a particular sense of
achievement in acting as if one were at home wherever one happens
to be."[18] I find Said's words true in describing how he felt about exile
and how he defined exile as a displaced scholar. The last line in the
quote above, when he says that he is at home wherever he happens
to be, is worth pausing over. Said expresses the same sentiment in his
memoir *Out of Place* when he writes, "I have learned actually to prefer being not quite right and out of place" (295). It is clear from his
writings that Said never felt "at-home" despite his claims to being "at-
home" with his nomadic life or "at-home" as an exile in the space of
exile. The pleasure of exile and being at-home in being dislocated is
an illusion he creates for himself. The contradictions in his perception
and definition of exile and homelessness in his scholarly work and his
memoir reveal this to us.

Said's memoir then becomes a chronicle of a search for home
that he never finds, at least not in the traditional sense, because
of an absence of "tradition, family, and geography" in every new
home he settles into. He was also not an authentic exile in the literal sense despite his conflated idea of an exile and his attachment
to a sense of metaphorical exile. In reality, his identity crisis as a
transnational subject produces similar angst as that of an exile who
is forced to leave his homeland to lead an unsettled life forever. Said's
very last line in "Reflections on Exile" is prophetic of his true displaced

condition: "Exile is life led outside habitual order. It is nomadic, decentered, contrapuntal; but no sooner does one get accustomed to it than its unsettling force erupts anew."[19] In his parting words on his meditation on exile, Said contradicts himself again, finally admitting to never being at-home even in exile. I propose that it is not his so-called exilic life away from Palestine that has decentered him, but his life as a transnational subject that prevents him from having a sense of being at-home in his new homes.

At the time of the publication of *Out of Place*, intense criticism was leveled against Said on his claim to being a Palestinian exile. Ioana Luca, in "Edward Said's *Lieux de Mémoire*: *Out of Place* and the Politics of Autobiography," focuses on the debate that surrounded the publication of *Out of Place*. She writes that Justus Reid Weiner launched one of the worst attacks against Said, arguing that Said over-stated his and his family's connections to Palestine. In attacking Said's connection to Palestine, Weiner questions the very essence of Said's Palestinian identity. Weiner claims Said exaggerated to make himself appear more Palestinian, more of a victim of the fall of Palestine in 1948 than he was.[20] Another critic, Geoffrey Wheaton, accuses Said of being a man of the West. He states, "The accidents of his birth are irrelevant to the real truth, that Edward Said is a man of the West, and to the larger truth that the world we live in today had been made by Europe. Do I need to add, for the better or worse?"[21] It goes with-out saying that Wheaton's remarks verbalize Orientalist attitudes. Not only does he take away Said's right to name himself, he disregards and disallows Said's heritage, but also takes on the act of naming the other in his own shadow. By calling Said a "man of the West," Wheaton nul-lifies the Palestinian Said, the Christian Arab Said, and the American Arab Said. In the midst of such accusations, another Palestinian critic Meron Benvenisti views Said's memoir as the "portrait of a privileged family and a pampered youth in the midst of great suffering and great destruction."[22] He does not deny the condition of the Palestinians, but denies Said the right to speak on behalf of the victims, because of Said's distance from the lower-class Palestinians who suffered the most and because Said was physically absent from Palestine in 1948. It is as if Said is doubly marked for being wealthy and absent, and for not being an "authentic" exile. The criticism leveled against Said reveals the complexities that Said himself went through in life in determining who he was, and who he was speaking for.

In her essay, Luca lists the various accusations directed toward Said and his memoir. She responds by writing that "Said's memoir was one way or another denied authenticity and truth-value and accused of 'non-representability.' "[23] Luca's assessment of the situation is helpful in understanding the struggle Said had taken on in his writing by being a Palestinian exile and speaking for the Palestinians. Luca's essay, which so marvelously captures the crisis embedded and surrounding *Out of Place*, ends by suggesting that we should read Said's memoir based on Pierre Nora's notion of *lieux de mémoire*—sites of memory. Luca is astute in recognizing the personal crisis that permeates *Out of Place*, but she doesn't dwell on this important aspect of the memoir any further. She writes, "given that he [Said] fulfills his mission to narrate, it does function as remedy. Healing. Healing at the individual level. [. . .] Also, healing worked in the sense of commemorating and being able to leave an account of those remote times and places, facing loss and forgetting."[24] Again, Luca picks up on the sense of loss, but her analysis deviates from a deeper examination of the loss, and instead, focuses on what Said himself writes that his memoir is "account of those remote times and places" (xii). Luca also suggests that *Out of Place* ultimately occupies a third place, a Deleuzian "AND," a space of continuous becoming. She writes that the book becomes "a minefield like mobile territory of constant clashes and negotiations" and a space which is a "dangerous, uncomfortable location. It marks points of *crisis*, spaces where *conflicting* values, ideas, and beliefs converge only to diverge anew along lines that construct even wider splits and conflicts."[25]

Luca is perceptive concerning the crises that surround Said's *Out of Place*, as well as those that are in the memoir and those that emerge out of the memoir. She writes, "Said's memoir opens up in-between spaces where new forms of art, experience, and political action emerge."[26] (141). For my purpose here, Luca stops short of the moment of an epiphany. She recognizes the loss, but does not explore the loss or the implications of what a loss of home does to identity. She sees the in-between space as a productive space for new art and action, and I disagree with this analysis. For Said or any transnational subject, to be in a perpetual state of conflict in the third space or in an in-between space is disastrous to their sense of being. I interpret the metaphorical exile as being akin to disaster, and I believe that we should rethink *Out of Place* as more than a testimony, more than a site of memory, or more than a third space.

REREADING SAID AS A TRANSNATIONAL

Reading Said as an exilic writer is insufficient in understanding Said's sense of crisis at the end of his life. Exile understood as forced expulsion is not the way Said articulates his relationship with Palestine. Said never claims to have been forced from Palestine or later from Egypt. He moved away from Cairo to pursue higher education in America. Other Palestinians in his community may have moved away from Palestine and later from Egypt due to hostilities, but it was not the case for him. It may be better to examine Said through the lens of dislocation and displacement instigated by economic mobility. In a physical sense, with each move, he or his family stood to gain monetarily because of business opportunities or higher education. Said's father had his son's future planned out so that he would receive the best education from the best institutions in the world. Although Said was very young when his path in life led him away from Palestine and Egypt, nonetheless, Said's separation from his native land was a matter of choice and not coercion, just as his colonial education, his piano classes, and vacations to Dhour were.

Barbour's essay "Consolations and Compensations of Exile" is particularly helpful in my suggestion that Said's memoir should be reread as that of a transnational identity in crisis rather than that of an exile. Barbour points out that Said in "Reflections on Exile" criticizes a heroic or romantic notion of an exile. And yet, as Barbour points out, Said himself creates a heroic, romantic, lonely, and alienated vision of an exile. Said's contradictory notions on exile permeate his rhetoric in "Reflections on Exile." Barbour continues to critique Said's claim that violence and suffering ensues when people feel that they have a God-given right to a land, and yet, "in *Out of Place*, the way in which Said portrays exile shows certain affinities to the idea of sacred space. His depiction of the metaphorical space of exile reveals not only his secularist and humanistic values and commitments, but also an orientation that resembles the religious perspective of diasporic peoples."[27] As Said explains in the preface to *Out of Place*: "The main reason, however, for this memoir is of course the need to bridge the sheer distance in time and place between my life today and my life then [...] as I have set about reconstructing a remote time and experience" (xii). And at the end of his memoir when he writes, "Better to wander out of place, not to own a house, and not ever to feel too much at home anywhere, especially in a city like New York, where I shall be until I die" (294). In both these examples we can read how Said understood and made meaning of his life as never really being at-home. He remains homeless throughout without a concrete sense of belonging. I think Said avoided admitting the one great need that remained unfulfilled in his life, that of being rooted in a place called at "home." When he creates his identity in America as a postcolonial scholar, as a passionate

Palestinian advocate, and as an exile, he is in fact bemoaning the loss of his country and of never being at-home. Barbour is also attuned to this aspect of Said. He writes, "In contrast to his theoretical works, the autobiographical writing of *Out of Place* reveals Said's yearning *to belong to a particular homeland* as well as his desire to cross over to other places, both geographical and metaphorical."[28] Said is indentured to an identity characterized by his transnational life; his identity ruptured at every geographical and metaphorical crossing.

Said's memoir narrates the story of a man journeying away from home. Each departure makes the return even more implausible, if not impossible. While having the possibility of a return, Said is still denied this possibility because with each new chapter of his life he further removes himself from his homeland of Palestine and later that of Egypt. Said dwells on this idea of an impossibility of a return home in his memoir when he talks about his experience as a 12-year-old at summer camp at Lake Maranacook. On an overnight trip during camp, Said canoed with another camper while a counselor named Andy stretched the length of the canoe between the two manning the boat. What Said found intriguing and worth noting about this seemingly mundane canoe trip from his adolescence was the fact that Andy, who lay in the canoe reading a book, would tear out the page of the book as he finished reading it. Andy would then proceed to crunch it up into a ball and throw it into the lake. As a 12-year-old, Said attributed this odd behavior to some unknown aspect of American life that he did not understand. But reflecting on it later, Said views the incident differently. He writes, "I remember reflecting afterward that the experience took its significance from the desire to leave no traces, to live without history or the *possibility of return*" (138, my emphasis). The act of throwing away an already read page becomes symbolic of leaving no trace, to live without history, to eradicate history, undo a past without a possibility of return. There is no undoing the triple dislocation of the word from the page, and of the page from the book, and then the page into the lake. This is not the only time Said views his frequent dis-/re-locations as terminal events that cannot be undone. Said goes into great detail over the political issue of losing his homeland, Palestine. It can even be said that while he not only feared not returning as discussed earlier, he does in fact goes through life never being able to return "home."

When Said returns to Camp Maranacook 22 years later as an adult and asks around about the camp, he finds out that no one had ever even heard of the camp or remembered it. Similarly, when he revisits his old school, Victoria College in Egypt, in 1956, it is nothing like what he remembered. It had been nationalized by the government and renamed Victory College. This was the school that had expelled him once as a young boy, and on this revisit, he is once again expelled, accused of being a trespasser. The old British system that had expelled him before was now replaced by a Muslim authority, and this time too, he was thrown off the school premises. Said's attempt to revisit his past proves futile, there is almost no possibility of a return. The metaphorical tearing and throwing of the page from Said's childhood memories echo his literal permanent dislocation. This impossibility of a return can be read as the condition of being in exile, as Said himself saw his condition. And while I distinguish the condition as that of physical and forceful banishment, it may be helpful to consider Ketu H. Katrak's idea of "emotional exile" versus "literal political exile." In "Exilic Homes: The Legacy of Edward Said," Katrak doesn't elaborate the coinage of "emotional exile," but it can be deduced that he saw Said's "nomadic and contrapuntal" life and his sense of loss akin to emotional trauma or exile. Katrak writes, "Said's notion of the intellectual as exile, as marginal and as an outsider had a personal valence different from his discussion of the 'Other.' "[29] Here the term "exile" is used to portray ways that make it less than the condition of banishment and deportation. Said concurs with this assessment of himself as an outsider in his adopted homes without the possibility of a return home. Said's memoir becomes the space that enacts the despair and crisis of being never-at-home, of not belonging. However, I prefer to read the crisis of Said's life as that of a transnational rather than that of an emotional exile.

Said experiences the impossibility of a return home again and again in his life. He laments the loss of Palestine to Israeli occupation and, later, he laments his inaccessibility to Egypt because of legal and political complications. His diagnosis of cancer in 1993 furthered his alienation from home. He could not return to a state of healthiness; much like his parents, he knew he was moving further away from life itself. When he was diagnosed, he considered all the "places" where he would like to die. He contemplated returning to Boston, a place he had enjoyed living in as a student to spend the rest of his life, but he rejects that idea. He writes, "So many returns, attempts to go back to life, or people who are no longer there: these constituted a steady response to the increasing rigors of my illness" (215). He could not bring himself to actually return to a past that no longer existed. The question that arises after reading about Said's repeated failed attempts at returning to a place he called "home" is that perhaps Said's search for a "place" to return to was misplaced. It is apparent throughout

Out of Place that Said never felt at home in any one place. He always felt like an outsider, a foreigner, an "other" at every destination. So, if a "place," a city or a country, a land, or a nationality could never be his home, then to what did he view himself as "belonging"?

The question of what to belong to permeates Said's memoir. Said writes very clearly from the very beginning that his memoir "*Out of Place* is a record of an essentially lost or forgotten world" (ix). For him, Palestine symbolizes that lost and forgotten world. That is the first displacement and loss he mentions in the memoir. The focus he places on the loss of a geographical location encompasses his text, but this is not the only displacement we can trace in the text. Said fails in his attempt to remember history and reconstruct his sense of himself through his past. But one thing he may not have been as aware of is that his memoir is a search for "home" in the midst of all the transitory homes. And he does that very successfully, although they are not the "homes" grounded in a place or a specific land in a traditional sense. It is clear from his writing in *Out of Place* that Said re-locates his "home," as well as his sense of belonging in the absence of a rootedness to a homeland, in the figure of his mother and in the various educational institutions he was associated with all his life. Together, they "ground" him and tie him temporarily to an alternative sense of self. Said's transnational identity remains in a state of crisis despite all his attempts to find a place to belong, as his memoir stands as a testament to his anguish and despair at being dislocated from his home.

NOTES

1. Edward W. Said, *Out of Place: A Memoir* (New York: Knopf, 1999). Hereafter cited by page in the text.
2. Asaad Al-Saleh, "Displaced Autobiography in Edward Said's *Out of Place* and Fawaz Turki's *The Disinherited*," *Arab Studies Quarterly* 33.2 (2011), 79.
3. Ibid., 80.
4. Qtd. in Al-Saleh, "Displaced Autobiography," 80, italics mine.
5. Ibid., 81.
6. Ibid., 84, italics mine.
7. Moustafa Bayoumi and Andrew Rubin, "Introduction," in *The Edward Said Reader*, ed. Moustafa Bayoumi and Andrew Rubin (New York: Vintage, 2000), xvii.
8. Ibid., xviii.
9. Said, "Reflections on Exile," in *Reflections on Exile and Other Essays* (Cambridge, MA: Harvard University Press, 2000), 173.

10. Ibid., 174.
11. Ibid.
12. Stephen Vertovec, *Transnationalism* (New York: Routledge, 2009), 4.
13. Said, "Reflections on Exile," 181.
14. Ibid.
15. John D. Barbour, "The Consolations and Compensations of Exile: Memoirs by Said, Ahmed, and Eire," *Journal of the American Academy of Religion* 79.3 (2011), 709.
16. Said, "Reflections on Exile," 184.
17. Ibid., 186.
18. Ibid.
19. Ibid.
20. Ioana Luca, "Edward Said's *Lieux De Memoire: Out of Place* and the Politics of Autobiography," *Social Text* 24.2 (2006), 131.
21. Quoted in Luca, "Edward Said's *Lieux De Memoire*," 132.
22. Ibid., 133.
23. Ibid.
24. Ibid., 140.
25. Ibid., 140, my emphasis.
26. Ibid., 141.
27. Barbour, "The Consolations and Compensations of Exile," 712.
28. Ibid., 713, my emphasis.
29. Ketu H. Katrak, "Exilic Homes: The Legacy of Edward Said," *Amerasia Journal* 31.1 (2005), 34.

CHAPTER 7

DE-ORIENTING AESTHETIC
EDUCATION

Cameron Bushnell

We position ourselves in the physical world using frames of reference such as those designated by the compass, North–South–East–West, which supply the scientific, mathematical, and technological coordinates of orientation. But, as Octavio Paz suggests in a poem used by Henri Lefebvre as the epigraph to *The Production of Space*, these coordinates can sometimes appear as the four walls of a prison from which one writes messages, but receives no reply.[1] In various ways these cardinal points motivate epistemology, reflect history, and ultimately situate us and what we know. As such, though we use these directions to chart our external *geospace*,[2] they might be conceived as self-referential and inward-looking human constructions, which are at times, as we see for Paz, imprisoning. Bernard Stiegler identifies them as part of the standard operating system for spatial location; these orientation-markers of the compass are "geographic givens," assumptions that license our positioning in the world, technologies "already there" that function as foundations of spatial knowledge and insight.[3] Henri Lefebvre remarks in *The Production of Space*, "there is no stage [of human development] at which 'man' does not demarcate, beacon or sign his space, leaving traces that are both symbolic and practical." Lefebvre suggests that from an early stage of social reality, which he identifies as primitive and calls anthropological, humans mark spaces and orient themselves through route making, boundary marking, herding, migrations, and so on. Although these pastoral spatiotemporal determinants recede in social importance with modernization, "changes of direction and turns in this space always need to be represented, and ['man'] meets this figurative need either by taking his own body as a centre or by reference to other bodies (celestial bodies for example)."[4] This marking of space, as Lefebvre sees it, underpins parallels between physical geography and human symbols, ideas, and beliefs. Such human propensity for developing presuppositions from positioning invests spatial representations with entrenched senses of rootedness.

In our global era, we rely on systems of orientation that emerged alongside the technology of the compass, which identified magnetic north as "the means of orientation for mapmakers."[5] The compass arrived in Europe from China in the twelfth century, but solidified in the fifteenth-century Age of Discovery.[6] Placed in the world, our geographic location governs the norms, rituals, traditions, and understandings of relations between sexes, classes, generations, and races that we accept or reject. Experience and imagination arise in response to the city and nation to which we belong or from which we come. These external frames that shape our assumptions about ourselves and others confront our mental frames, shaped by ego, intelligence, stupidity, self—notions that Gregory Bateson categorizes loosely as "heuristic concepts," interior explanatory notions that also organize data according to beliefs and presuppositions, but these are obtained from societal kinships, communities, and institutions.[7] Orientations—whether externally derived or internally devised—provide frameworks that order our world and, in turn, direct our thinking. Our most sophisticated comparative thinkers acknowledge the intellectual debt to the geography of their upbringings. As Edward Said admits, "Much of the personal investment in [*Orientalism*] derives from my awareness of being an 'Oriental' as a child growing up in two British colonies."[8] These deeply grounded mental foundations are necessary to thought, but also potentially detrimental to open-mindedness. Gayatri Spivak suggests that, especially in the West, we tend to think that our nations and cultures alone are progressive and resourceful and that we can "know" others by "reading up" on them. She proposes an aesthetic education, training the imagination in play, in order to escape the habit of cultural arrogance and appropriation, and she suggests that we must "bequeath a geography to it."[9]

In this essay, I want to begin by asking what might comprise such a geography of aesthetic education, and further, how do we orient ourselves in a geographic space of literary imagination? The essay then ventures into a reconsideration of spatial relations through literary consciousness to ask how we might rethink the very basis on which spatial, and thus human, relations emerge as situated in the world. If placement operates as a closed system—within the quadrants of cardinality, within a logic of character determined by direction—then is it possible to open this system by cultivating a sense of being displaced through the medium of literature? And if so, does this sense of displacement require a correlate physical experience? That is, can there be a geography when the "place" of displacement does not involve relocation, when our surroundings remain stable, and rootedness is not at stake? In short, can we, as readers and students of humanities, step outside the quadrants of the map we carry in our heads?

In this chapter, I investigate how we might interrogate cardinality (standard orientation) as a presupposition, which in turn allows us to question the values imposed through the spatial coordinates of the globe. My aim is to demonstrate not only the difficulty of throwing off the frames of reference in which we operate, but also the desirability of locating other methods of orienting ourselves that leave us not in Paz's self-referential four corners with our backs against the stony West wall, but rather learning from literary imagination strategies for spatial positioning. Both of the novels considered in this essay—Mohsin Hamid's *The Reluctant Fundamentalist* and Salman Rushdie's *The Ground Beneath Her Feet*—demonstrate the double bind of multiple geographies offering conflicting instructions for being and behaving in the world that we will investigate below through Spivak. These novels also allow us to examine other strategies for interrogating orientation, for questioning the scientific certainty of our conceptions of the compass by presenting us situations of catastrophe, serial heterotopia, and refigured orientation-markers, conditions in which the traditional sense of orientation is suspended, and thus achieving through what Gaston Bachelard might term a "*productive* imagination," the conditions for acquiring new knowledge.[10] The points of the compass have obtained an unwarranted ability to identify and characterize people, have become an unquestioned source of social knowledge, produced by ideologically laden experience of direction.[11] As Said ably demonstrates, the East as the Orient becomes shorthand for stereotype. This essay questions the assumptions of "orientation" itself in seeking a less certain geography in light of an aesthetic education that assists us in strategies for temporarily suspending our existing frames of self-positioning and for imaginatively attuning ourselves to less stable, even false, orientation-markers.

Cultural and national habits of mind are continually enforced by having been born in a place and by continuing to live in that place. In other words, it is not that we should eschew traveling, living abroad, or reading culturally different texts, but in order to avoid the pitfall of reconciliation, the resolution of difference into the firm frames of reference that accommodate difference or isolate it, I propose that we look to literary examples for models of how to suspend, not just disbelief or beliefs, but rather deeper assumptions based in the geographic and technical foundations of orientation itself. I point to the efforts of two novels to elide the sense that we know where we are and thus from whence we speak. Orientation is never as straightforward as the science, mathematics, and technology of orientation would have us believe. While I would never say that we don't absolutely depend on the compass (and its technological advancements in GIS and GPS systems) for negotiating the real world, I want to assert that we might develop the habit of suspending orientation in our literary imaginations to forestall the comfort of knowing our minds by knowing our place in the world.

I examine the geography of aesthetic education as it is created in literary imagination through the intellectual and emotional effort of authors and their readers. I am concerned not with real-world landmasses and oceans, or peoples and their economies, politics, and ethical relations, but rather the art, literature, and compositions about these locations, people, and relations. I focus on geography associated with literary works arising from conceptions of place and how they develop in reading, in imagination, in mind. Rising from a correlation to Said's notion that all physical spaces have their mental counterparts, I think of geography in aesthetic works as "material" territory that rises as a counterpart to writers' and readers' imaginations; that is, those places that form in imagination based in part on lived experiences. Geography appears in literary works as descriptions of scenes or symbolic figurations, so that the landscape of the English moors may be green and rolling, but may also be, in British gothic sensation fiction, shrouded in fog and coursing with shrieking winds. Literature depicts and symbolizes the real-world geospace, so that, as we learn from Lefebvre, *representations of space* spring from *representational space*, the latter including not only the land, but also the signs, images, and symbols generated by inhabitants.[12] Each of the two kinds of space, the " 'ideal' space of mental categories and 'real' space of social practice," Lefebvre insists, "involves, underpins and presupposes the other."[13]

THE DOUBLE BIND

In *An Aesthetic Education in the Era of Globalization*, Spivak suggests that the geography of aesthetic education is a negative one, requiring displacement of entrenched belief systems onto imagination through play training and close reading. Spivak's interest lies in the human dimensions of geography, less in the earth's "physical features or characteristics," or in the "topography of a place or region," and more in "human activity as it affects and is affected by these." She suggests two modes of imaginative engagement with our positions on earth: displacement and deep language learning. *Displacement*, in Spivak's view, shifts belief onto imagination, unseats the constraints of Enlightenment through subalternity, and of monocultural certainty with linguistic diversity. Her notion of displacement arises, in part, from her own experience of voluntary uprootedness, not only in her initial move from Calcutta to New York, but also in her continued traversal between continents. What Spivak refers to as *deep language learning* has the ability to motivate "epistemic performance for the rearrangement of desires,"[14] and she suggests that systems of knowledge might be stimulated, "put on the run," by intense close reading of the type necessary for translation. Deep language learning cultivates desire for active engagement with the world, in turn promoting interrogation of one's own assumptions and encouraging other-oriented thinking.

Spivak suggests that "learning to live with contradictory instructions" produces Bateson's "double bind." We can develop this habit of thought in "play training," where play invites thinking about an action differently. From Bateson, we learn that play, as well as threat and histrionics, are contexts in which acts and events stand in for that which they are not. Bateson observes two chimps, one nipping at the other; the nip stands in for the aggressive bite, but taken as play, the nip "does not denote what would be denoted by the bite."[15] That is, the nip is a bite, but it isn't interpreted as a bite when the understanding between the two chimps is that they are playing. What this involves is an understanding of the metacommunication that occurs in this scenario: the rules governing the actions ("this is play") are implicit in the interaction itself. With Bateson's monkeys, the statement "this is play" produces a paradox where the same sign is both play and fight. (This happens often enough between boys who are play-punching; when one lands a fist too hard, the other cries to his mother, "Billy's fighting"). What we see in this example is not a change in practices (the nip is the same in both instances); what changes instead is the governing context.

In *The Ground Beneath Her Feet*, Rushdie depicts a more extreme case through a game of cricket, where competing geographic contexts change not the rules of the game, but the political valences in which we interpret the scene. Just after the birth of his second set of twin sons, Ormus and Gayomart, Sir Darius Cama, Rushdie's Anglophile figure of the late-Raj period, leaves the hospital to play in an All-City cricket tournament. Although the game in Bombay is played by the rules from London, in Bombay the game is more than a simple competition among national teams. There, British, Hindu, Pakistani, and other ethnicities, such as Parsi, are separated into leagues, demonstrating directly the geopolitical divisions of post-independence India. Additionally, when Sir Darius lobs a cricket ball squarely into the forehead of one of his first set of twin sons, he renders him not immediately, but gradually, completely mute. While on one level the hit is just a poor effort in an important, but not world-ending, game, on another level, the strike transforms the cricket ball into a symbol of cultural silencing, representing the end of a certain world: the Parsi father, with his deep allegiance to all things British, first silences one of the twins and then is silenced himself by the other (who becomes a mass-murderer suffocating his victims by pillow). That is, the silencing the colonial generation inflicts on the subsequent postcolonial generation returns with a vengeance.[16]

Play, as we see in Rushdie's game of cricket, divides two logical schemas according to geography, resulting in paradox. On the one hand, the game in England proceeds as direct signals between teams; on the other hand, the game in India plays out the postcolonial struggle left in the wake of partition. This paradoxical thinking—that is, the framing of both an action and its rules of play or of both a discourse and its rules for reading—is the kind that Spivak wants to inculcate in readers. Rushdie's example demonstrates geography's role in cultivating differing frames of interpretation for the same action or discourse; this vacillation in framing is training in "play."

In addition to play training of the imagination, Spivak instructs in accessing geography (and history) through close reading, specifically the deep, inquisitive, and investigative type necessary for translation. Spivak theorizes that, through literature and the arts, we can "train [...] the imagination in [...] an indefinite series of mutual reflections" in order to provide a critical means to cast off the habit of neglect toward premises and assumptions and to engage in the production of "intended mistakes" that allow us to "learn to learn."[17] That is, we can examine what we view, read, hear in exchanges with others and with texts and, rather than continuing to look, think, listen as we have always done, we might revisit the rules of the game and refuse our assumptions their grant. Immersion into foreign texts occurs at its deepest level during the process of translation; translation calls for the translator to "[g]rasp [...] a writer's presuppositions, [...] as they inform his or her use of language, as they develop into a kind of singular code," making translation "the most intimate act of reading, a prayer to be haunted."[18] In presuppositions lie history and geography; reading in such a way as to discern the writer's presumptions results again in displacement of beliefs, not so much onto imagination, as Spivak prescribes in play, but displacement by supplementation, where the translator makes room in her thinking for the addition of other (the writer's) cultural, linguistically conveyed perspectives.

In ways that are resonant with Spivak's argument, Thomas Keenan argues for unseating an "authoritative cognitive position" by developing habits of reading focused not on a canon, but on "strategies, difficulties, and conditions" of reading that pursue experiences of responsibility. That is, reading itself becomes "not a moment of security or of cognitive certainty," but rather a strategy that "comes with the removal of grounds, the withdrawal of the rules or the knowledge on which we might rely to make our decisions for us."[19] This kind of reading-as-responsibility occurs when we find ways to evade or weaken conceptions of the subject, agency, and identity as grounds for our actions, as instructions for what we should do, as directions for our decisions. Keenan calls for reading that does not return us even to a sense of "self," but instead exposes us to the openness of the other.[20]

Hamid's *Reluctant Fundamentalist* offers an opportunity for and exemplifies such a reading by presenting a literary consciousness living between worlds—Pakistan and the United States—experiencing not the double bind of double consciousness, wherein one mind receives contradictory direction from disparate sources. Instead, this literary consciousness collapses two urban perspectives into a single aspect, such that the visible directives from the distinct locations—Lahore and New York—present to him as a single text. New York looks like Lahore in terms of its vehicle-deterring traffic,[21] its cold, disapproving doormen (49), and its multiplicity of medium-toned skin colors (33), so that even though this Pakistani exchange student and rising financier, Changez,[22] considers himself an outsider in New Haven, he feels himself to be "*immediately* a New Yorker" (33). When he begins to date Erica, a former classmate, he finds her room "the socioeconomic equivalent of a spacious bedroom in a prestigious house in Gulberg [a neighborhood in Lahore], such as the one in which [he] had grown up" (50–51). When he returns to Lahore, Changez recalls to an unknown interlocutor that he meets for conversation in the old town square, a home in New York that resembles his home in Lahore.

However, Lahore turns out to be the palimpsest upon which his New York is written. Changez's younger self slips through the new practices of New York mannerisms and habits. Changez willingly extends himself toward his American colleagues, absorbing the creed of his new employer, Underwood Samson. He brushes aside the insults to Muslims made by Erica's father, even forgives Erica the distance she keeps in their intimate relations. Hamid's literary consciousness is explained in part by turning to Bateson's idea of "mind," which describes an extension and diffusion of self. Opposing Freud's model of the mind that imagines its interior structures motivated by energies (drives), Bateson considers the mind a system that not only includes the body, but also the environment in which the body circulates: "A mind can include nonliving elements as well as multiple organisms, may function for brief as well as extended periods, is not necessarily defined by a boundary such as an envelope of skin, and consciousness, if present at all, is always only partial."[23] Rather than Freud's hierarchy of mental governance—superego, ego, and id—Bateson understands mind, body, and environment as comprising an interdependent ecosystem. Such an ecology is designed to be "vertiginous, [to] challeng[e] familiar habits of mind." According to Bateson, "processes of knowing: perception, communication, coding and translation" (that is, the positive acquisitions of knowledge) form a feedback loop with the knower herself, and this "relationship between the knower and the known" provides a place in which new knowledge can become "knowledge of an expanded self."[24] In such a system of mind, the self can never attain complete self-knowledge because it makes available both material from the world and material from the mind for intellectual and emotional interpretation. Hamid's novel presents an exemplar of self studiously willed toward the other. This model is also instructive for readers. The literary figure is entirely sympathetic: the scrappy underdog at the firm who excels in the competitive environment; the handsome cosmopolite who knows instinctually that his embroidered kurta will be just the right garb to impress the girl's parents; the lover who loses his girl not to neglect or boredom, but to an unassailable opponent, the perpetual mourning for the boyfriend who has died. Hamid's literary figure demonstrates a method for extending the mind's purview, for attenuating self-certainty through an expanded self-conception that diffuses mind itself in the process.

To understand how this conception of mind helps us in conceiving a geography, we might consider the realities of travel, but not the usual sense of modern travel that involves the pre-scripted journey, the pre-planned itinerary, and the agenda of daily events. Rather, as Matt Gross of the *New York Times* writes of his own itinerary-free travel, he "will let the place itself guide [him]," with the hopes that he will be "caught up in moments [he] never could have imagined."[25] Gross avers that he has simply never been lost in almost 30 years of traveling abroad, but he thinks he (and we as fellow travelers) have lost something in not ever getting lost. He suggests breaking free of "the constraints of modern travel, of a culture in which every minute is rigorously planned." Looking ahead to a series of future travels, Gross has decided that rather than plan an itinerary, he will "surrender to the whims of [his] limbs," letting his feet decide. And yet, he understands this experience is arrived at only by radical change in his modes of travel. He will make no hotel reservations, he will hire no guide, he will consult no guidebook, but rather he'll wing it. Even so, he counts on that sense of inner orientation that means he is never lost. We might say that his sense of mind includes cues from the environment; mind and matter work together. Gross's ability is not unlike the skill Fredric Jameson describes as "an aesthetic of cognitive mapping": the ability to carry an image of ourselves as placed, within a social and cultural grid, among ideologies and institutions of the places we know. Whereas Gross wishes to foil a directed journey by "going with the flow" of the city through labyrinthine medina and isolated casbah, Jameson seeks a new mechanism of orientation itself, one that would shake up our interior assuredness and certainties, even as it allows us to resituate. Jameson challenges us to invent a new mental projection, a new mode of representing the world space of multinational capital.[26] Although Jameson's notion of such a projection aims at representation that allows us again to place ourselves in the world, to regain capacity for political action and struggle, and to avoid a paralyzing and undecidable "social confusion," he also advocates undoing our frames of reference in order to resituate ourselves.

A recent critic challenges Jameson, suggesting that the whole "cartographic paradigm" itself must be replaced. Dave Ciccoricco suggests that orienting ourselves by territorial map misses an opportunity to learn from dynamic, unmappable *network* texts. Reading Brian Massumi's account of being lost in his own office,[27] Ciccoricco poses proprioception, in which "bodily memory forms a mode of orientation that we tend to take for granted, one based not on vision but rather on movement."[28] This is Gross's plan for getting lost in the city. Proprioception is, according to Ciccoricco, self-referential and "directly registers [...] displacements of the parts of the body relative to each other." With the self at center, proprioception allows for orientation in a system in flux. He suggests we locate ourselves not in the panoptical sense of cognitive mapping, but in the sense of being on tour, or, turning to texts, in making our way through a novel. Mobile network texts require this moving through what Ciccoricco identifies as a continually changing topology. With Bateson, we might understand proprioception as a physio-imagistic compass. If body is part of mind moving us through experiences that collect into an expanded self by means of perception and knowledge, real or read, then this interleaving of body, mind, and environment, creates a self-made geography. In attempting orientation, an environment of transit emerges, and this environment comes to be part of the mind. Orienting oneself in hypertext and network topologies, proprioceptively, becomes a model for orienting oneself more generally whether reading a text or negotiating the streets of a city. In moving through the world, the perceiver himself simultaneously creates in the journey the mind and the world he traverses that, while not eschewing cardinal directions, complicates them with a fifth centralizing point of orientation.

CATASTROPHE

As much as proprioception seems to elide standard systems of geographic orientation, in a way it simply solidifies a sense of self rather than uprooting it. It reaffirms the subject as the center of orientation and ensures the authoritative ground from which one might speak of experience. Following Keenan, we see that literature exempts us from this authority, even as it might seem to concretize it: language, as found in literature (or rhetoric, text, fable) produces an "elsewhere" that reminds us of empirical reality and history but also, he notes, constitutes an "alterity that precedes [subjectivity] and that [the subject] cannot understand." That is, "others and their traces are always working within us already, in a space and time that cannot be reduced to that of consciousness or self-presence."[29] Thus literature, featuring worlds with which we are unfamiliar, may provide us situations of unplanned itinerary through uncharted terrain, a site of reading without advance organization or settled theoretical approach to the text's complexities. Hamid and Rushdie accentuate the unplanned, portraying it in its most extreme case, catastrophe.

Hamid's narrator, as we have seen, straddles US and Pakistani territories, but sees their similarities as globalized, cosmopolitan urban centers . . . that is, until such a view is permanently marred by catastrophe. The destruction of the World Trade Center's two towers acts as the pivotal moment of this book, just as it occurred in the middle of Hamid's writing of the novel. Beginning the book in the summer of 2000, Hamid was writing "an utterly minimalist account of a Pakistani valuation expert who decides to return to Pakistan despite loving New York."[30] After multiple rejections, Hamid's narrative is jarred by the catastrophe that strikes the world: 9/11 suspends the usual modes of orientation through the visual and psychological collapse of New York's financial signature, the Towers.

The novel itself stages the horrific destruction as the culmination of disorientation, suggesting that when disorientation intensifies it reaches a point when orientation dissipates and no longer functions as a way of knowing ourselves (safe, powerful, leading, benevolent) by our location (in the United States). Just pages before the narration of the disaster, Changez confesses that his extraordinary success at Underwood Samson was at times plagued by "moments when [he] became disoriented" (66). Changez is with the firm on his first overseas assignment in The Philippines. At a stop sign, he is suddenly conscious of a Filipino bicyclist pulled up beside them. The bicyclist glares when they catch each other's eye, and in that moment Changez realizes that, in Pakistan, he would certainly be that local bicyclist. He turns his gaze back to his fellow American limousine passengers and thinks, "they are so foreign." In traffic in East Asia, in transit via elite US business transport, Changez suddenly recognizes that he is neither a New Yorker nor a Filipino. Rather than identifying with one or the other, he is conscious of being neither, neither the common man-on-the-street of Bangkok, nor the chauffeured US businessman. He *feels* his "Pakistaniness" though it remains invisible as he later sits in the bar with his cohorts; his suit, expense account, and companions cloak his ethnic identity (71). While in the United States, Changez had been able to balance the paradox of place by claiming the simultaneity of Lahore and New York; abroad the façade of Americanness begins to crumble. He knows himself as belonging neither to the West nor to the East; the ground of his identity shifts with the change of locations, which we often understand as a positive result from travel. However, the sedimentary, tectonic plates that form the basis of Changez's identity begin to shift, fracturing a self-image built upon a sense of congruent metropoles. 9/11 completely shatters this illusion of singularity, which Changez compensates by intensifying orientation toward the East, a point to which we return below.

Hamid catapults disorientation into confusion, not by the usual depiction of chaos and disaster, not by inconsolable weeping or utter bafflement, and not only by separating Changez from the whole first-hand experience though he lives in Manhattan at the time, but also by depicting the cataclysm not as disaster, as expected, but as an occasion for celebration, though fleeting, of the fall of Western power. In 2006, when the novel was finished, discussion of 9/11 brought an expectation of the language of grief, tragedy, and trauma. The few dissenting voices were immediately and publicly derided. Hamid dared to depict a character who smiled, not at the fate of the victims, but at the symbolism of the fall (70). This smile also indicates, perversely, pleasure in a certain self-destruction. If Changez's identity is cached in the sediment of Lahore and New York, then the devastation to New York translates into severe personal injury. The ground of self-secure knowledge is destabilized by the destruction of the World Trade Center, destabilized by the exposure of the gaps of personal and national self-knowledge, including knowledge of others.[31] The novel depicts the split in the cemented foundation of Changez's personality when the West is prized from the East. Any sense of being Western is exposed as illusory as Changez makes his hugely more complicated way back to New York, separated from his US compatriots by airport security, passenger scrutiny, and strangers' stares. The novel characterizes 9/11's fault lines between the East and the West, denying the very continuity that it had carefully constructed in portraying Lahore and New York as palimpsests. With the irruption of 9/11 mid-novel, a period in which the ordered sense of orientation, separated into identifiable quadrants of the earth, is thrown into tumult by airborne terrorists in an attack that reverses geopolitical power arrangements with the intrusion of the East into the West.

The novel further stages this geopolitical reversal in the formal presentation of its plot. It frames Changez's US experience within a conversation between Changez and an unknown interlocutor in a teashop in the Old Anarkali plaza of Lahore. The unknown man may be CIA, but the novel denies assurances; we never know for certain who the man is, not because he is not described, but because we never hear anything that he says. He is a mute figure to readers. We hear only Changez who offers us unflattering portrayals of the man as uneasy, alarmed, armed, and salacious in gazing at the young female art students who walk by. Thus, what begins as a world we know—America's largesse in inviting foreign exchange students to learn at our institutions of higher education and to assume positions with large salaries at high-profile firms, both underscored by Changez's willingness to see New York as his home through similarities with his own home—capitulates with catastrophe that collapses the charted spheres of the globe, deconstructing global power at a local level by asserting an Eastern voice that dominates a changed geopolitics.

Rushdie's *The Ground Beneath Her Feet* employs catastrophe to disrupt the narrative almost as soon as it starts, before the plot unfolds. The novel opens with a distortion of fact and time: the Category 10 earthquake of September 19, 1985, in Mexico City, is reset to coincide with Rushdie's personal earthquake, the Ayatollah Khomeini's *fatwah* against him issued on February 14, 1989. The co-protagonist, a rock singer of worldwide fame, Vina Apsara, dies in this earthquake. She is far from home on her first solo tour without her costar, Ormus Cama, and has just spent a compensatory night of rough sex and hard drugs after a mediocre concert in Mexico City. In a compromising position after her sexual partner for the evening nearly dies, Vina calls on her doting friend, photo-journalist Umeed Merchant (better known as Rai), who drops everything, as usual, and rushes to her side. The occasion without Ormus allows Rai and Vina to become lovers (something he has always wanted). The earthquake disrupts the short-lived bliss of new love; Rai sends Vina off by helicopter to a coastal resort, promising to join her; even though she begs him to come with her, he insists upon staying to record the destruction of the earthquake. They never meet again. Vina's helicopter crashes and, since it is never found, is presumed swallowed by an open crevice in the earth's surface. Vina disappears into an underworld where manmade parameters of orientation hold no purchase. With her demise, Ormus and Rai lose orientation in a more metaphorical sense; she is their East. This catastrophe initiates the novel's continuing interrogation of orientational systems. The trajectory of global connectedness that the rock stars inscribe on the earth's surface in their globe-trotting lifestyles, based on an itinerary of worldwide tours that leap from one metropolitan center to another, is challenged, suspect in the face of this opening disaster. At any time, the ground might shift, obviating, at least temporarily, the need for orientation as it has been known.

SERIAL HETEROTOPIA

The Ground Beneath Her Feet is all about how a trio of Bombay youths locates its place in the world, ordered around a traditional sense of cartographic concepts. Recalling the importance of the East to medieval maps and to Christian narratives, Rushdie claims a positional preeminence for the East: "Ask any navigator; the east is what you sail by. Lose the east and you lose your bearings, your certainties, your knowledge of what is and what may be, perhaps even your life.

Where was that star you followed to that manger? That's right. The east orients. That's the official version. The language says so, and you should never argue with the language."[32]

Rushdie takes us back to the etymology of orientation. This linguistic starting point recalls Said's similar academic beginning in *Orientalism*, which firmly demarcates the Orient, describing it from multiple disciplines and perspectives. The ways in which the "Orient" became constituted as a foil to the "Occident" directed much of Said's own scholarship, as well as that of many a subsequent scholar. But if charting the East orients navigators, real and metaphorical, in multiple dimensions, spatial, etymological, existential, Rushdie is not so sure it is a worthy goal. Laying out the benefits that the East provides in allowing us to become oriented, he immediately dares us to give it up: "What if the whole deal—orientation, knowing where you are, and so on—what if it's all a scam?" (176). "What if home, kinship, the whole enchilada is only brainwashing; what if daring releases you to live your own life; what if you have to get lost, venture into chaos and beyond, accept loneliness and the wild panic of losing your moorings before your life is your own" (177). To lose the East is to be not only disoriented, but also and more so, *de*-oriented. Only in risking loss of the East, in abandoning a particular direction conventionalized by centuries of mapmaking and orientating tools,[33] can you hope to truly live.

The Ground Beneath Her Feet portrays in two different figures how de-orienting might occur and how to compensate such a condition. The novel presents, on the one hand, a literary consciousness that deals with a series of material losses of secure location, and on the other, another literary consciousness that locates a directional substitute, a new figure of the East. The first strategy we might conceive of as a serial heterotopia; the second as a refiguration of the markers of orientation. It is Ormus who is trapped in a series of heterotopic locations. While Vina travels the world on the power of her four-octave voice and high-octane rock performances, and while Rai chases photographic catastrophes around the globe, Ormus, suffers agonizingly long transitions that go nowhere, plotting a random, serial heterotopography. If, as Michel Foucault suggests, heterotopias exist in society as "something like counter-sites," like mirrors to society, which are "at once absolutely real" and "absolutely unreal,"[34] then these spaces of crisis and deviation marginalized by society are the locations in which Rushdie's character careens. Ormus experiences episodes in underground, off-ground, off-shore, and out-of-body situations in locales where cartography has no purchase, locations where mapping by cardinal orientation-markers makes little sense. As Foucault notes, hospitals, prisons, cemeteries are "not freely accessible like a public space," but rather remain outside society's navigable throughways, having their own particular navigation systems that include orientation-markers encountered in no other, except like spaces.[35]

The series of heterotopic episodes for Ormus begins, vis-à-vis the plot, after the earthquake, but chronologically in the earliest years of his life when as a boy he travels to the underworld, propelled by deep meditation, seeking his twin brother, Gayomart, who has died in childbirth. Ormus runs through the levels of the underworld—what turns out to be a kind of writer's hell with unfinished characters waiting to be brought to life—trying to catch up with the ever-elusive Gayo, who runs ahead leaving in his wake melodies without words, songs which Ormus hears only as nonsense syllables dressed in tunes that turn out to be early rock hits, like Peter, Paul, and Mary's "Blowin' in the Wind." Rushdie suggests that Ormus, like his mythological analog Orpheus, will live between spheres, but Ormus's divided world is not only above and below ground, but rather his existence on earth also takes place in de-oriented places. Heterotopias multiply: Ormus departs Bombay and arrives in London only after a preternaturally long flight, during which he is talked into eschewing land for four months at sea; he debarks the plane, only to be immediately set adrift, marooned on a radio boat in the English Channel. (We remember that Foucault calls the ship the "heterotopia *par excellence*.") Thereafter, Ormus spends two years in a coma; several years performing in a glass silo, a coffin-like case lowered over him on stage, sealing him off from fans, and nearly a decade holed up in a twilit video studio seeking glimpses of Vina on dozens of televised video feeds from around the world, hoping against hope that Vina still lives since although she disappeared in the earthquake, her body was never found. Thus, even though Rushdie instructs us to give up orientation altogether, at least one result of such non-directedness is paralysis. The novel seems to affirm Jameson's notion that politics require located-ness: Ormus, without the "ground beneath [his] feet," and left in a series of unstable places—flight cabin to video chamber—is isolated, vulnerable to fantasies, unable to act.

REFIGURED ORIENTATION-MARKERS

Rushdie gives us some hope beyond ungrounded paralysis by suggesting that the Orient comes in many forms; the East is not an absolute truth. We already understand this notion from the dichotomy

of norths: "true north" guides us toward the North Pole, while "magnetic north" pulls us toward a shifting geomagnetic center located
at various, shifting points in northern Canada ("Wandering"). Thus,
when Rai must finally give up Vina, he finds Mira, the woman who
tries and fails to be a Vina-impersonator. Unlike Ormus, who can find
no substitute for Vina, who never regains his place in the world, and
who, instead, is assassinated John Lennon-like as soon as he steps from
his isolation chamber, Rai reorients toward another figure of the East,
toward an imitation of Vina, an imitation of the East. Rai transfers orientational value to Mira, who is simultaneously a fake Vina, a "mira"
(mirror) of Vina, but also a real self, another form of orientation
for Rai. Thus, the novel not only questions a singular conception of
the East, and by extension other cardinal directions, but also demonstrates the value in trusting other orientation-markers, even false ones.
Neither a particular signal of orientation, nor a singular orientational
system, needs to dominate our sense of place in the world.

   The Reluctant Fundamentalist takes the opposite tack: the East
dominates the protagonist's sense of orientation, but it is a thick,
complex, and complicated East. It is multipart and difficult, incorpo-
rating the West and complicating direction. In contrast to *The Ground
Beneath Her Feet*, Hamid's novel not only re-establishes the East,
but also insists upon it as the only marker of orientation. We read
Hamid's depiction of a Pakistani-American dialogue in which the
Pakistani voice is the only one heard as a critique of US imperialism
and as an assertion of Eastern views in the world. Oddly enough, the
mute American may also be read as having expected political recognition and prominence. That is, the novel may indicate that the most
powerful figures among us need not talk at all to be heard. In this
novel, the East orients, but the West hidden within the East never
relinquishes orientational authority. Hamid poses *The Reluctant Fundamentalist* as an American post-9/11 allegory. We see it particularly
in the scenes that occur after Changez graduates Princeton; he moves
into Western life, winning a position at a prestigious financial services
firm, Underwood Samson (an exemplary figure of the United States)
and falling in love with Erica (linked with her namesake, Am-erica).
She can never fully allow herself to love Changez because she mourns
the death of her boyfriend from high school, Chris (Christian, in our
morality tale). Immersed in Western culture and, increasingly, in capital (he is well paid in the United States), Changez assumes a Western
identity.

   Unlike Rushdie's character, who substitutes one East for another,
Hamid's protagonist, Changez, keeps the East firmly in sight, even

among a greatly increased anti-Muslim sentiment after September 11, 2001; despite the "reluctance" in the title, the novel is a radical orientation to the East, creating a sense of single-mindedness that is disorienting in its ever-multiplying Easts. The novel's present occurs wholly in the East, narrated by Changez, now a professor in Lahore and a potential terrorist on US watchlists. The novel's past also establishes touchstones of the East in the United States: not only does Changez locate a Pakistani deli and work at Princeton's East Asian library, but also, more importantly, he presents his past within the frame of the East, part of the present-moment teahouse dialogue. On one hand, then, the present directly challenges any claim to predominance on the part of the West by silencing the Western voice. Readers never "hear" the voice of the unnamed interlocutor. On the other hand, the (CIA) man retains his anonymity, so that the violence portended at novel's end has no known agent. The perpetrator (or victim . . . it is never completely clear) retains his cover. Since the visible signals are all one-sided, readers are oriented by Changez, by the East; however, the Western figure retains a certain power under cover of and camouflaged by the East. The East becomes a refigured palimpsest; in this case it is not Lahore barely detectable through the image of New York, but the reverse in which the West is visible and audible only in traces of the prevailing East. The Orient as an East that is no longer purely East becomes a mode of de-orientation. The Orient itself de-orients.

CONCLUSION

These novels, while reconsidering the assumptions of cardinality undergirding geography, do not completely dispense with the conception of orientation, but they change our approach to it. Rather than the four cardinal points equipoised and present to direct our travel, our gaze, our pursuits of knowledge, these novels suggest we may think differently about global positioning. Although there are places on this planet that we know by empirical data and observation that cannot be denied, Said directs us to "imaginative geographical and historical knowledge," which create a sense of "something *more* than what appears to be merely positive knowledge."[36] This something more is often what cannot so easily be charted. If literary texts provide sites that train the imagination, they also produce an "elsewhere," an alternative empirical reality and history that questions the societal conventions, ideologies, disciplines of "here." Keenan advises difficult reading so that the text itself may cease to be a moral authority conveying lessons for human relations. Paying less attention to what establishes us in what we know and more attention to sense-defying elements of language, we might uproot our assumptions, making of literature that place of undecidability, chance, and risk, where undecidability is not uncertainty or "a fog of confusion," but rather a frontier that necessitates passage "from one side to another, to the other."[37] That is, language puts responsibility to the other in play in the literary text; the literary text "reintroduce[s] the complexity and the difficulty of the rhetorical into the theory and practice of politics," undermining self-certainty in recognizing what François Lyotard calls "the silence of the other inside us."[38]

Thus, literature and literary pedagogy have not only the task of presenting us unfamiliar realities from other worlds, but also the much more difficult work of destabilizing the frames of reference into which we pigeonhole experience, of instilling openness to the other that resides as a "second existence" (Lyotard) within us. The world literature classroom becomes a site where mental compasses might be recalibrated. Aesthetic education might be conceived as offering sites off the cartographic grid where we might practice repeatedly repositioning ourselves; this essay rehearses possibilities: letting place guide exploration (Gross), recognizing double binds rather than reconciling them (Spivak), developing a dyslexia of place to see its pluralities (Hamid), de-orienting through heterotopic episodes (Rushdie), and refiguring cardinality (Rushdie and Hamid). Geography of aesthetic education in Spivak's sense would certainly include world literature as a site of play training and exercise in conditions of the double bind. However, literature also offers us geographies for imaginative traversal for which the standard compass simply does not apply. World literature is the broad terrain on which we must de-orient the geographies we encounter in our aesthetic educations, find new modes of orientation, and gain bearings that avoid the quadrangular arrangement of self-referential knowledge that we think we know.

NOTES

1. See Henri Lefebvre, *The Production of Space*, trans. Donald Nicholson-Smith (Oxford: Blackwell, 1991), v.
2. Geospace refers to "the real, physical space, which can be described geographically and represented cartographically, with measurable distances between any desired points." It contrasts virtual "textual space," which is figured in language and often represents geospace. See Anne-Kathrin Reuschel, Barbara Piatti and Lorenz

Hurni, "Modelling Uncertain Geodata for the Literary Atlas of Europe," in *Understanding Different Geographies*, ed. Karel Kriz, William Cartwright, and Michaela Kinberger (Berlin and Heidelberg: Springer-Verlag, 2013), 138.

3. See Bernard Stiegler, "Introduction," in *Technics and Time, 2: Disorientation*, trans. Stephen Barker (Stanford: Stanford University Press, 2009), 1–13. Other systems preceded the current one established by the technology of the compass, including the well-known system of orientation provided by medieval T-and-O maps depicting *orbis terrarium* as a circle incised by a T, in which Asia is placed above the crossbar and this top of the map is East; Europe and Africa occupy either side of the vertical bar, and Jerusalem is at the intersection, as the center of the world. See Robert T. Tally, *Spatiality* (London: Routledge, 2013), 20, 158.

4. Lefebvre, *The Production of Space*, 192.

5. Tally, *Spatiality*, 21.

6. Paul Gans, "Compass," *The Medieval Technology Pages* (October 8, 2002) http://scholar.chem.nyu.edu/tekpages/compass.html. [accessed May 5, 2014].

7. Gregory Bateson, "The Science of Mind and Order," in *Steps to an Ecology of Mind* (Chicago and London: University of Chicago Press, 2000 [Orig. 1972]).

8. Edward W. Said, *Orientalism*, 25th anniversary ed. (New York: Vintage, 1994), 25. The line is also quoted in Gayatri Chakravorty Spivak, *An Aesthetic Education in an Era of Globalization* (Cambridge, MA: Harvard University Press, 2012), 458.

9. Spivak, *An Aesthetic Education in an Era of Globalization*, 20.

10. Bachelard quotes the lessons of Jean Lescure: "Knowing must therefore be accompanied by an equal capacity to forget knowing. Nonknowing is not a form of ignorance but a difficult transcendence of knowledge." See Gaston Bachelard, *The Poetics of Space*, trans. Maria Jolas (Boston: Beacon Press, 1969 [Orig. 1958]), xxviii–xxix.

11. Bernard Stiegler, in a complex argument, proposes that technics (technology and techno-science) disorient worldviews through processes of innovation and invention that precede social change, thus becoming the "engine of all motivation." Further, cardinality, though established in a highly stable period, provided the scaffolding for "geographic givens" still in use today, even though the directions of East–West now have associations that produce "particular experiences of disorientation." See Stiegler, "Introduction," 2–3.

12. Lefebvre, *The Production of Space*, 38–39. Lefebvre is concerned particularly with the production of social space; space is both "a *product* to be used, to be consumed, [and] it is a *means of production;* networks of exchange and flows of raw materials and energy fashion space and are determined by it" (85). Although he is suspicious of literature's ability to theorize the disjunction of physical, mental, and social space,

he does credit "literary authors" who have "written much of relevance, especially descriptions of places and sites" (14); he does note
that "an already produced space can be decoded, can be *read*" (17).

13. Lefebvre, *The Production of Space*, 14.
14. Spivak, *An Aesthetic Education in an Era of Globalization*, xxx.
15. Bateson, "The Science of Mind and Order," 180.
16. See Salman Rushdie, *The Ground Beneath Her Feet* (New York and
    London: Henry Holt, 1999), 27–30, 45–47. See also Cameron
    Bushnell, *Postcolonial Readings of Music in World Literature: Turn-
    ing Empire on its Ear* (New York and London: Routledge, 2013),
    163–165.
17. Spivak, *An Aesthetic Education in an Era of Globalization*, 9.
18. Ibid., 257.
19. Thomas Keenan, *Fables of Responsibility: Aberrations and Predica-
    ments in Ethics and Politics* (Stanford: Stanford University Press,
    1997), 1.
20. Arguing for a relinquishment of the "immodest self-certainty of one
    who resets content in the good sense of a responsibility properly
    assumed," one who speaks from "an authoritative cognitive position,"
    Keenan offers us "no one," open to differences and alterity within,
    the subject resisting subjectivity by means of "constant, recurrent
    exposure to risk," the risk found in literature. See Keenan, *Fables of
    Responsibility*, 176.
21. Mohsin Hamid, *The Reluctant Fundamentalist* (New York: Harcourt,
    2007), 32. Hereafter references to this novel will be given in the text.
22. Sumood Almawaoshi has brought it to my attention that the name
    Changez, while ringing in English and French ears with the idea
    of change, also alludes to Genghis, particularly Genghis Kahn,
    thirteenth-century founder of the Mongol Empire, whose territorial
    expansion was accomplished through wholesale slaughter of the van-
    quished, but who also united warring Mongol tribes and brought
    Eastern and Western civilizations into contact while building the
    largest contiguous landed empire in history. David Gay also notes that
    in Urdu, Changez is pronounced "Chun-gaze," the name for Genghis
    Kahn; see Gay, "Confronting Myths of Difference: Fundamental-
    ism, Religion and Globalization in Mohsin Hamid's *The Reluctant
    Fundamentalist*," *Religious Studies and Theology* 30.1 (2011), 58.
23. Mary Catherine Bateson, "Foreword," in Gregory Bateson, *Steps to an
    Ecology of Mind* (Chicago and London: University of Chicago Press,
    2000 [Orig. 1972]), x–xi.
24. Ibid., xii–xiii.
25. See Matt Gross, "Lost in Tangier," *New York Times* Reprint. Septem-
    ber 9, 2010, *NYTimes.com* [accessed April 2, 2013].
26. See Fredric Jameson, "Postmodernism, or, the Cultural Logic of Late
    Capitalism," in *The Jameson Reader*, ed. Michael Hardt and Kathi
    Weeks (Oxford and Malden, MA: Blackwell), especially 231–232.

27. Massumi recounts taking a path through the building that makes him think that he sees North from his window, when in reality it is East. The recognition of his mistake is disorienting. See Brian Massumi, "Strange Horizon: Buildings, Biograms, and the Body Topologic," in *Parables for the Virtual: Movement, Affect, Sensation* (Duke University Press, 2002).

28. Dave Ciccoricco, "Network Vistas: Folding the Cognitive Map," *Image [&] Narrative* 8 *Melanges/Miscellaneous* (May 2004), n. pag.

29. Keenan, *Fables of Responsibility*, 66.

30. Hamish Hamilton, "Interview with Mohsin Hamid on *The Reluctant Fundamentalist*," May 12, 2014. http://www.mohsinhamid.com/interviewhh2007.html [accessed May 12, 2014]. See also Gay, "Confronting Myths of Difference," 62.

31. Spivak identifies a similar irruption between epistemology and ethics, where the epistemological attempts "to construct the other as object of knowledge [...] in order to punish or acquit rationally," and the ethical, in contrast, "listen[s] to the other as if it were a self, neither to punish nor acquit." See Spivak, *An Aesthetic Education in an Era of Globalization*, 374.

32. Rushdie, *The Ground Beneath Her Feet*, 176. Hereinafter cited parenthetically in the text.

33. Tally discusses centuries of mapmaking, including the *mappamundi* and T-and-O maps of Medieval cartography, which "combin[e] religious instruction and geographic information" (20–21), as well as the "portolan charts" made by early fifteenth-century Mediterranean navigators to detail coastlines and harbors (25).

34. Michel Foucault, "Of Other Spaces," trans. Jay Miskowiec, *Diacritics* 16.1 (1986), 24.

35. Ibid., 26.

36. Said, *Orientalism*, 55.

37. Keenan, *Fables of Responsibility*, 12–13.

38. Qtd. in Keenan, *Fables of Responsibility*, 189.

CHAPTER 8

DANGEROUS INSIGHT: (NOT) SEEING AUSTRALIAN ABORIGINES IN THE *NARRATIVE* OF *JAMES MURRELLS*

Kristine Kelly

Concluding his brief account of castaway James Murrells's (also spelled Morrill) return to Australian settler society in 1863 after living with Aborigines for 17 years, popular colonial chronicler James Bonwick notes that this man's insight into Aboriginal life rendered him surprisingly ineffectual as a mediating influence between Aboriginal Australians and British colonial settlers. Bonwick writes, "The blacks mistrust the deserter of their camp fires; and the whites threaten him already with deadly hostility for supposed confederation with the natives to the injury of the flocks."[1] Bonwick admits his regret over the failed connection. Nevertheless, first-hand accounts of lost-and-found travelers like Murrells become, despite their failure at promoting cultural negotiation, the basis for Bonwick's subsequent ethnographic account of Aboriginal manners and customs. For Bonwick, the preservation of such ethnographic insights offers a response to what was believed to be the imminent disappearance of Aboriginal peoples.

In another account of Murrells's failure as a mediator, an 1870 article in the Sydney *Empire* ends by noting, "It is a great pity that the experience and intelligence of this man were not made available, as he was anxiously desirous that they should be, for the purpose

of bringing about a better understanding between the frontier settlers and their men and the aboriginal tribes." Such an understanding
might, this report suggests, have intervened on the "the wanton and
cruel attacks upon the blacks by the Native Police." Written seven
years after Murrells's 1863 return to settler society and five years after
his death, this report contends that Murrells's advocacy of making
Aboriginal rights visible "gained him few friends and many enemies."
Following this opening statement on failure, the writer moves on to
the tale of shipwreck and the plight of the survivors, omitting any
further description of Murrell's 17 years living among Aborigines.
This posthumous report recognizes lost opportunities, but ultimately
it sidesteps that topic as it foregrounds lost sailors and castaways for
readers desiring a good story.[2] During his years among the Aborigines, Murrells had gained an extraordinary knowledge of Australian
flora and fauna, geographical routes, and Aboriginal culture. As such,
he should have been an excellent source for cultural insight. This
chapter questions why Murrells seems to be recalled often as the man
who failed at mediating between frontier settlers and Australian Aborigines and thus explores the cultural and literary contexts in which
his narrative was produced.

Murrells's story belongs, in part, with those colonial accounts in the
mid-nineteenth century that seem typically to hover at the frontier of
settlement and wilderness or at the boundary between "us and them."
This active state of inhabiting liminal space between home and away
becomes a feature of a complex and brutal negotiation of national
identity for British colonial settlers. Speaking of exile and nationalism, Edward Said suggests that they are constituting oppositions as
"All nationalisms [...] develop from a condition of estrangement."
In Britain's settler colonies, this connection between exile and nationalism became multilayered as emigrants exiled from their homeland,
voluntarily or by compulsion, clung to the places from which they
(were) cast away, while also claiming another geographical place both
as a new, other world and as an extension of home. In the process of
their exile, colonial emigrants, as is well known, displaced indigenous
inhabitants causing another trend of exile. Within this multilayered
space of exclusion and re-association, the colonial settler inhabited
what Said suggests is "the perilous territory of not-belonging" that lies
"just beyond the frontier between 'us' and the 'outsiders.'"[3] In this
dangerous place, the usual organizing effects of borders don't apply
and established hierarchies are unstable. Here, in this imagined and
geographically-real, in-between space of not quite home and not quite
exile, colonial Australian writers, like Bonwick, show both fascination

with the Aboriginal other and recognition of this other's influence on British colonial identity, *even and especially in his corporeal absence.* That is to say, even as British colonists claimed the land and extended the frontier, the recognition of failed negotiation with the Aboriginal people, who they instead confronted, killed, displaced, assimilated, or exiled, becomes a component factor in the colonists' tenuous sense of place. This condition of being "exiled-to-home" engendered a kind of colonial literature that sought literally to write out the presence of Aboriginal peoples.

For those castaways, convicts, or free settlers exiled to colonial Australia, travel from Great Britain to colony involved embracing or resisting a transformation of identity with regard to a new geographical orientation. Insomuch as this transformation involved cultural exchange, resistance occurred through various strategies both outright and roundabout. James Murrells's story in the *Narrative of James Murrells' ("Jemmy Morrill") Seventeen Years' Exile among the Wild Blacks of North Queensland, and His Life and Shipwreck and Terrible Adventures among Savage Tribes; Their Manners, Customs, Languages, and Superstitions; also Murrells' Rescue and Return to Civilization,* transcribed and edited by colonial journalist Edmund Gregory, offers a conflicted presentation of both the castaway's transformation and the transcriber's resistance that illuminates the unsettling condition of colonial exile. The *Narrative* demonstrates an effort both to see and not to see the Aboriginal people accounted for. This castaway tale demonstrates some of the rhetorical strategies that colonial writers made in claiming colonial space and disclaiming Aboriginal tenure.[4]

In this essay, I reread Murrells's narrative of shipwreck and return as it is prefaced and retold by Gregory in the revised edition of 1896 to show how transcriber and subject differ in their attitudes toward cultural integration as they narrate the dangerously transformative nature of colonial space. Their efforts either to represent or resist the changes caused by radical displacement contribute to a text that is uneven and lacking in ideological coherence even while it presents a fairly straightforward narrative sequence in which Murrells is lost at sea, found by Aborigines, and then finds his way home. This uneven narration, and Murrells's interruptions to his transcriber's conventional story (about the castaway's resistance to and rescue from savagery), illustrate how for many colonial writers, coping with exile involved a rhetorical strategy that dismissed Aboriginal presence. As such, the *Narrative of James Murrells* offers a point against which to read other colonial accounts, such as those penned by Englishman and emigration advocate Samuel Sidney or those of writers like Bonwick who wrote of Australian colonial history, to show how cultural negotiation was actively resisted or benignly overlooked by a rhetorical strategy of not seeing Aboriginal presence (even contradictorily when it was seen). By unraveling the threads that contribute to Murrells's story and untangling the dual discourses within the story itself, I hope to show how this castaway narrative demonstrates a fairly consistent resistance to the insight it offers. Because of Murrells's very efforts to provide knowledge about Aboriginal culture, his narrative as transcribed by Gregory exemplifies how colonial writers and activists wrote to erase Aboriginal presence from their stories and histories so as to overwrite their ethical obligations and, perhaps, to divert attention from their role in the forcible exile of Aboriginal people.

SPEAKING OF ABSENCE: HOW COLONIAL WRITERS AVOIDED (IN)SIGHT

Australian colonists and colonial officials explained the decimation of the Aboriginal population using various rhetorical formulations. Because of the need to justify the actual and potential disappearance of a race in the face of colonial settlement, this absence, itself, becomes a defining characteristic of settler identity. For instance, commenting on the vehement racist rhetoric common among frontier settlers, historian Henry Reynolds explains that the terms in which settlers consistently, especially after 1840, depicted blacks, such as "merely brutes" or "ungrateful, deceitful wily, and treacherous" (despite various philanthropic and fair-minded voices that refuted such characterization), coincided with frontier settlers' need to claim the geographical and political landscape.[5] To facilitate colonial land acquisition and to define the terms of nation building, many frontier settlers maintained a militantly derogative attitude toward the Aborigines whose lands they annexed as if they were uninhabited. The frontier was, as Reynolds notes, typically a space in which settlers resisted negotiation or integration. Describing the brutality with which settlers at the frontier hunted down and massacred Aborigines, Reynolds writes that, "Racism was as functional for the frontier squatter as the Colt revolver. One cleared the land, the other cleared the conscience." Racist discourse in which Aborigines' humanity was negated was directed not to control the other, but to erase the other's claims "to the full rights and privileges of humanity" and thus to minimize the colonizers' moral accountability with regard to their removal.[6] Racist language served to distract attention from settlers' own violent behaviors; by dehumanizing victims, anti-human behaviors become less recognizable. The identity of the "frontier" was formed not only by emphasizing difference but also by the forceful denial of Aboriginal presence as a "real" issue of human engagement, and as such, the liminal place of the frontier is both acknowledged (as a space of confrontation) and denied (as a space of potential sociocultural engagement). It is a conflicted space of both presence and absence. In reading colonial stories like Murrells's, one sees a derogatory language inscribed into the overlying fabric of the text, almost exclusively at points in the text in which Gregory's overseeing hand is emphasized or his revisions offer subtle shifts in descriptive emphasis regarding the habits of Aborigines. However, such language is also resisted by Murrells's voice as he consistently emphasizes the humanity of his adopted tribesmen and his own pleasure in seeing them.

A key component of settler identity, then, might be conceived as this (desire for a) clear view over the landscape that elides over a humanly real Aboriginal presence. The Australian stories of Samuel Sidney offer some further insight into how such clarity was written into the colonial story. An emigration advocate and a prolific writer, Sidney published a variety of works throughout the 1840s and 1850s on this subject including, *Sidney's Australian Handbook* (1848), *Sidney's Emigrant Journal* (1848–1850), and *The Three Colonies of Australia* (1852). He addressed the question of emigration "from an emigrant's point of view, and...[sought] to give such practical advice, founded on [his] large experience of the emigrating classes."[7] Sidney had not, himself, been to Australia, and for much of colonial knowledge, he relied on his brother, John Sidney, who had spent six years in New South Wales, and on the work of other advocates of working-class emigration. Sidney wanted to make the Australian colonies inviting to working-class people, who, before efforts such as his and those of other advocates, "were merely shovelled out on the shores, like so much live stock to find their own way to market—to service, to marriage, to sin, or death."[8] Sidney assisted the working-class emigrant in finding his place in the distant Antipodes, and in effect, he wrote to thwart the alienating, antinationalistic effects of exile and to construct the identity of Australian settlers as heroes of the Empire who worked hard to extend the borders of home.

His tales of adventure in the Australian outback published in his own *Emigrants' Journal* and subsequently in Charles Dickens's weekly journal *Household Words* (1850–1859), illustrate the work of settlers claiming land and often battling Aborigines in the process. Typically, his subjects are rough, working men whose quests for decent living conditions are hindered by arbitrary colonial policies, by the greed of so-called "gentlemen," and by debased and war-mongering natives. In making the unknown colonial space known through his contributions to a popular magazine like *Household Words,* Sidney addresses the journal's readers' misconceptions (and underestimations) of the value and relevance of the colonial settler. He wrote to increase the visibility of settlers as core players in colonial expansion.

The stories in which he narrated settlers' confrontations with Aborigines not only present the excitement of conquering an alien land and people, but they also reinforce racial hierarchies necessary to delineate Britain's own working classes from "real" savages abroad and were thus didactic prescriptions for colonial attitudes. For instance, in the story, "An Exploring Adventure" (1850), Sidney's narrator recounts his experience in claiming farmland despite resistance from "wild" Aborigines. In this account, the narrator searches for new pastures for his livestock under the threat of impending drought, but while exploring, he and his fellow settlers have two unhappy encounters with Aborigines. In the first, they come upon a station run by an English "gentleman" who "had sought to make his fortune in Australia" but who lacked the discipline to clear the land and who instead has made his station the meeting place of "a tribe of tame blacks." By associating familiarly with the local Aborigines, this gentleman becomes, readers are told, utterly degraded—"unwashed, uncombed, pale-faced and red-eyed, surrounded by half-a-dozen black gins (his sultanas), a lot of dogs, poultry, a tame kangaroo, and two of his men." He has clearly crossed the border of the frontier and taken a place among a motley crowd where beast and human are contiguously linked, suggesting little differentiation. This fear that coexistence with indigenous peoples might lead to degeneracy is a common theme in both colonial and metropolitan literature about the colonies, and the abruptness with which the adventurers of "An Exploring Adventure" leave this scene gives the author an opportunity to remind his readers that such a coexistence is neither desirable nor acceptable.[9]

Leaving behind this scene of racial and social degeneracy, the narrator describes the vastness of the land to which they travel. After crossing a "dividing range," the adventurers are "rejoiced by the sight of the wished-for land," a vast, verdant pasture for the cattle. The landscape is a "delicious prospect," connoting the narrator's voracious appetite and his eye toward consuming the space. He claims it despite clear evidence in the crisscrossing paths that this land is being well traveled by Aborigines. As he marks his possession of the newly found station hut by tracing his initials, he speaks as though he doesn't see the evidence of Aborigines' habitation even though he acknowledges *their* traces in the footprints on the ground. That is, this narrator both looks at and overlooks the evidence; he creates an absence in the face of noted presence, suggesting a kind of uneven double vision that is, I would suggest, characteristic of many accounts of settler interactions with Aborigines.[10]

On their return across the border of the frontier, the explorers relax at the newly built hut of the stockman when, for no apparent reason, a troop of marauding Aborigines attack but are repelled and mostly killed by the trekkers' bullets. The explorers are unscathed save for the unfortunate Irish stockman. These events explain and justify the narrator's initial complaints at the story's opening about "blacks" as among the major nuisances of the bushman at the border along with droughts, dogs, and fire. To stress the arbitrary violence of these Aborigines, the narrator notes how the dying stockman testifies that "he had never wronged any of the blacks in any way." Hence, in the end, the gun-wielding trekkers have clear possession of the land and, like the stockman, clear consciences.[11]

"An Exploring Adventure" begins with the narrator's prediction that the "blacks soon tame or fade before the white man's face," and his story describes this *fading* into almost absence through the militant, but presumably just, actions of frontiersmen. He assures readers that this small victory by honest, sober settlers leads to a future of peaceful colonial elegance, and he concludes his story noting that, "A handsome verandah'd villa now stands in place of the slab hut. Yellow corn waves over the Irishman's grave and while cattle and sheep abound as well as white men, women, and children, there is not a wild black within two hundred miles." The story, written for British audiences and prospective colonists, presents an exemplary instance of the duplicitous rhetoric of visual and ideological dismissal: it affirms an absence of Aboriginal people from the settlement and their looming absence from Australia even as it acknowledges their presence on the land. Although their traces underpin the narrative movement, they are for the most part buried in the text. As such, the author both emphasizes the civility of the rough-but-honorable, working-class settler and presents him not as an exile from home but as a visionary with a clear view of colonial space.[12]

This language of absence as a fading from view also underlies colonial predictions of the Aboriginal peoples' demise as a result of evolutionary pressures. In a less directly violent, but potentially more sinister discourse envisioning Aboriginal absence, Bonwick refers to their then-presumed evolutionary destiny of extinction, and he evokes a language of both nostalgia and relief for a lost chance at peaceful coexistence. This rhetorical usage of evolutionary destiny is duplicitous as it both heralds the end of Aboriginal existence and looks back to a more pristine past, pointing to a kind of painful pleasure in the present. As such, this forward/backward vision, also, works to excuse the role of colonists in the damage apparent in their present. For instance, Bonwick introduces the ethnographic section of *The Wild White Man and the Blacks of Victoria* with a vignette in which he shows ambivalence in regard to British "civilizing" efforts. He depicts four Aboriginal people all rather haphazardly dressed in European clothes and engaged in trade for European goods: an old man, his wife, a motherless, mixed race child, and their companion, a man described as "the last of his family"; Bonwick depicts a "family" dispute in which the old man and woman argue over her fidelity using "oaths" borrowed "from the classic tongue of the English" until he begins to beat her without restraint. With them, the child, fathered by a white settler who has no interest in her, cries hopelessly, and Simon, the companion, sits by "ill, melancholy, and without hope" as he grieves over the death of his tribe and sees the growing absence of black people on the land. "Such," comments Bonwick, "the march of improvement from contact with the civilised white man!" As an onlooker to this scene of colonial failure, Bonwick voices both hopelessness for the social development of the Aborigines (who can't dress so well or control their emotions) and also his criticism of the colonists (who bring alcohol, vulgarity, and unrestrained sexual desire), suggesting that his own position on the border between settlers and Aborigines lacks any ideological certainty. He is caught in a double bind of hopelessness and advocacy.[13]

Bonwick ends this anecdote by expressing his sorrow over the forthcoming loss of what he believes to be a dying race that *might have been* a strong ally for British settlers. In his last words to this preface, Bonwick repeats the oft-iterated belief that "there is no shadow of a hope of perpetuating the race" and hence he feels the burden of "gather[ing] a few records of their history" before it is forever lost.[14] Patrick Brantlinger calls this an "expectation of extinction theory," a popular belief that "developed in correlation to white settlement and also to declining faith in attempts to civilize aboriginals." Brantlinger notes the "ideological usefulness" of the extinction of a race as an evolutionary certainty as the colonial, and then federal, governments could overlook any Aboriginal claims to land, cultural independence, or social services. The idea of racial extinction also, suggests Brantlinger, reinforced colonial expansion on a global scale with a conviction that Aboriginal peoples were all "doomed" to disappear. This theory, thus, allowed colonial settlers a rhetorical means to allay feelings of guilt over this pending doom by deferring to natural forces or, as Brantlinger writes, by emphasizing the persistence of degenerate "savage customs" like cannibalism and thus identifying "causes other than white conquest or colonization."[15] Insights into Aboriginal life and customs, like Bonwick's ethnography and his accounts of "wild white men," served the interests of those who desired to see a brutal colonial history through a comforting lens.[16] Such nostalgia offers a painful pleasure that incorporates foresight of absence and hindsight of imagining a once-possible harmony, but that also overlooks the writer's present vision of failed negotiation. By displacing the Aborigine into a rhetoric marked by terms like "faded" images and "shadows," the colonial writer only vaguely sees the other at all, and that is, perhaps, the greatest comfort.

In comparison to works like Bonwick's or Sidney's, the *Narrative of James Murrells* presents an anomaly and underscores the dissonance in their colonial stories. As an editor and a scribe, Gregory works to limit Murrells's story into a rigid framework of tragic loss and joyful return to civilization; his eye is always on emphasizing the strength of Murrells's link to settler society. However, Murrells's positive and sometimes whimsical narration of his life among the Aboriginal people who took him in spills over the edges of this frame and offers insight both into Aboriginal culture and into settler attempts to contain and suppress it. This excess becomes compelling particularly as the narrative reveals the struggle between the castaway's recognition of Aboriginal humanity and his editor's attempt to overlook it.

JAMES MURRELLS'S STORY OF LOSING HIS WAY AND FINDING HIS PLACE

In 1863, James Murrells appeared at a settlers' outstation in Queensland after having been shipwrecked 17 years earlier and having since lived among Aboriginal people in New Cleveland Bay.[17] He was reportedly met with great astonishment at the station but the settlers eventually welcomed his return to civilization. Murrells was the sole survivor of the shipwreck of the freight ship the *Peruvian* in 1846. Originally, Murrells, the ship's captain, his wife, and a ship boy had found their way to shore and were taken in by different Aboriginal tribes. Murrells's three fellow survivors died within two years of this rescue. His story was recorded, edited, and published by journalist Edmund Gregory in 1863, using, he claims, Murrells's own words and, on occasion, adding clarifications and evidence of his own—the result is, as writer Charles Barrett suggests, a gathering of "many fragments of a wonderful history which he skillfully pieced together."[18] The resulting story is not seamless despite (or, perhaps, due to) Gregory's apparent attempts to provide narrative continuity with a thread emphasizing Murrells's persistent gaze homeward. Gregory claims that he published the 1863 version to satisfy "urgent public demand" to know the story and to generate some income to support Murrells in his reclaimed civilized life.[19] In his preface to the 1896 edition, Gregory notes that this reissue of the pamphlet should be of interest to "a new generation" of Australians as "it must ever remain the sole available record of one of the most thrilling and astounding incidents in early Australian history." Here, he frames Murrells's narrative with a nostalgic reference to earlier colonial days before "the Burdekin blacks have been civilized out of existence" and before any form of peaceful interaction with other Aboriginal groups was not possible.[20] On the one hand, Gregory's reissue of Murrells's narrative reminds late-century, pre-Federation readers of lost possibilities, but, on the other, it underscores colonial settler identity as shaped by the quality of being in-between worlds—of being castaway and claiming home. In this 1896 edition, the Aborigine exists as a trace from an earlier printing, and the return of the castaway is foregrounded.

Gregory recognizes the value of the story of homecoming to Australian identity as the colony is on the brink of independence. However, suggesting that the castaway offers a metaphor first for colonial displacement and then for postcolonial instability, Michael Titlestad and Mike Kissack write in "The persistent castaway in South African writing" that "accounts of shipwreck commonly enquire into versions of settler identity, posing, among others, the possibility of assimilation [...], presenting the threat of barbarous violence or demonstrating the resilience of the colonial project." Because European castaways taken in by indigenous others underwent, at least in written accounts, a profound transformation during the time of their captivity, the castaway symbolizes the anxieties *or* the desires of settler communities. Titlestad and Kissack further note that, with regard to the organizing effects of borders between settlers and indigenous peoples, "The narratives, in other words, present an inversion, albeit evanescent and contingent, of the epistemic hierarchy that situates Western reason above corporeality [...], and, in its anthropological projection, Western colonisers above 'savages.' "[21] That is to say, the castaway narrative unsettles colonial orders of civility and savagery and renders established borders and their corresponding ordering function slippery and chaotic. Murrells's narrative offers this kind of chaotic insight into a world across the border of the frontier replete with thrills and wonders for the pamphlet's readership, but written under the guidance of Gregory's point of view, it also offers a comforting affirmation of borders reestablished and of Aboriginal presence fading into a geographical and historical background.

Also, noting the significance of castaway and captivity narratives to nation building, Kay Schaffer's *In the Wake of First Contact*, a study of castaway Eliza Fraser's story, explains how in the colonial context, castaway stories are "performative acts of nation," in which "a passage from old world to new" is enacted and affiliations among settlers are affirmed. The "exclusionary effect" achieved by the juxtaposition of civilization and savagery or white and black offer opportunities to define and to extend the "imagined community" of nationhood. In addition, Schaffer suggests that "the rescue mission" becomes a symbolic gesture by which to set straight geographical borders and cultural orders.[22] As textual figures, reclaimed castaways offer parables of restoration of appropriate colonial hierarchies, and they also offer an opportunity to define the extended borders of "home." Such restoration seems to be the case in Murrells's story as Gregory underlines the order to which Murrells's life was put on his return to settler society, including a baptism, a meeting with the Governor, a steady job, and marriage. Murrells's insights into Aboriginal life and his positive descriptions of his experiences contradict the urgency of this movement toward reestablishing colonial social orders.

In the *Narrative of James Murrells*, the castaway's first-hand descriptions of his experiences among Aborigines show a cautious but intriguing cultural integration, a welcoming embrace of the castaways by their Aboriginal rescuers. For instance, describing when the castaways were first brought to the Aborigines' camp, Murrells narrates how he was led to group of what looked like chiefs and how he feared that his fate was "to be killed, cooked, and eaten." He invokes cannibalism, a well-known stereotype for categorizing the indigenous other, and he tells how he at first resisted, but then reflected, "how small the fire was, and that they had no weapons." He *sees* these others in their context and responds to the available evidence rather than rendering them invisible through a dehumanizing colonial discourse. Remarkably, he explains how seeing that he was afraid, "They warmed their hands at the fire, rubbed them over my face and body to reassure me, seeing which I took heart again."[23] This gentle contact signified by the comforting hands suggests cultural bridging and a rebuttal to imagined fears of cannibalism that enable a dismissal of insight.

Such vivid representations of cultural contact occur in many of the scenes that Murrells describes and on various levels of his discourse. At their first meeting, Murrells tells how the Aborigines take from them all the objects that identify the castaways' place of origin, their culture, and their customs. Exposed and vulnerable, the loss of the castaways' belongings signifies a loss of cultural belonging; stripped of possessions, they are displaced. Later, however, at a gathering of various tribes, a corroboree, these articles of European civilization, clothes, books, tools, *and* fully dressed castaways, become objects of display as they are taken from their original contexts and re-presented in an unusual fashion. Murrells explains: "Some of them dressed themselves very fantastically, with shirts, trousers, coats, &c, which we had saved from the wreck, and a more ludicrous scene could not be imagined; one with only the sleeve of a shirt on, another with a pair of trousers—his legs put through the bottoms, and another hind part before. They tore the leaves out of the books and fastened them in their hair and on their bodies."[24] Objects signifying their links to their home culture are seen anew in the Aboriginal context. The meaning of the items becomes dual, and from one angle, one might see this duality as celebratory; after all, the scene is a part of celebration and the castaways are at the center.

As a part of this spectacle, the claimed castaways are put on display night after night. Murrells explains how they were hidden beneath dry grass at the center of a circle and the oddly dressed Aborigines jumped into the circle and "danced one of their dances" while telling onlookers how they discovered the castaways. Then, presumably at the climax of the story, they reveal the concealed white people themselves to the amazement of the gathered tribes.[25] While Murrells notes that this repeated performance was exhausting, and that it would seem a bit bizarre to readers, I would suggest that it also shows an occasion of integration. The castaways become part of another's collection of stories. Objects, like clothes, books, tools, and language, which mark their connection with Britain, get put to use in other contexts (not wholly unlike the ethnographies written of Aboriginal manners and customs). Murrells's account of this castaway-lost-and-found-by-Aborigines story within Gregory's larger castaway narrative framework suggests another telling from an Aboriginal frame of reference in which the castaways' appearance (both physical and on the scene) occasions a performance that interprets and preserves it. The transposition and transformation are unsettling, to be sure; however, the movement is seemingly integrative, not destructive. As such, in losing their belongings, these exiles come to belong in another's story.

DUAL NARRATION: INSIGHT AND OVERSIGHT

In the 1863 and 1864 editions of Murrells's narrative, authorship is attributed solely to James Morrill and the story and ethnographic sections are told completely in first person; despite Gregory's transcription, the narrative presents what appears to be only first-hand experience. However, in the 1866 and the 1896 reprints, authorship is attributed to Edmund Gregory. In the 1896 edition, Gregory added a preface and a chapter of background on Murrells and the crew of the *Peruvian*. Additionally, Gregory re-edited both the narrative of shipwreck and return and the account of Aboriginal manners and customs, most notably in this latter section by shifting to a third-person impersonal rather than first-person narration.[26] While the reasons for this shift in authority might be practically associated with the posthumous publication of the booklet, the double attribution also suggests a degree of instability. The challenge in reading either version of the narrative seems to be disentangling the insight of Murrells from the oversight of Gregory. In this regard, this castaway narrative calls for what Said terms a "contrapuntal reading," an approach that recognizes a duality of voice and diverse interests and that explores both the logic of the text and the contexts in which it was produced and read. In regard to the texts on British colonial expansion, Said, thus, advocates a reading that "must take account of both processes, that of imperialism and that of resistance to it."[27] The effect of this double, sometimes mixed-up, language of colonial conquest and cultural exchange is confusion as to whether Murrells's ultimate repatriation with British settlers is a movement of return or of further exile.

In the story of shipwreck and survival, Murrells seems to have narrative control. After an introductory biographical sketch, Gregory tells readers that the following pages are "as nearly as possible in [Murrells's] own words—in narrative form,"[28] suggesting some limitations on Murrells's autonomy and Gregory's oversight as a story crafter. Within these shaky limits, Murrells's story shifts between descriptions of kinship with his Aboriginal rescuers and competing interjections of dejection at his exile from his countrymen. Despite his articulations of a feeling of belonging among his tribesmen, his look toward "home" and his fellow Britons offers a persistent refrain throughout the story. At several points, Murrells tells of sighting ships or of receiving word that white settlers had been spotted. Each instance is framed by statements that underscore his sense of his place among his tribe and on the land. For example, Murrells explains how, after the death of the last of his shipwrecked companions, he "lived on year after year in the tribe as one of themselves." In the following sentence, he counters this acknowledgment with a note of a sighting of a distant reminder of the home: "On one occasion when I was on the coast fishing, I saw a barque going northwards [...], but, of course, she was too far out [...] Oh, how my heart sank within me as I beheld her retreating from my gaze!" The next sentence then again blends his everyday activities with a report of another ship sighting: "When I was on Mount Elliott looking for honey and breadfruit, which was not quite ripe at the time, a report was brought to me that a vessel had been seen on the coast."[29]

The back and forth of this discourse suggests both a comfortable insight and an anxious look outward. Murrells has a productive role among his tribe, and he knows how to work the land. The interjection of the readiness of the breadfruit, for instance, is unnecessary at the moment of this telling (except perhaps as a way to offer a vague sense of timing) but intriguing in the casual insight it offers to his everyday life. However, his persistent, fruitless search for rescue, while quite possibly genuine, also suggests a formulaic response, a feigned excess of anxiety. Speaking of the double condition of the exile in "Reflections of Exile," Said notes that "both the old and the new environments are vivid, actual, occurring together contrapuntally." However, such a contemporaneous vision does not offer harmony or coexistence, because, as Said explains, "Exile is never the state of being satisfied, placid, secure."[30] Murrells looks both inside and outside with seemingly equal interest in this narrative, but his story seems always to be pulled more deliberately toward a look to a home among the settlers. Perhaps it is Gregory's narrative-crafting hand that insists on reiterating discontent with this exile's expressions of ease and belonging.

In another instance, Murrells tells how his Aboriginal fellows kept a lookout for white men, and in one case, he explains how, spotting a ship off the coast, they made an effort to tell the sailors about Murrells. Not understanding their language, the crewmen became alarmed and pursued the entreating Aborigines. Here, Gregory overtly interrupts Murrells's first-person account by interjecting with a "report of the proceedings of the Government schooner 'Spitfire' in 1860 [that] will explain this matter." The report contends that the natives were aggressive despite the sailors' friendly overtures, and that in their attack, the sailors only broke a canoe and frightened the natives. Gregory disclaims: "Nothing [...] is mentioned in this report about shooting the natives." Murrells then resumes narrative control and explains how "one stout able-bodied black fellow, however, was shot dead by someone in a boat, and another was wounded." The two narrators' accounts are written side by side, alternating passages, as it were, and drawing attention to an incompatibility between inside and outside. Murrells notes other incidents in which Aborigines were shot by frontiersmen, but, then, even as he tells these tales, he interjects how, hearing word of cattle-tracks while with "with one of the blacks—a brother-in-law of mine—making possum-skin rugs," he "began to think of the possibility of rescue." The rhetorical pull between accounts of violence, mentions of kinship and industry, and the professed desire for rescue becomes unwieldy. Finally, in this section, after another account of 15 of his tribesmen being shot, Murrells suggests that he needed to return to the white settlement not so that he might be rescued but so that he "might be the means of saving their lives."[31] For Murrells, despite the refrain about having an eye toward rescue, returning among his countrymen is less about crossing the border to home than about offering himself up as a tool to protect Aboriginal claims to home.

In the last part of his story before his return to settler culture, Murrells describes his final leave taking, noting: "There was a short sharp struggle between a feeling of love I had for my old friends and companions, and the desire once more to live a civilized life, which may better be imagined than described." And for the most part, after this moment, Murrells no longer describes his own life. Gregory inserts the details about his getting a job on the docks, his marriage, and the birth of his child. He then appends a newspaper account, describing Murrells's illness before his death on October 30, 1865, and the attendance at his funeral. In this account, without his first-person control, Murrells is used to symbolize colonial resistance to the seduction of the native and the report insists on not seeing the Aborigine. It describes how "during his late illness, when his mind passed as in a dream through the scenes of misery and care of his exile, he always returned to his wife and child, and his only care seemed to be how they should in future be provided for." As such, the "feeling of love" for the Aboriginal people among whom he lived is overlooked and buried in the underside of his consciousness. The report overwrites his past with the more conventional happy ending of marriage. The description of his funeral, too, is an occasion for the rhetorical fading of Aboriginal presence in this story. Many settlers and notable citizens came to mourn his passing as he was "a general favourite in the district." The reporter contends that, "Could the Mount Elliott blacks learn that their pale-faced brother was dead, what howling and woe there would be," but, the reporter claims, their sorrow "could not be more serious or deeply felt than is that experienced by the people of Bowen."[32] Even as this reporter notes Murrells's kinship with the Aborigines, he dismisses it as superficial and insubstantial—all noise with little depth.

The rhetorical effort to render Aboriginal absence is emphasized by comparing the last words of the account in 1864 and the edited version in 1896. In the earlier edition, Morrill completes his first-person account of Aboriginal customs, with an appeal to the colonial government to stem the genocidal violence against the Aboriginal people and to allow his tribe to retain an expanse of land "which was no good to anybody but themselves—the low swampy grounds near the sea coast."[33] By 1896, Gregory has changed the narration of this section to third person and simply omitted this final appeal. As such, it seems that he has rhetorically performed an act of making Aborigines disappear and deleted Murrells's efforts at mediation from the text. Insomuch as it is contained in the *Narrative,* this moment in Australia's story is literally erased from historical memory.

In another example of how Murrells's insights were sidelined, emigrant and journalist Marcus Clarke in 1873 calls Murrell "The First Queensland Explorer" and thus credits him for his insights and travel among the Aborigines; however, he then proceeds to all but dismiss this insight. The bulk of Clarke's lengthy account focuses on telling a good story about the shipwreck and the plight of the castaways. Clarke summarizes a few details of the manners and customs section of the narrative, adding jovial sketches on the strangeness of Aboriginal habits. He explains, for instance, the coming of age rituals of Aboriginal boys, which "[consist] principally in undergoing various torments designed to test courage." Completing his sensational description of these "torments," Clark notes how "in happy Europe, the 'heir' only gets drunk" and thus successfully renders the account of the rite as an opportunity for derision and dismissal. Clarke comments that this custom differs only in degree from "the many unpleasant ceremonies practiced by all savage tribes."[34] His comment invokes what Simon Ryan explains as "colonial discourse's need to create the Aborigine as entirely known and familiar" and thus to invoke colonial stereotypes as a means of categorizing all indigenous peoples and dismissing

their autonomous presence.[35] Murrells's Aborigines are like indigenous people everywhere and thus already known. In a final turn away
from Murrells's insight, Clarke tells that when Murrells returned to
the settlers' hut after bidding farewell to his tribesmen, "he was fed,
and clothed, *and returned to his right mind*," thus, it seems, leaving behind a skewed, unsettling perception of the world.[36] As such,
Clarke, like Gregory, virtually erases Murrells's insights in favor of
telling a more acceptable story of loss and return.

REAPPEARANCES

The *Narrative of James Murrells*, full of unrealized possibility for cultural negotiation, demonstrates the rhetorical moves by which colonial
writers dismissed or effectively repressed recognition of Aboriginal
presence. However, the traces of that presence remained and resur-
faced in various literary works. Notably, David Malouf's 1993 novel
Remembering Babylon uses Murrells's story as the base on which it
builds its fiction and interrogates the interstices between storytelling
and history. In this novel, Malouf is concerned with exploring how
colonial settlers might have responded to the arrival of a man like
James Murrells. Malouf's character, Gemmy Fairley, is shipwrecked,
taken in by Aborigines, and on finding his way back to the settlement, is deemed a "black white" man. He disturbs the settlers as he
represents "a mixture of monstrous strangeness and unwelcome likeness" that puts into question not only their racial identity but also the
fragility of their place in the colonial landscape.[37] As such this fictional
castaway is emblematic of racial conflict and a crisis of belonging.
Commenting on Gemmy's ineffectiveness as a symbol for the negotiation of racial identity, Penelope Ingram in her essay "Racializing
Babylon: Settler Whiteness and the 'New Racism' " argues that though
Gemmy is "a hybrid figure," Malouf's novel "does not create a new
hybrid Australian identity." Instead, Ingram contends the narrative
works to racialize and "problematize whiteness," and thus it offers an
interrogation of the privileges associated with a white racial identity.[38]
As an in-between character, Gemmy traverses shifting and reversing
boundaries of cultural inside and outside throughout the novel, and
the certainty of his belonging with either the white settlers or Aborigines who adopted him is questioned and reassessed. Indeed, the novel
offers a thought-provoking critique on the "Colonial fairytale"[39] of
exile and return Gregory tried to privilege in the *Narrative of James
Murrells*.

As a critique, *Remembering Babylon* refuses to see the process of colonization and settlement in benign terms, but also refuses to see clearly the Aborigines who hover at the fringe of the novel's plot. For instance, when Gemmy walks with the minister through the bush teaching him the names and properties of indigenous plants, the narrator explains how: "Once or twice on these outings, [Gemmy] saw blacks who were unfamiliar to him standing frozen in the brush [...] On other occasions he saw nothing but felt the presence of watchers [...] Mr Frazer saw nothing at all. Even when they were meant to be seen, he did not distinguish them from the surrounding vegetation or the play of light and shadow."[40] Gemmy notices them because of his unusual insight, but, otherwise, they do not (except on one occasion) cross the border fence into the settlement or into the narrative. Malouf's novel recognizes an absent-presence of the Aborigine, showing both recognition and staged blindness that reflects the kind of colonial not-seeing described in this chapter. In an interview with Nikos Papastergiadis, Malouf responds to a query about the lack of Aboriginal perspective in the novel by noting his own hesitation to represent Aboriginal experience: "partly because I don't have the knowledge to do that, and I don't think anyone has the knowledge to do that, except those people themselves who perhaps don't have the voice or the words to do it."[41] He does, however, turn the perspectival tables slightly, noting that those shadowy Aborigines also see Mr. Frazer as a trace and an absence: "a shape, thin, featureless, that interposed itself a moment, like a mist or cloud, before the land blazed out in its full strength again and the shadow was gone."[42] Malouf's retelling of Murrells's story taps into a desire to see anew that cultural presence which has been hidden from view or erased from rhetoric.

At another point in this interview, Malouf notes his effort to represent a "language of silence" as a kind of understanding of the world and engagement with others that exists outside the mediating influence of words.[43] One might consider how his 1993 retelling of Murrells's story of being lost and found tries to get around language, to get out from beneath the thumb of an oppressive rhetoric that insists on the absence of Aboriginal presence even while it clearly acknowledges the traces on the landscape (and the page). Indeed, in the *Narrative*, Murrells, too, tries to find his way around an authoritative language that intervenes on his story and counters his mission to bring to sight the presence and the place of his Aboriginal fellows. His narrative speaks to an Aboriginal humanity that colonial writers and readers didn't want to acknowledge and to a negotiating impulse that is recognizable mostly when one reads his narrative as, on one hand, an exchange between competing worldviews and desires and, on the other, a mission to rescue Aborigines from a rhetorical absence.

NOTES

1. James Bonwick, *The Wild White Man and the Blacks of Victoria* (Melbourne: Fergusson and Morre, 1863), 17.
2. "James Murrell" [*sic*], *Empire* [Sydney, NSW: 1850–1875], (Friday, July 29, 1870), 4.
3. Edward Said, "Reflections on Exile," in *Reflections on Exile and Other Essays* (Cambridge: Harvard University Press, 2000), 176, 177.
4. Edmund Gregory, *Narrative of James Murrells' ("Jemmy Morrill") Seventeen Years' Exile among the Wild Blacks of North Queensland and His Life and Shipwreck and Terrible Adventures among Savage Tribes; Their Manners, Customs, Languages, and Superstitions; also Murrells' Rescue and Return to Civilization* (Brisbane: Printed by Edmund Gregory, 1896). The narrative was originally published in 1863. This 1896 revised edition is the one to which I will refer in this essay unless otherwise noted.
5. Henry Reynolds, *Frontier: Aborigines, Settlers, and Land* (New South Wales: Allen and Unwin, 1996), 104, 108. See also Chapter 4, where Reynolds details opposition to frontier abuses of Aboriginal people.
6. Ibid., 104.
7. Samuel Sidney, *The Three Colonies of Australia: New South Wales, Victoria, South Australia; Their Pastures, Copper Mines, and Gold Fields* (London: Ingram, 1852), viii–ix.
8. Ibid., 160.
9. Samuel Sidney, "An Exploring Adventure," *Household Words* (June 27, 1850), 418–420, 418, 419.
10. Ibid., 419.
11. Ibid., 418, 420.
12. Ibid.
13. Bonwick, *The Wild White Man and the Blacks of Victoria*, 18.
14. Ibid. (my emphasis). In the sections that follow this introduction, Bonwick composes a history made up of various travelers' and settlers' accounts of contact with Aboriginal tribes. He takes a positive, if highly sentimentalized, stance on Aborigines as enjoying a rather pristine existence before colonization.
15. Patrick Brantlinger, *Dark Vanishings: Discourse on the Extinction of Primitive Races, 1800–1930* (Ithaca: Cornell University Press, 2003), 122, 130, 137.
16. See also Mary Louise Pratt, "Scratches on the Face of the Country; or, What Mr. Barrow saw in the land of the Bushmen," in *Defining Travel: Diverse Visions*, ed. Susan L. Roberson (Jackson: University

Press of Mississippi, 2001), 132–152, 133. Pratt discusses how ethno-graphers' language of manners and customs serves as "a normalizing discourse, whose work is to codify difference, to fix the Other in a timeless present" that is unaffected by the observing eye of the explorer. Under the weight of this discourse, difference and distance become fixed and stable concepts.

17. Gregory, *Narrative*, 5. Gregory explains that Murrells at first mis-remembered his name as James Morrill but that after some research into his origins, he discovered that his name was Murrells and that "It will not be considered anything very extraordinary, after reading this narrative of suffering and hardship resulting from seventeen years' isolation in the bush among the aboriginals [. . .] that there had been taken from him the power accurately to recall his own name."

18. Charles Barrett, *White Black Fellows: The Strange Adventures of Europeans Who Lived among Savages* (Melbourne: Hallcraft Publish-ing Co., 1948), 39.

19. Gregory refers to: James Morrill, *Sketch of a Residence among the Aboriginals of Northern Queensland for Seventeen Years: Being a Nar-rative of My Life, Shipwreck, Landing, on the Coast, Residence among the Aboriginals, with an Account of Their Manners and Customs, and Mode of Living; together with Notices of Many of the Natural Produc-tions, and of the Nature of the Country/by James Morrill* (Brisbane: Courier General Printing Office, 1863).

20. Gregory, *Narrative*, iii.

21. Michael Titlestad and Mike Kissack, "The persistent castaway in South African writing," *Postcolonial Studies* 10.2 (2007), 191–218, 192, 197.

22. Kay Schaffer, *In the Wake of First Contact: The Eliza Fraser Stories* (Cambridge: Cambridge University Press, 1995), 49, 50.

23. Gregory, *Narrative*, 19, 20.

24. Ibid., 20.

25. Ibid., 18.

26. James Morrill, *17 Years Wandering among the Aboriginals* (Australia: David Welch, 2006). This edition contains a reprint of the origi-nal 1864 edition of *Sketch of a Residence among the Aboriginals of Northern Queensland for Seventeen Years* by James Morrill.

27. Said, *Culture and Imperialism* (New York: Knopf, 1993), 66.

28. Gregory, *Narrative*, 10.

29. Ibid., 23.

30. Said, "Reflections on Exile," 189.

31. Gregory, *Narrative*, 25, 27.

32. Gregory, *Narrative*, 30–31, 33.

33. Morrill, *17 Years Wandering among the Aboriginals*, 71.

34. Marcus Clarke, "The First Queensland Explorer," *The Queenslander* [Brisbane: 1866–1939] (Saturday, December 20, 1873), 7.

35. Simon Ryan, *The Cartographic Eye: How Explorers Saw Australia* (Cambridge: Cambridge University Press, 1996), 137.
36. Clarke, "The First Queensland Explorer," 7 (my emphasis).
37. David Malouf, *Remembering Babylon* (New York: Vintage, 1993), 43.
38. Penelope Ingram, "Racializing Babylon: Settler Whiteness and the 'New Racism' ": *New Literary History* 32 (2001), 157–176, 159, 161.
39. Malouf, *Remembering Babylon*, 19.
40. Ibid., 68.
41. Nikos Papastergiadis, "David Malouf and Languages for Landscape: An Interview," *Ariel: A Review of International English Literature* 25.3 (July 1994), 83–94, 92.
42. Malouf, *Remembering Babylon*, 68.
43. Papastergiadis, "David Malouf and Languages for Landscape," 91.

CHAPTER 9

EXILIC CONSCIOUSNESS AND ALTERNATIVE MODERNIST GEOGRAPHIES IN THE WORK OF OLIVE SCHREINER AND KATHERINE MANSFIELD

Elizabeth Syrkin

In a 1938 article on New Zealand literature, Robin Hyde suggests an intriguing source for a type of exilic critical consciousness she observes in her fellow New Zealand writer Katherine Mansfield. Hyde begins by describing Mansfield's sense of alienation as a trigger for her emigration to England: "People say K. M. ran away from New Zealand, but if you could see and understand her exact environs, you might sympathize with the belief that she ran away from a sham England, unsuccessfully transplanted to New Zealand soil, and utterly unable to adapt itself to the real New Zealand."[1] A prolific author herself, Hyde writes out of her personal experience of New Zealand settler reality, and concludes that it is precisely these conditions—Mansfield's enclosure behind doors in "the heavy, conventional well-to-do household around her"—that generated her ability "to look out of windows" and craft her most celebrated modernist tales.[2] Mansfield herself seemingly negates Hyde's interpretation with a 1922 letter to Sarah Gertrude Millin, in which she describes how in the preceding five years of her life, her most productive years, her thoughts and feelings would always "go back to New Zealand—rediscovering it, finding beauty in it, re-living it." She concludes the letter by stating, "I am sure it does a writer no good to be transplanted [...] I think the only way to live as a writer is to draw upon one's real *familiar* life—to find the treasure in that as Olive Schreiner did. Our secret life, the life we return to over and over again, the 'do you remember' life is always the past."[3] The stifling and alienating landscape, whose transplanted English values simply do not fit in the colony, as described by Hyde, transforms here into a site of longing, a treasured past to be excavated, remembered, and written. Together, Hyde's article and Mansfield's letter gesture to the significance of both a homeland and an exilic consciousness to a writer's craft and development. Their apparent contradiction can be resolved by invoking Edward Said's call in *Orientalism* for the need to be separated, physically or metaphorically, from one's cultural home in order to acquire the ability to assess the world "with the spiritual detachment *and* generosity necessary for true vision."[4] This chapter responds to Said's call by considering the ways in which their colonial homelands, often deemed peripheral to their modernisms,[5] helped constitute the fiction and thought of Katherine Mansfield and Olive Schreiner, the author Mansfield invokes in her letter.

Katherine Mansfield and Olive Schreiner made the "voyage in" from their native New Zealand and South Africa at an early age, becoming central figures in English modernism and feminism. Their lives and writing contain remarkable similarities: both became absorbed in the London intellectual society of their time, even while England never came to feel like "home"; both led nomadic lives and had unconventional marriages; and both depicted their families and homelands in their fiction. As early as 1894, Schreiner's novel *The Story of an African Farm* (1883) was recognized as "the forerunner of all the novels of the Modern Woman," and her heroine Lyndall is often hailed as "the first wholly feminist heroine in the English novel."[6] At the same time, Mansfield, whose writing often reflects Schreiner's feminist concerns, is celebrated as a pioneer of the modernist short story.[7] My analysis takes direction from Hyde's suggestion that the exportation of the rigid boundaries and domestic standards of Victorian England to the empire's peripheries fostered a feeling of displacement, evocative of Said's critical "detachment *and* generosity." This critical perspective, I argue, was generative for the creative development of both writers in the colonies. By considering the striking parallels in Schreiner's and Mansfield's writing—accounts of the collisions and transplanted values their colonial homelands negotiated—this chapter explores how modernist themes developed not only within an alternative geographic space, but also as an alternative to a particular kind of colonial reality. In what follows, I begin by examining Said's theory of exile, together with his profoundly grounded approach to space and empire, with an eye especially to the domestic sphere and the exportation of Victorian values from the empire's center. I then continue by situating Schreiner's and Mansfield's writing within the context of a European domesticity imposed on the colonial periphery, first by taking a closer look at Schreiner's formation of New Woman subjectivity in *The Story of an African Farm*, and later at Mansfield's early writing in order to set the stage for a close analysis of "The Woman at the Store" and "Prelude."

EXILE, EMPIRE, AND THE CULT OF DOMESTICITY

Said's theory of exile negotiates the slippage between an exile's isolation and the concurrent formation of an exilic critical consciousness, nourished by a deep affection for a native place.[8] His understanding of exile is closely entwined with his conceptualization of what he terms a text's "worldliness": the ways in which texts and writers are "always enmeshed in circumstance, time, place, and society."[9] While Said never discounts the often traumatic nature of exile for displaced persons and refugees, he also reconfigures it as a state of mind or subjectivity characterized by "originality" and "plurality" of vision attuned to the relationship between historical processes and contemporary realities.[10] Mansfield and Schreiner's creative development can be read in terms of Said's theorization of such a critical consciousness and its relation to a writer's position in the world. In this sense, a Saidian lens helps delineate the ways in which conditions in their countries of birth fostered an exilic consciousness even *before* Schreiner and Mansfield departed to England, a consciousness that was generative for their creative development and writing. As I try to show in this chapter, their "nomadic, decentred, contrapuntal" exilic perspectives, to use Said's words,[11] are reflected in their affinity for the undomesticated wilderness of South Africa and New Zealand, etched in their fictional settings both explicitly and in hints and hauntings.

The transplantation Hyde speaks of in the lines quoted above introduces a concurrently spatial and cultural struggle in the colonies, also addressed by Said. Taking direction from his *Culture and Imperialism*, this chapter undertakes a type of "geographical inquiry into historical experience"[12] by focusing specifically on the spaces described in Schreiner's and Mansfield's writing. While empire is fundamentally a struggle over land, which involves exploring, charting, and bringing spaces in the world under control,[13] Said offers a model that negotiates the vital dialectic between this cartographic struggle and the simultaneous struggle "about ideas, about forms, about images and imaginings."[14] He contends that geographical transformations and conflicts permeated and were in turn affected by the narratives and debates of the cultural sphere. The importation of European classifications and codes to the empire's peripheries in an attempt to, in Elleke Boehmer's words, make the foreign landscape of the colonies more "homely,"[15] constituted one such simultaneously geographical and cultural struggle. As Boehmer explains, these classifications and codes were then "matched to people, cultures, and topographies that were entirely un-European."[16] Among them was the transportation and sedimentation in the colonial landscape of European flora and fauna,[17] as well as the Victorian middle-class home structure, which turned the colonial space into a "theater for exhibiting the Victorian cult of domesticity."[18] In this context, the settler woman was not only confined to the home, but her greatest social value at the height of empire became the production of more male bodies to populate the expanding territories.[19] These Victorian conceptions of family, privacy, and domesticity were inherently spatial, concerned as they were with securing boundaries and distributing bodies.[20] In Karen Chase and Michael Levenson's apt phrase, Victorian society was "tidily distributed according to function and fortune."[21] Such distinct gender, class, and racial hierarchies and the rigid boundary between private and public were in turn adapted to the South African and New Zealand landscapes Schreiner and Mansfield confronted.[22]

Images and critiques of such domestication pervade both Schreiner's and Mansfield's fiction, aligning their writing with literary modernism's preoccupation with and critical response to the traditional structure and function of domestic and private spaces. Indeed, as Victoria Rosner suggests, such spatial concerns, particularly what she calls the "dismantling of the traditional home," can be characterized as a "modernist gesture that ineluctably and materially links feminism to modernism."[23] This chapter similarly proposes and extends this link between Schreiner and Mansfield's emerging modernisms and their feminist preoccupations, particularly their concern with a stifling and imposed domesticity in the colonies.[24] Furthermore, it engages alternative modernist trajectories by following Said's contention that while "the most prominent characteristics of modernist culture" often tend to be derived from purely internal Western dynamics, they also "include a response to the external pressures on culture from the *imperium*."[25] His gesture toward colonial influence on Western cultural production can be taken further by considering how ideas that have come to be associated with the metropolitan center developed *within* the periphery itself and were only later transported by expatriate writers to England. At its core then, and in the words of Patrick Williams, this chapter addresses "modernism from the empire," exploring the possibility he raises in his work that, in making the "voyage in," writers like Mansfield and Schreiner carried modernism with them.[26]

THE NEW WOMAN IN AFRICA: OLIVE SCHREINER

Born into an English family in colonial South Africa in 1855, Schreiner was brought up in strict accordance with English standards and values,[27] causing what Anne McClintock calls a "lifelong sense of exile" from thinking herself a "colonial intruder in a foreign land."[28] Restless and unsettled, Schreiner described her state in a letter to her husband in 1914: "No one wants me. I'm in no relation with the life or thought in England or Africa or anywhere else."[29] Yet, throughout her life and writing, it is the South African landscape to which Schreiner consistently turned for strength, inspiration, and as a setting for her stories: "I love the Karoo. Do you know the effect of this scenery is to make me so silent and strong and self-contained."[30] *The Story of an African Farm*, which details the lives of three childhood friends on a remote South African farm, is set on Schreiner's beloved karoo.[31] Published two years after her move to England in 1881, this novel transformed Schreiner into a leading feminist and intellectual of her time.

On one hand, *The Story of an African Farm* is a distinctly South African novel, one Doris Lessing called "the first 'real' book I'd met with that had Africa for a setting [...] reflecting what I knew and could see."[32] However, the novel also anticipates, and even participates in the English modernist tradition, with its stylistically "modern" elements of narrative fragmentation, shifts in point of view, a focus on interiority, and a nonlinear structure that incorporates letter writing, narrative interjections, and dreamscapes.[33] The vast landscape of the karoo, with which Schreiner opens the novel, is both a refuge for the children on the farm and a silent witness to personal and historical struggles. When they find preserved ink markings, drawings of "grotesque oxen, elephants, rhinoceroses, and a one-horned beast, such as no man ever has seen or ever shall,"[34] Waldo remarks how sometimes the stones speak to him of things that history books "never tell" (18). He continues: "It was [...] one of these old wild Bushmen, that painted those [...] To us they are only strange things, that make us laugh; but to him they were very beautiful [...] Now the Boers have shot them all, so that we never see a little yellow face peeping out among the stones [...] and we are here. But we will be gone soon, and only the stones will lie on here, looking at everything like they look now" (19–20). The karoo here has agency in its inaction, inhabited yet resistant, constant among a layering of historical atrocities and occupations. And the farm of the novel's title is presented as a claustrophobic intrusion, a transient new layer on this unconquerable and unconquered karoo. The homestead's rigid boundaries are emphasized by the narrative's continual reference to its thatched roof, square red-bricks, and stone-walls, in direct opposition to the karoo's open spaces. As J. M. Coetzee describes it: "the farmhouse is at war with nature [...] set down in the midst of the vastness of nature, living a closed-minded and self-satisfied existence."[35] The farm and its European values yield nothing, Coetzee continues, thereby suggesting their "unnatural and arbitrary imposition on a doggedly ahistorical landscape. Schreiner is anticolonial both in her assertion of the alienness of European culture in Africa and in her attribution of unnaturalness to the life of her farm."[36] While Coetzee rightly points to the "alienness" of transplanted and "unnatural" European values and structures on this landscape, his description of the karoo as "ahistorical" misleadingly bespeaks its remoteness from the events it witnesses. While seemingly adhering to no temporality, the landscape does register, however silently, a European intrusion. The marks it bears remind its current inhabitants of an impenetrable yet tangible history from which Waldo is able to draw inspiration, in a way similar to Mansfield's generative connection to the mysterious New Zealand bush explored in the next section. Within the karoo's unchanging nature exists a liberating force for its inhabitants' imaginations, evident in the Bushman's ability to imagine a beast "no man ever has seen or ever shall."

The markings Waldo describes are haunted by colonial violence and intrusion, of which the farm is the foremost symbol. The novel's heroine Lyndall, whose heightened feminist rhetoric has led some to call her the first real "New Woman,"[37] is introduced as the narrator zooms in on her isolated sleeping form within this farm, thereby foregrounding what Lyndall intuits early on in the novel: the connection between enclosed spaces and opportunities available to her as a woman. As she tells Em, her cousin and heir to the farm: "If I were you, when I get this place I should raise the walls. There is no room to breathe here; one suffocates" (191). Lyndall repeatedly rebels against the farm's confining spaces, at one point almost burning it down while attempting to escape her locked room. She imagines that the reality outside the farm is not as restrictive and convinces her aunt Tant' Sannie to send her to boarding school. Once there, however, Lyndall is confronted with the same conventions she sought to escape, concluding that these "finishing schools" merely function as "machines for experimenting on the question, 'Into how little space a human soul can be crushed?'" (194). Four years of schooling only further reinforce for Lyndall the spatial and metaphorical constrictions that plague women. She explains to Waldo:

> They begin to shape us to our cursed end […] when we are tiny things in shoes and socks. We sit with our little feet drawn up under us in the window, and look out at the boys in their happy play. We want to go. Then a loving hand is laid on us: "Little one, you cannot go […] your little face will burn, and your nice white dress be spoiled." […] [W]e kneel still with one little cheek wistfully pressed against the pane […] It finishes its work when we are grown women, who no more look out wistfully at a more healthy life; we are contented.
>
> (199)

The image of a girl pressing against a window and looking out onto a world not available to her recalls Mansfield's stories of women at thresholds and similar windows: a seemingly fragile boundary through which they can see, yet which they cannot quite penetrate.[38] The glass, while fragile, remains unbroken according to Lyndall, because women are indoctrinated into their position from such an early age that they accept it fully, seeing it as natural and unalterable.

In response, Lyndall requests a separate room at boarding school, a refuge to which she retreats to explore texts untaught in the classroom. On one hand, this need for self-exile can be read as a demonstration of the limited options available to women at this time; however, at the same time, as Rosner suggests, in the Victorian period "the spaces of reading and writing are associated with a privilege and power that is exclusively masculine."[39] Lyndall's room can be read as an instance of a woman appropriating the traditionally autonomous male space of the study for herself, prefiguring the usurpation of the creative privileges the study space affords by female modernists, most famously articulated in Virginia Woolf's *A Room of One's Own* (1928). Schreiner nevertheless problematizes this appropriation of private space as it appears to merely reinforce limits imposed on Lyndall. In Schreiner's unfinished novel *From Man to Man*, a similar improvised study space only emphasizes the protagonist's repression. In a room not larger than a closet built within her children's bedroom, Rebekah keeps a collection of personal belongings, books, and fossils. She retreats to this space to sew, write, and meditate, yet it is more a prison than a refuge, evident in her pacing like an animal unable to break out of its minuscule cage.[40] "The room is all too clearly and pathetically the embodiment of her femaleness" through its direct link to her children's room, according to Elaine Showalter: it is, in effect, a "womb with a view."[41] Rebekah and Lyndall remain locked within their respective roles as procreators, with Lyndall's pregnancy revealed only a few chapters after her return from boarding school.

Lyndall's uncompromising and self-assured actions and rhetoric are consistently contrasted with Em's submissiveness and acceptance of a traditional role as wife and mother. Em's expanding body and antic-ipation of marriage recall the popular notion of the "Angel in the House" and prefigure Tant' Sannie, herself a grotesque caricature of women in the domestic sphere, whom Schreiner uses to discredit "tra-ditional forms of female survival" by showing monstrosity arise out of domestic confinement.[42] However, it is Tant' Sannie and Em who survive and continue life on their respective farms at the novel's con-clusion, while Lyndall and the baby she has with an unnamed Stranger both die. Lyndall rejects marriage when she is confronted with her pregnancy, preferring instead to become the man's mistress. When the Stranger leaves, Lyndall finds herself in another isolated room, with Gregory Rose appropriating the role of mother by dressing as a woman and acting as her nurse. This switch in traditional roles high-lights their inherent arbitrariness; Gregory's pronounced success as a nurturer, and Lyndall's failure, suggest that the purportedly natural role of women as mothers is an imposed construct that perpetuates female imprisonment in the home. Lyndall's death, following as it does her extended rhetoric on women's issues and her expressed desire to escape female repression, is often read as a failure of *The Story of an African Farm*.[43] While she is able to articulate the underlying causes of female suffering—the undervaluing of intelligence, a lack of interest-ing work or alternatives to marriage, being judged by appearance—she is unable to either imagine or enact changes within her own life.[44] Dying the death of a Victorian fallen woman and unable to act beyond the confines she denounces, her death can nevertheless be seen as generative to Schreiner's feminism as it suggests that her contempo-rary society cannot assimilate an approach to sexuality that does not include marriage. Any answer to the question posed by Lyndall's situa-tion (that is, how does one *house* an unwed mother and her illegitimate child?) remains as transient as the hotel room in which she lives out her last days. Through what can be read as a self-inflicted deterioration, "a radical refusal to continue bearing the race,"[45] Lyndall is able to definitively break the chains of Victorian domesticity imposed on her. After eight years in England, Schreiner synthesized her argument in *The Story of an African Farm* in a short allegorical tale published in a collection titled *Dreams*, the same title she gave to the chapter that immediately follows Lyndall's death, and which considers the importance of imagining alternative futures. The tale "Three Dreams in a Desert: Under a Mimosa Tree" charts the process of female emancipation and explicitly aligns the formation of New Woman subjectivity with a colonial landscape. Depicting a bounded space—a parched, and hostile African plain—Schreiner places her narrator "on the border of a great desert,"[46] effectively a stage whose delimited space foregrounds the restricted possibilities for the enactment of female subjectivity. The narrator dreams of a bound woman on the ground, weighed down by the "Inevitable Necessity" of bearing "men in her body" (68–70). The earth witnesses her struggle: "the ground was wet with her tears and her nostrils blew up the sand" (70); her oppressed and bound body acts both as a symptom and a cause of her condition. In the second dream, "Reason" explains to the now standing woman that in order to reach the "Land of Freedom," she must not only endure suffering and labor, but also abandon the child nursing at her breast (76). This New Woman's need to reject her offspring, much like Lyndall's rejection, suggests the need for a violent rupture with the Angel in the House tradition in order to delineate possible alternatives and create a social system fit for future children. The woman is a revolutionary leader driven by a vision of the "thousand times ten thousand and thousands of thousands" of feet following in her footsteps (81–82). She is able to envision transformed relations within society between all men and women, depicted in the tale's final dream: a land in which "walked brave women and brave men, hand in hand," a collective ideal of equality that Reason explains lies in the future (84).

Schreiner's vision of feminist progress, though lacking any clear political or social plan of action, was nevertheless appropriated by the English suffrage movement, with her writing regularly drawn upon "as a source of inspiration" in suffragette memoirs and in *Votes for Women*, the newspaper of the Women's Social and Political Union.[47] *Woman and Labour*, her treatise on women's rights published in 1911, was called "a prophecy and a gospel" of the movement in an early review,[48] while one Lancashire working-class woman described the impact of *The Story of an African Farm* by saying: "I read parts of it over and over [...] I think there is [*sic*] hundreds of women what feels [*sic*] like that but can't speak it, but *she* could speak what we feel."[49] Lyndall's struggle in the colony showed English women that the oppression of *their* lives existed thousands of miles away in the empire's peripheries. *The Story of an African Farm* was read not as defeatist, but rather as an account of suffering shared across boundaries of gender, race, and continents. By depicting the impractical and restricting application of British codes to the isolated landscape of the karoo, the embedded unnatural, performative, and exclusionary practices of the Victorian domestic ideal were exaggerated. Schreiner emphasized through her characters' struggles the profoundly limited number of choices available to women. Isolated from any feminist European causes, she nevertheless drafted versions of foundational feminist texts as a colonial woman, motivated by her own personal sense of gendered injustice. As Lyndall declares to Waldo: "If women were the inhabitants of Jupiter, of whom you had happened to hear something, you would pore over us and our condition night and day; but because we are before your eyes you never look at us" (197). Staging the "Woman Question" in a South African context was akin to staging it on Jupiter, highlighting all the muted struggles of the English woman at the center of the empire.

NASCENT MODERNISM IN NEW ZEALAND: KATHERINE MANSFIELD

Katherine Mansfield's New Zealand, the transplanted "sham England" intimated in her family's strict adherence to English standards of respectability,[50] engendered a sense of isolation reminiscent of Schreiner's in South Africa three decades previously. Biographical accounts have persuasively argued that her sense of dissatisfaction with New Zealand's backwardness drew Mansfield to immigrate to London at age 19,[51] a perspective that in turn underemphasizes the centrality of her affection for New Zealand to her craft. Numerous factors, such as her husband John Middleton Murry's editing of her journals after her death, have generated an image of a purely metropolitan and European Mansfield, opening a lacuna noted by Saikat Majumdar of her relationship to her native country's history and landscape.[52] Her noticeable turn to New Zealand as a setting for her later stories is attributed to nostalgia triggered by her brother's death in 1915 and her own failing health, suggesting the primacy of her *distance* from New Zealand to her emergent modernist form. This form is characterized by a type of free indirect discourse—in Sylvia Berkman's words, "the fluid combination of inner and outer 'view' "[53]—that constructs life episodes as a mosaic of fragments and perspectives, exemplified in her 1918 story "Prelude."[54] Essential to its development, however, in Mansfield's own description in an oft-cited 1916 journal passage, is her desire to bridge that distance and reanimate her former life in New Zealand: "Oh, I want for one moment to make our undiscovered country leap into the eyes of the Old World. It must be mysterious, as though floating. It must take the breath."[55] In this way, Mansfield's relationship to New Zealand, with its preeminence in her writing, closely echoes Schreiner's affection for South Africa.

By considering Mansfield's early writings in light of the restricting imported codes described by Hyde and McClintock,[56] I place my argument within recent critical trends that recognize the continuities between her New Zealand and English writing.[57] Her early stories, for instance "Die Einsame," written when Mansfield was 15 years old, with its exploration of a lonely and unsettled consciousness in a dialectic relationship with a surrounding wilderness, bear the marks of her most celebrated later stories.[58] Mark Williams suggests that her 1907 trip through the Ureweras, shortly before her emigration, exposed the young Mansfield to the effects "of settlement and isolation on domestic lives, particularly of women," and "the massive collisions" of divergent traditions within the landscape.[59] Through a short account of this trip, I set the stage for an exploration of how such local tensions translate into Mansfield's domestic scenes in later stories, culminating in a close reading of "The Woman at the Store" and "Prelude," the latter often considered her first great modernist story. I suggest that her exile's "originality" and "plurality" of vision, theorized by Said, was formed not only by Mansfield's physical exile to England, but also in response to settler realities she encountered in New Zealand.

Mansfield's trip through the Ureweras is documented in a notebook striking in its alertness to the landscape's complexities. Her obvious fascination with the people and places she encountered in some ways recalls the exotic tales of a far-flung empire written by adventurists like Robert Louis Stevenson and H. Rider Haggard. At the same time, her emphasis on the land's mystery and generative power suggests Schreiner's connection to the South African karoo. Mansfield's narrative eye in the notebook unceasingly turns to the wild and untamed sights: "the valley—the air—the shining water [. . .] it is so passionately secret [. . .] And always through the bush the hushed sound of water running on brown pebbles—It seems to breathe the full deep bygone essence of it all."[60] The bush she describes is haunted by an inaccessible undercurrent of mystery, of bygone histories, and refuses to reveal its secrets—like Waldo's karoo and the Bushman's undecipherable carvings, the bush carries hidden within it secrets unrecorded in history books. Mansfield senses these reminders and remainders of colonial violence perpetrated on the land. She feels stirring within her "visions of long dead Maoris—of forgotten battles and vanished feuds" as they approach the site of an 1866 conflict between native and British forces (37). Mixed with this visceral unsettlement is a sensory celebration; stepping into a clearing, she cries out at "the river—savage, grey, fierce rushing tumbling" (73–74). Hearing the "thunder" of the water, observing the "vivid orange sky," smelling greedily "a handful of pine needles," and feeling the sun "scorching her skin" (74–75), her immersion bespeaks a sensual and bodily awakening. It is such corporeal experiences that are stifled by a domesticated land and people in Mansfield's later stories like "The Woman at the Store." Suggestions of a celebratory sensuality are extinguished in favor of a purely reproductive sexuality: rapture is replaced with the bearing of children to populate the colonies.

Mansfield's textured description of the Ureweras, which evoke color, sound, touch, and movement, coupled with the tension inherent in the dual nature of the land—its vast power and the violence lurking underneath—translate into her fictional writing. In a short sketch published in the same year as her trip, titled "In the Botanical Gardens," Mansfield recreates her impressions in the form of a conflict between "the smooth swept paths," surrounded by beautiful (though imported) flowers, of a well-tended New Zealand garden and the "bush, silent and splendid," discovered by the narrator after wandering along a side path.[61] The settler figure has a vivid encounter with the native landscape: the "strange indefinable scent," the bright colors, the silent mystery of the land make the narrator feel "old with the age of centuries, strong with the strength of savagery." And here again hints of violence emerge as the narrator looks up and imagines seeing "vague forms lurking in the shadow staring at me malevolently, wildly, the thief of their birthright [. . .] through the bush, ever in the shadow, [I] see a great company moving towards me [. . .] passing, passing, following the little stream in silence." The narrator's awakening at the hands of an undomesticated wilderness to an existence in tune with nature is ruptured by the land's intruding colonial past, the "great company" advancing to domesticate the bush. One of the story's final images captures the nature of this intrusion: people "crowding the pathway, looking reverently, admiringly, at the carpet bedding, spelling aloud the Latin names of the flowers." The desire to name, conquer, and categorize, to chart the spaces of the empire in the way described by Said, eradicates those spaces conducive to the full, textured experience of the narrator, whose own culpability in the violence is suggested by the "vague forms" staring from the shadows.

This unsettling divide between nature and an intruding civilization is staged within the domestic sphere in Mansfield's 1912 story "The Woman at the Store." When three travelers encounter the proprietress of a store on their journey through the New Zealand frontier, she is no longer the pretty "wax doll" of one traveler's memory from a trip four years previously.[62] Her body carries signs of toil and suffering, from her hands scarred by work, to her knocked out teeth, which suggest physical abuse, presumably at the hands of her absent husband. Domestication and violation, rather than being written on the landscape, are inscribed on the woman's body. She implicates domestic values in her degeneration, explaining that she has had four miscarriages in her six years of marriage, failing in her role to produce children to populate the colony by bearing only a "kid" with a "diseased" mind (274). The woman, however, has not "gone native" through the influence of her savage surroundings, as Lydia Wevers contends when she states that the woman represents a colonized colonizer turned into a "savage."[63] Rather it is suggested that physical and emotional abuse, as well as her unnatural domestic role have turned the ideal of a strong settler woman in a domestic haven into a monster who, it is revealed, murdered her husband to combat the abuse. The woman, confined within an isolated space and existence, appears misplaced in a sphere reminiscent of Hyde's unsuccessfully transplanted England. While her walls are "plastered with old pages of English periodicals [depicting] Queen Victoria's Jubilee" (270), she is not their intended audience, unable as she is to successfully perform the Victorian values they represent. According to Miles Fairburn, New Zealand settlers often surrounded themselves with English periodicals and scenes of England as a reaction to the lack of social interaction in the colony.[64] This tendency was not only limited to New Zealand, emerging as it does in Gregory's room in *The Story of an African Farm*, with his "walls profusely covered with prints cut from the 'Illustrated London News'" (178).

Entering the woman's house, the travelers see the manifestation of her unsuccessful attempt to construct an idyllic feminine domestic sphere: "a table with an ironing board and wash tub on it—some wooden forms—a black horsehair sofa, and some broken cane chairs pushed against the walls. The mantelpiece above the stove was draped in pink paper, further ornamented with dried grasses and ferns and a coloured print of Richard Seddon [...] and bundles of dried clover were pinned to the window curtains" (270).

The ironing board, a symbol of a standard domestic task, is surrounded by the detritus of English modernity and New Zealand life. Her dirty child, the flea-bitten dog, and these broken remains of imported and disintegrating traditions, highlight the conflict between the social role the woman is assigned and the realities of her everyday life. The scene is at once an emblem of her failure to enact a Victorian ideal of a tidily distributed and strictly regimented domestic space, and also the failure of this very same ideal to sustain and protect the woman from the traumas of her existence. "Imagine bothering about ironing," thinks the narrator, "*mad*, of course she's mad!" (271, emphasis original). The woman's gendered performance is out of place, like the dolls in Mansfield's later story "The Doll's House," whose "stiff" bodies are "really too big for the doll's house. They didn't look as though they belonged."[65] This scene of her fellow settler woman's ramshackle room has a profound effect on the narrator, one of the three travelers, revealed to be a woman toward the end of the story. Sitting in her room, she reflects: "There is no twilight in our New Zealand days, but a curious half-hour when everything appears grotesque—it frightens—as though the savage spirit of the country walked abroad and sneered at what it saw. Sitting alone in the hideous room I grew afraid" (271). The narrator projects her unease with the woman's struggle onto the landscape and her own room, deeming them grotesque and hideous. The recurrent contention that "The Woman at the Store" describes "the terrible power of an uncivilised territory to undo the civilisation the white man brought with him from his country of origin"[66] disregards the role of this very civilization in forcing an unnatural isolation on the woman. The sneering "savage spirit of the country" acts as a critical eye on misplaced importations. It harbors the critical spirit of the malevolently staring forms in Mansfield's "In the Botanical Gardens," suggesting that the settler's presence is ultimately an invasion.

Mansfield's explicit engagement with her homeland's unsettling, and at times hostile, forces is muted in her later stories, which, though frequently set in New Zealand, often only indirectly evoke its wilderness. Yet her localized settler impressions and intuitions, evident in these earlier stories, continue to form the basis of her later writing. Most notably, "Prelude," published in 1918 and often considered key to Mansfield's development as a modernist writer, evinces the unstable foundations on which colonial society is built, particularly the effects of imported values on women within the domestic sphere. "Prelude" recounts the Burnell family's move from Wellington to a new house on the outskirts of the city. The mother Linda embodies all the restrictions placed on the settler woman in the colonial sphere. She is imprisoned within the confines of her house, weighed down by the burden of having to bear children she does not want, and denied autonomy over her body by her husband. An unnatural mother, Linda, like Schreiner's Lyndall or Mansfield's unnamed woman at the store, is unable to perform the imposed role of nurturer and is continually plagued by visions of things expanding and "coming alive."[67] As she traces a poppy with "a fat bursting bud" on the wallpaper in her bedroom on her first morning in the new house, "under her tracing finger, the poppy seemed to come alive. She could feel the sticky, silky petals, the stem, hairy like a gooseberry skin, the rough leaf and the tight glazed bud" (68). This grotesque yet sensual image of fecundity, emanating from the very walls that imprison her, suggests Linda's complete physical and mental entrapment in her imposed role as a procreator.

Linda's condition is crystallized in the aloe plant at the center of her garden, itself divided between "a tangle of tall dark trees and strange bushes" on one side, and a "high box border" and paths with "box edges" on the other (72). The aloe grows at the center, perched on an island between these cultivated smooth paths and the untamed bush, reminiscent of Mansfield's "In the Botanical Gardens." This "fat swelling plant with its cruel leaves and fleshy stem" (73) embodies Linda's ideal of an autonomous existence. While it is swelling and fertile, it is isolated within itself, not letting anyone penetrate inside: "She particularly liked the long sharp thorns" (87). While the aloe is able to isolate itself from others, Linda's form of self-protection is a persistent detachment from her family. With her mind fixated on the plant, she has a vision of her own escape: "the high grassy bank on which the aloe rested rose up like a wave, and the aloe seemed to ride upon it like a ship with the oars lifted [. . .] She dreamed that she was caught up out of the cold water into the ship with the lifted oars and the budding mast [. . .] They rowed far away over the top of the garden trees, the paddocks and the dark bush beyond. Ah, she heard herself cry: 'Faster! Faster!' " (86–87). Linda imagines abandoning her house and children, trading her tended garden for the wilderness, the dark bush of "In the Botanical Gardens." Yet, just like the aloe, she remains rooted to the ground, suspended somewhere between her domestic haven and a wilderness perpetually out of reach. Sarah Ailwood rightly points out that, even for all their "self-defence measures," neither Linda nor the aloe is able to escape their "reproductive role: the aloe has buds, and Linda is already aware of her new pregnancy."[68] Indeed, much as the aloe fosters a dream of escape in Linda, it also

makes her acutely conscious of her inevitable fate: "What am I guard-
ing myself for so preciously? I shall go on having children and Stanley
will go one making more money and the children and the gardens will
grow bigger and bigger, with whole fleets of aloes in them" (88). The
singular, autonomous aloe becomes "whole fleets of aloes" and Linda,
like Schreiner's Lyndall, realizes her inability to escape her prescribed
fate and the dissolution of her individuality into membership in a fleet
of colonial mothers.

Unlike Schreiner, Mansfield was not directly engaged with political causes like the campaign for women's suffrage. Her ambivalence
about this latter movement is suggested in her story "Being a Truthful Adventure," which exposes it as a fad that transforms its advocates
into moral crusaders who uphold essentialist and traditional views of
women as mothers.[69] Mansfield's suspicion may be attributed to the
fact that New Zealand was the first country to enfranchise women
and, in the process, as Richard Evans explains, engendered an almost
complete end to its feminist movement as further demands were
abandoned.[70] Mansfield's stories nevertheless expose the gendered
injustices of her time, with her signature characters—the often isolated
and wandering female outcasts whose sexuality and bodies have been
repressed—evident from her first published collection, *In a German
Pension*, to her last completed story "The Canary."[71] It is this central
concern with sexual and domestic freedom throughout her writing
that clearly engages the very impulse that drove feminist thought and
action, and, in this way, Mansfield's stories extend the crucial role of
feminism and gender to modernist writing.

CONCLUSION

I return in closing to Edward Said, whose theorization of the enabling
"detachment *and* generosity" inherent in an exilic critical consciousness has informed my approach in this chapter. My attempt to, in
some ways, triangulate modernism, empire, and feminism by invoking
Said's thought is complicated, however, by his often unacknowledged
silence on gender. Boehmer provocatively outlines this elision, stating that "Said's silence on feminism whether as theory or as politics
of resistance is deafening."[72] This "occlusion," she continues, extends
to both theorists of Said's work, as well as to the broader field of
mainstream postcolonial studies.[73] Yet this does not preclude Said's
paradigms from being usefully applied to both the study of empire
and questions related to women and gender. Indeed, invoking his
work has allowed me to bring into sharp relief the textured realities

and the myriad echoes and complexities connecting the work of two colonial writers rarely thought together.

While there is no evidence to suggest that Schreiner and Mansfield ever met, and while there is also a marked difference in their political and aesthetic ambitions, their writing emanates from the spaces they inhabited and the "outsider" critical dispositions these fostered. Their burgeoning feminist ideas, and with them an evolving modernist form, are colored by both writers' acute sense of the local contradictions and limitations of empire, limitations that were often gender inflected. In her letter to Sarah Gertrude Millin, Mansfield sees Schreiner as a model for a writer's relationship to a homeland because of the latter's ability to "find the treasure" in the seemingly bounded spaces of her South African past. Most tellingly, Mansfield goes on to conclude that by describing "this which seems to us so intensely personal, other people take it to themselves and understand it as if it were their own."[74] As this letter proposes, rather than expressing a parochial loyalty to their homelands by drawing on these personal and familiar spaces, Schreiner and Mansfield take on and extend into the realm of fiction the role of the intellectual described by Said: to represent and "universalize" human experiences, sufferings, and crises.[75]

ACKNOWLEDGMENTS

For their encouragement and feedback on earlier versions of this chapter, I would like to thank Elleke Boehmer, Janet Wilson, Florian Klaeger, Klaus Stierstorfer, and Jeffrey Hole. My deepest thanks also to James Sweetman for his unwavering support and keen critical eye. I gratefully acknowledge the financial support provided by an EU-funded Marie Curie Initial Training Network (ITN), Diasporic Constructions of Home and Belonging (CoHaB) fellowship at the University of Muenster during the writing of this chapter.

NOTES

1. Robin Hyde, "The Singers of Loneliness," in *Disputed Ground: Robin Hyde, Journalist*, ed. Gillian Boddy and Jacqueline Matthews (Wellington: Victoria University Press, 1991), 354–355.
2. Ibid.
3. Mansfield to Sarah Gertrude Millin, "March 1922," in *The Collected Letters of Katherine Mansfield*, Vol. 5, ed. Vincent O'Sullivan and Margaret Scott (Oxford: Oxford University Press, 2008), 80.

4. Edward Said, *Orientalism* (London: Penguin, 2003), 259, emphasis original.

5. Emphasis is instead often placed on their social and geographical marginalization as colonial women in exile in England; see, for instance, the two extant comparative analyses of the two authors: Cherry Clayton, "Olive Schreiner and Katherine Mansfield: Artistic Transformations of the Outcast Figure by Two Colonial Women Writers in Exile," *English Studies in Africa* 32.2 (1989), 109–119; and Ruth Parkin-Gounelas, *Fictions of the Female Self: Charlotte Brontë, Olive Schreiner, Katherine Mansfield* (London: Macmillan, 1991).

6. W. T. Stead, "The Novel of the Modern Woman," *Review of Reviews* 10 (1894), 64; Elaine Showalter, *A Literature of Their Own* (Expanded edition) (Princeton, NJ: Princeton University Press, 1999), 199.

7. Sydney Janet Kaplan, *Katherine Mansfield and the Origins of Modernist Fiction* (London: Cornell University Press, 1991), 5.

8. Said, *Culture and Imperialism* (New York: Vintage, 1994), 336.

9. Said, *The World, the Text, and the Critic* (London: Faber and Faber, 1984), 34–35.

10. Said, "Reflections on Exile," in *Reflections on Exile and Other Essays* (Cambridge: Harvard University Press, 2000), 186; see also *Representations of the Intellectual: The 1993 Reith Lectures* (New York: Vintage, 1994), 60–61.

11. Said, "Reflections on Exile," 186.

12. Said, *Culture and Imperialism*, 7.

13. Ibid., 225–226.

14. Ibid., 7.

15. Elleke Boehmer, *Colonial and Postcolonial Literature: Migrant Metaphors* (Oxford: Oxford University Press, 2005), 17.

16. Ibid.

17. See Alfred Crosby, *Ecological Imperialism: The Biological Expansion of Europe, 900–1900* (Cambridge: Cambridge University Press, 1986), especially 196–216.

18. Anne McClintock, *Imperial Leather: Race, Gender and Sexuality in the Colonial Contest* (London: Routledge, 1995), 34.

19. Anna Davin, "Imperialism and Motherhood," *History Workshop* 5 (1978), 14.

20. Karen Chase and Michael Levenson, *A Public Life for the Victorian Family* (Princeton, NJ: Princeton University Press, 2000), 143.

21. Ibid., 154.

22. McClintock, *Imperial Leather*, 36.

23. Victoria Rosner, *Modernism and the Architecture of Private Life* (New York: Columbia University Press, 2005), 14.

24. On links between modernism, feminism, and gender, see also Marianne DeKoven, "Modernism and Gender," in *The Cambridge*

Companion to Modernism, ed. Michael Levenson (New York: Cambridge University Press, 1999); Bonnie Kime Scott, *The Gender of Modernism: A Critical Anthology* (Bloomington: Indiana University Press, 1990); and Ann L. Ardis, *New Women, New Novels: Feminism and Early Modernism* (New Brunswick, NJ: Rutgers University Press, 1990).

25. Said, *Culture and Imperialism*, 188.
26. Patrick Williams, " 'Simultaneous Uncontemporaneities': Theorising Modernism and Empire," in *Modernism and Empire*, ed. Howard Booth and Nigel Rigby (Manchester: Manchester University Press, 2000), 25.
27. Ruth First and Ann Scott, *Olive Schreiner* (London: Andre Deutsch, 1980), 196.
28. McClintock, *Imperial Leather*, 265.
29. Schreiner to Samuel Cronwright-Schreiner, November 30, 1914, in *The Letters of Olive Schreiner*, ed. S. C. Cronwright-Schreiner (London: T. Fisher Unwin, 1924), 343.
30. Schreiner to Havelock Ellis, April 5, 1890, in *Olive Schreiner Letters: Volume I: 1871–1899*, ed. Richard Rive (Oxford: Oxford University Press, 1988), 168.
31. Defined in the novel's glossary as "[t]he wide sandy plains in some parts of South Africa"; note the modern spelling of "karoo," I retain Schreiner's spelling when citing textual passages.
32. Doris Lessing, "Afterword to *The Story of an African Farm* by Olive Schreiner," in *A Small Personal Voice*, ed. Paul Schlueter (London: Flamingo, 1994), 162–163.
33. Carolyn Burdett, for example, calls Schreiner a "colonial proto-modernist," see *Olive Schreiner and the Progress of Feminism: Evolution, Gender, Empire* (London: Palgrave, 2001), 9.
34. Schreiner, *The Story of an African Farm* (Oxford: Oxford University Press, 1998), 13; all subsequent references in text.
35. J. M. Coetzee, *White Writing: On the Culture of Letters in South Africa* (London: Yale University Press, 1988), 65.
36. Ibid., 66.
37. See Miriam Wallraven, *A Writing Halfway Between Theory and Fiction: Mediating Feminism from the Seventeenth to the Twentieth Century* (Würzburg: Königshausen & Neumann, 2007), 127.
38. See, for instance, Mansfield's 1908 story "The Tiredness of Rosabel," in *The Collected Fiction of Katherine Mansfield, 1898–1915* (Vol. 1), ed. Gerri Kimber and Vincent O'Sullivan (Edinburgh: Edinburgh University Press, 2012), 133–138.
39. Rosner, *Modernism and the Architecture of Private Life*, 93.
40. Schreiner, *From Man to Man* (London: T. Fisher Unwin, 1926), 171.
41. Showalter, *A Literature of Their Own*, 202.

42. Sandra Gilbert and Susan Gubar, *No Man's Land: The Place of the Woman Writer in the Twentieth Century*, Vol. 2: *Sexchanges* (New Haven: Yale University Press, 1989), 60.
43. Showalter, *A Literature of Their Own*, 202.
44. See the novel's fourth chapter in Part II, titled "Lyndall" (190–213).
45. Gilbert and Gubar, *No Man's Land*, 62.
46. Schreiner, *Dreams* (London: T. Fisher Unwin, 1897), 67–68; all subsequent references in text.
47. Kate Flint, *The Woman Reader, 1837–1915* (Oxford: Oxford University Press, 1993), 242.
48. Ibid.
49. First and Scott, *Olive Schreiner*, 121, emphasis original.
50. Claire Tomalin, *Katherine Mansfield: A Secret Life* (London: Viking, 1987), 8–9; see also note 1.
51. Biographers often cite her personal writings, for instance a letter written on January 8, 1907, which describes her isolation in New Zealand and her longing for London; see *Collected Letters* (Vol. 5), 21.
52. Saikat Majumdar, "Katherine Mansfield and the Fragility of Pākehā Boredom," *Modern Fiction Studies* 55.1 (2009), 122.
53. Sylvia Berkman, *Katherine Mansfield: A Critical Study* (London: Oxford University Press, 1952), 49.
54. On "Prelude" and Mansfield's developing modernism, see Kaplan, *Katherine Mansfield and the Origins of Modernist Fiction*, 104.
55. Journal entry, January 22, 1916, in *The Letters and Journals of Katherine Mansfield: A Selection*, ed. C. K. Stead (London: Allen Lane, 1977), 65.
56. See notes 1 and 18.
57. See Janet Wilson, " 'Where is Katherine?': Longing and (Un)belonging in the Work of Katherine Mansfield," in *Celebrating Katherine Mansfield: A Centenary Volume of Essays*, ed. Gerri Kimber and Janet Wilson (London: Palgrave Macmillan, 2011), 175–188; and Boehmer, "Mansfield as Colonial Modernist: Difference Within," 57–71 in the same volume.
58. "Die Einsame," published in the *Queen's College Magazine* in March 1904; see *Collected Fiction*, Vol. 1, 20–22.
59. Mark Williams, "Mansfield in Maoriland: Biculturalism, Agency and Misreading," in *Modernism and Empire*, 256.
60. *The Urewera Notebook*, ed. Ian A. Gordon (Oxford: Oxford University Press, 1978), 55; all subsequent references in text.
61. "In the Botanical Gardens," published in the Melbourne periodical *The Native Companion* in December 1907; see *Collected Fiction*, Vol. 1, 85; all subsequent references to this page.
62. "The Woman at the Store," published in *Rhythm* in Spring 1912; see *Collected Fiction*, Vol. 1, 272; all subsequent references in text.

63. Lydia Wevers, "How Kathleen Beauchamp Was Kidnapped," in *Critical Essays on Katherine Mansfield*, ed. Rhoda Nathan (Oxford: Maxwell Macmillan, 1993), 44.

64. Miles Fairburn, *The Ideal Society and Its Enemies: The Foundations of Modern New Zealand Society 1850–1900* (Auckland: Auckland University Press, 1989), 202–203; see also Mansfield's 1913 story "Millie," in which a print on a bedroom wall titled "Garden Party at the Windsor Castle" only highlights a settler woman's isolation; in *Collected Fiction*, Vol. 1, 326–330.

65. "The Doll's House," in *The Collected Fiction of Katherine Mansfield, 1916–1922*, Vol. 2, 415.

66. See, for instance, Wevers, "How Kathleen Beauchamp Was Kidnapped," 44.

67. "Prelude," published by the Hogarth Press in July 1918; see *Collected Fiction* (Vol. 2), 68; all subsequent references in text.

68. Sarah Ailwood, "Anxious Beginnings: Mental Illness, Reproduction and Nation Building in 'Prelude' and *Prelude to Christopher*," *Katherine Mansfield Studies* 2 (2010), 28.

69. "Being a Truthful Adventure," *Collected Fiction*, Vol. 1, 229–234. Mansfield's ambivalence is further indicated in her letter to Garnet Trowell on September 16, 1908, which ridicules the suffragettes, *Collected Letters*, Vol. 1, 59–61; on Mansfield's feminism, see also Kaplan, *Katherine Mansfield and the Origins of Modernist Fiction*, 118–144.

70. Richard Evans, *The Feminists: Women's Emancipation Movements in Europe, America and Australasia 1840–1920* (New York: Routledge, 1977), 63, 233–234.

71. See, for instance, "Miss Brill" or "Bliss"; from *In a German Pension*, see "A Birthday" or "Frau Brechmacher Attends a Wedding."

72. Boehmer, "Edward Said and (the Postcolonial Occlusion of) Gender," in *Edward Said and the Literary, Social, and Political World*, ed. Ranjan Ghosh (London: Routledge, 2009), 124.

73. Ibid., 124–125, 133.

74. *Collected Letters* (Vol. 5), 80.

75. Said, *Representations of the Intellectual*, 44.

CHAPTER 10

MUNDUS TOTUS EXILIUM EST:
REFLECTIONS ON THE CRITIC
IN EXILE

Robert T. Tally Jr.

Comparative literature has always presupposed transnationality, not only as it may be encountered in the circulations of texts and ideas, but also as it appears in the vocation of the critic. The critic engaged in a comparative study of literature, like Walter Benjamin's translator, is positioned outside of the national, linguistic, or cultural forest, desperately trying to catch echoes of the foreign utterances with more or less familiar resonances.[1] "National literature," as Goethe put it in the early nineteenth century, "is no longer of any importance; it is time for world literature, and all must aid in bringing it about."[2] In this view of *Weltliteratur*, a certain unfamiliarity or lack of homeliness is required. To forego the national in favor of some international or transnational vision is to embrace alterity, the estrangement that comes with being "out of place," which is also one of the most powerful experiences of the literary itself, as the great Russian formalists reminded us. To engage in the theory and practice of comparative literature is to confront this estrangement head on, not in order to make the transnational more familiar, but to marvel and delight in its implacable weirdness. In this sense, the critic approaches all texts as foreign, and criticism, rather than domesticating the strange experiences of the text, serves to evoke and even celebrate its foreignness.

Transnational literature necessarily involves displacements, border crossings, and translations (or, from the Latin root, the "carrying across") from one site to another. Although literary works commonly represent their time and place, sometimes embodying an *ethos* or identity of its local or national condition, more frequently literature wanders across boundaries, utters foreign words and speaks in strange accents, defamiliarizing things as it discloses to the reader novel ways of seeing, where even the most homey scene can become exotic, and the experience of reading not uncommonly involves metaphorical travels into foreign lands. In some respects, literature itself may be viewed as a form of exile. The literary critic, whose task is to make sense of all this, is thus engaged in another form of exile, moving beyond the familiar "homeland" and into the mobile and uncertain circumstances of a transgressive literariness. A transnational, or perhaps postnational, approach to that task seems altogether appropriate. In the critic's displacement, paradoxically, one finds that being "at home in the world" means being a stranger everywhere in it, which is also to say, one makes oneself at home by embracing one's sense of homelessness, at least with respect to literature and culture. For such a critic, the entire world is a foreign land: *mundus totus exilium est.*

In using this phrase, I am aware of performing a sort of rhetorical double-distancing, estranging its meaning from its own origins and projecting it into a world at large. Indeed, it is a quotation of a quotation, itself a metaphorical displacement reflecting the experience of exile itself, where one's very language is no longer tied to its native soil, and new meanings proliferate across permeable and shifting borders. Written in an archaic, even "dead," language, the phrase offers new life to an idea that seems particularly timely in our own age, this "borderless world" in the epoch of globalization, which, as jeremiad-shouting critics and starry-eyed cheerleaders alike now agree, apparently typifies our current condition. In its initial utterance by Hugh of Saint Vincent in the twelfth century, the phrase *mundus totus exilium est* put forward a philosophical position with respect to the *premodern* world, a worldly world seemingly at odds with a transcendental space in which the virtuous soul might properly feel "at home."[3] In its iteration by Erich Auerbach in his 1952 essay "Philology and *Weltliteratur*," the phrase is quoted to make the point that the *modern* critic of literature and language must not be tied to any national ground, but must accept that his or her "philological home is the earth; the nation it can no longer be."[4] And, in my own return to the expression, in this third moment of what still might be called *postmodernity*, I wish to register the meaning that both its original author and its philological patron assert: that, just as the "perfect" exile—one for whom the whole world is a foreign land—is better equipped to make sense of the world, the critic must adopt the symbolic or figural position of the exile in order to better grapple with the literary and cultural productions that are themselves principal means of making sense of that world.

The exile's sense of homelessness cannot but be a source of great anxiety. Yet, as Edward W. Said has argued in "Reflections on Exile," the critical insight and perspective of the exile produce a "pleasure" that may overcome "the grimness of outlook" occasioned by the experience of actual exile.

> While it perhaps seems peculiar to speak of the pleasures of exile, there are some positive things to be said for a few of its conditions. Seeing "the entire world as a foreign land" makes possible originality of vision. Most people are principally aware of one culture, one setting, one home; exiles are aware of at least two, and this plurality of vision gives rise to an awareness of simultaneous dimension, an awareness that—to borrow a phrase from music—is *contrapuntal*.[5]

Hence, the writer who remains "at home" may not be able to see the same things, or see them in the same way, as the writer in exile. As I have argued in another context and what may now seem a commonplace, the writer maps the world, producing a literary cartography that may offer a useful means of navigating the often chaotic or seemingly meaningless array of phenomena and experiences of the world.[6] In the case of the exile, the cartographic project would appear to be all the more urgent, since the chaos or senselessness is compounded by a foreignness as well. But, as with Said's reevaluation, the writer-in-exile is perhaps better able to produce this map by virtue of his or her "originality of vision." The critic who can "read" these imaginary or figurative maps may also benefit from that originality of vision whose provenance is exile.

Frank Kermode has famously noted that, if the task of the poet is to "help us make sense of our lives," the critic is bound "to attempt the lesser feat of making sense of the ways we try to make sense of our lives."[7] If the poet or literary artist maps our world, then the task of the critic is also cartographic, involving not just map-reading, but the drawing and redrawing of lines on the maps, marking this or that figure or *topos* for further elaboration or modification, and so on. The exiles, émigrés, nomads, renegades, and refugees who create our literary maps also call for a criticism attuned to the spatial peculiarities of the conditions of exile. The critic must approach the whole world as a foreign country, and then map it.[8] The experience of exile, then, requires the critic as well as the poet to create new maps, which in turn may transform the spaces that they attempt to represent.

In "Philology and *Weltliteratur*," Auerbach reflects on the project of literary criticism in the postwar period, and he calls for a return, albeit under novel conditions, to a medieval conception of *terra aliena* in order to make a case for a postnational theory of literature. Given the recent events, Auerbach's desire to transcend the nationalisms of the early twentieth century is completely understandable, but his broader argument about the importance of a postnational literary criticism bears directly on our own twenty-first-century condition, in an era of globalization, with even more urgency. In his concluding paragraph, Auerbach definitively places the nation in a subordinate, and even defective, position with respect to the principal task of criticism or philology. After discussing the study of world literature in his present moment, Auerbach concludes:

> our philological home is the earth: it can no longer be the nation. The most priceless and indispensible part of a philologist's heritage is still his own nation's culture and language. Only when he is first separated from this heritage, however, and then transcends it does it become truly effective. We must return, in admittedly altered circumstances, to the knowledge that prenational medieval culture already possessed: the knowledge that the spirit [*Geist*] is not national. *Paupertas* and *terra aliena*: this or something to this effect.[9]

Geist, "spirit" or "mind," is not national, and neither can its literary and cultural products be so limited. Indeed, Auerbach suggests that, to the extent that one's mind does remain fettered to its native land, the critic cannot "become truly effective," as nationality may blunt one's critical acumen. Also, the relationship between *paupertas* and *terra aliena* ("poverty" and "foreign land") designate the proper behavior of the critic: one should always behave as would a beggar in a foreign land: that is, with humility. For medieval theologians, the lesson is that one must not feel too "at home" in a place lest one forget that the only place that really matters is not of this world. After two world wars and particularly with respect to the reckless arrogance and bellicosity seemingly inseparable from any distinctively national identity, it is understandable that humility would reemerge for Auerbach as a supreme virtue for twentieth-century humanism. By returning to these premodern, medieval ideas in the context of the present, Auerbach reinvents the concepts and supplies them with added meaning for a world desperately wounded by the effects of heightened nationalisms.

Auerbach gives the twelfth-century theologian Hugh of Saint Vincent (also known as Hugo of Saint Victor) a final word, quoting in the original Latin a few lines from his *Didascalion*, including the phrase used as my title in the final clause. Here is the same passage in Jerome Taylor's English translation:

> It is, therefore, a great source of virtue for the practiced mind to learn, bit by bit, first to change about in visible and transitory things, so that afterwards it may be able to leave them behind altogether. The man who finds his homeland sweet is still the tender beginner; he to whom every soil is as his native one is already strong; but he is perfect to whom the entire world is as a foreign land.[10]

Auerbach then sums up, interpreting these lines from another epoch and giving them added significance for his own time: "Hugo intended these lines for one whose aim was to free himself from a love of the world. But it is a good way also for one who wishes to earn a proper love for the world."[11]

Auerbach's recasting of the concept—*mundus totus exilium est*—in the context of modernity offers a model for criticism in our own time as well. The critic must work through personal or cultural attachments to the native soil, detaching himself or herself from local prejudices and comforts, and engaging with one's place as a foreigner or exile, who can thereby map such spaces critically without the distortions or myopia occasioned by undue familiarity. Auerbach's own magnum opus, *Mimesis: The Representation of Reality in Western Literature*, was written while he was living in exile in Turkey, and he indicates in his preface that the work would not have been possible, in the form it took, without such admittedly uncomfortable circumstances. The conditions of Auerbach's exile, including such everyday matters as the availability of certain books, as well as more serious concerns, like the threat to his life and livelihood, explain the many limitations of the work, but these conditions also made possible the exhilarating sweep, the careful analyses, and the theoretical power of *Mimesis*.[12] To the extent that the poet or creative writer maps a world for his or her readers, making sense of and giving form to our experiences, the critic who can approach the entire world as a foreign land can also create new and more effective legends, interpretations, and supplemental maps.

In *The Theory of the Novel*, Georg Lukács argued that the age of the epic coincided with integrated or "closed" civilizations, in which "the starry sky is a map of all possible paths."[13] Still under the influence of Hegel and the Romantics, the young Lukács finds that the advent of modernity is marked by a profound break between self and world. Lukács gives this condition an evocative name, "transcendental homelessness," which figures forth the experience of living in "a world that has been abandoned by God."[14] Indeed, the notion that a kind of homelessness typifies the modern condition is felt strongly by the nineteenth and early twentieth centuries. Martin Heidegger, for example, emphasized in *Being and Time* that the existential condition of anxiety (*Angst*) was closely related to the experience of the uncanny (*unheimlich*), which itself is a pervasive feeling of "not-being-at-home" (*das Nicht-zuhause-sein*).[15] Yet, not surprisingly, Lukács is not mourning the loss of some idyllic golden age, and he does not call for a return to the epic past: "the great epic is a form bound to the historical moment, and any attempt to depict the utopian as existent can only end in destroying the form, not in creating reality."[16]

For Lukács, the "transcendental homelessness" makes possible the novel, a form that gives form to the world, establishing (if only, and necessarily) a provisional construction of a totality that can help us make sense of the vicissitudinous experience of our lives. The novel supplies a cartography for the existentially displaced or lost human subject a way of comprehending this condition, establishing a "you are here" in a spatial milieu that cries out for guideposts, landmarks, paths, and the like. In Lukács's estimation, the ancient epic represented a world that necessarily *was*, a world grounded in fate and utterly changeless in its stable identities: "Nestor is old just as Helen is beautiful or Agamemnon mighty."[17] By contrast, the novel represents a world that *may be*; it is a figural projection of a world that enables its inhabitants, along with its writers and readers, to shape their existence, create movements, and venture forth. "The novel is the epic of a world that has been abandoned by God," and thus, in Lukács's view, the novel is the preeminent literary form for exiles, for those who wander and who map, for those who transform spaces into *places*, as Yi-Fu Tuan would have it, by moving across them, coming to rest, and taking note.[18] Similarly, then, the critic, who takes note of these note-takers, adopts the vantage of the exile in order to see this new world anew.

If exiles, nomads, wanderers, or adventurers were already the archetypal subjects of a modern world abandoned by God, then the advent of modernism in the twentieth century enshrined them definitively. Perhaps not surprisingly, many of the key modernist artists, and many of their critics, were themselves exiles of one sort or another. In another famous image of "homelessness," George Steiner notes that much of the great literature of the twentieth century has often been produced by those who, like Conrad, Beckett, or Nabokov, write in the foreign language of their lands of exile, rather than in a native tongue associated with one's homeland. "It seems proper that those who create art in a civilization of quasi-barbarism which has made so many homeless, which has torn up tongues and peoples by the root, should themselves be poets unhoused and wanderers across language."[19]

Similarly, Terry Eagleton's early study of "English" modernism, significantly titled *Exiles and Émigrés*, notes that nearly all of the more influential literary artists of the period were not themselves English. As Eagleton puts it, "the seven most significant writers of twentieth-century English literature have been a Pole, three Americans, two Irishmen, and an Englishman. [. . .] With the exception of D. H. Lawrence, the heights of modern English literature have been dominated by foreigners and émigrés: Conrad, James, Eliot, Pound, Yeats, Joyce."[20] Eagleton's explanation for this is that the tumultuous experiences of the early twentieth century made it impossible for the traditional English novelist to achieve a sense of totality, as the English Romantics and later realists of Dickens's or Thackeray's stripe had been able to do in earlier generations, and that the perspective of the outsider, the writer-in-exile, allowed for the proper "originality of vision" (to insert Said's phrase here) to attempt to encompass a social totality at that historical moment. Eagleton adds that, by virtue of his working-class background, even Lawrence is a kind of outsider or exile with respect to the English tradition. Although Eagleton's use of the term "exile" is largely metaphorical—"I am concerned not so much with the work of 'literal' expatriates, but with the 'social' exiles"[21]—his point is similar to Steiner's: the writer-in-exile is more capable of understanding and representing the modern social condition than a native writer who feels "at home" in his or her world.

If this be the case for high modernism, in the era of monopoly capitalism in the age of imperialism, then how much more significant does it appear in the postmodern condition in the age of globalization? The cartographic aspect of literature and criticism becomes all the more urgent and desirable in an age when national identities and borders blur, and the shifting zones of metropolis and periphery become thoroughly entangled, through technology, industry, and culture. Fredric Jameson, in making his case for an aesthetic of cognitive mapping as a means to counteract the fundamental sense of placelessness or displacement in the postmodern condition, has pointed out that, in the era of modernism, it was already nearly impossible to coordinate one's existential situation with the realities of a global network of often invisible interrelations.

> At this point the phenomenological experience of the individual subject—traditionally, the supreme raw materials of the work of art—becomes limited to a tiny corner of the social world, a fixed camera view of a certain section of London or the countryside or whatever. But the truth of that experience no longer coincides with the place in which it takes place. The truth of that limited daily experience of London lies, rather, in India or Jamaica or Hong Kong; it is bound up with the whole colonial system of the British Empire that determines the very quality of the individual's subjective life. Yet those structural coordinates are no longer accessible to immediate lived experience and are often not even conceptualizable for most people.[22]

This leads to the paradoxical situation in which "if individual experience is authentic, then it cannot be true; and if a scientific or cognitive model of the same content is true, then it escapes individual experience."[23] Although not necessarily responding to the same conditions, Jameson's point complements Eagleton's, insofar as the seemingly "inauthentic" presence of the exile is better able to square the circle by attempting the totalizing representation afforded by that originality of vision.

Of course, not all "exiles" are the same. As Said observes, distinctions need to be made along this exilic continuum linking "exiles, refugees, expatriates, and émigrés." Whereas an exile may have been banished, he or she maintains a kind of nobility ("a touch of solitude and spirituality),'" while the "refugee" conjures up the image of helpless throngs ("large herds of innocent and bewildered people requiring urgent international assistance"). At the other end of the spectrum, expatriates are generally voluntary foreigners, who like Hemingway or Fitzgerald willingly choose to spend time in a foreign land. "Expatriates may share in the solitude and estrangement of exile, but they do not suffer under its rigid proscriptions." Similarly, the émigré may be anyone who has moved, voluntarily or otherwise, from one's native land to a foreign one, but the experience of exile varies greatly among émigrés. For example, many European settlers of Africa, Asia, Australia, and the Americas "may have once been exiles, but as pioneers and nation-builders, they lost the label 'exile.'"[24]

"Exile originated in the age-old practice of banishment," writes Said. "Once banished, the exile lives an anomalous and miserable life, with the stigma of being an outsider."[25] Think of Dante, cast out of his beloved hometown of Florence, *sub poena mortis*, and forced to lead a nomadic life. Such experience undoubtedly colors not merely the representation of the world, but also the poet's very perception. In Auerbach's astonishingly bold rereading, the author of the "divine" *Commedia* becomes the poet of the secular or worldly world (*die irdische Welt*). From his privileged perspective as a poet and critic in exile, Dante projects a vision of an otherworldly sphere that nevertheless functions as damning critique of his very real world of the fourteenth century. As Auerbach notes, "in truth the Comedy is a picture of earthly life. The human world in all its breadth and depth is gathered into the structure of the hereafter and there it stands: complete, unfalsified, yet encompassed in an eternal order."[26] An exile in body and spirit, Dante projects a sense-making order, a sort of transcendental map in its Lukácsean sense, that constrains and makes meaningful the chaotic, displaced, and rambling experience of daily life in which the whole world is like a foreign land. The joy and precision of the work of the exile-poet nevertheless also gives evidence of the pain, humiliation, and even righteous anger that accompanies the anguished homelessness of exile. As Said marvels, "Who but an exile like Dante, banished from Florence, would use eternity as a place to settle old scores?"[27]

But the bitterness of the anguished exile is in the end displaced by the remarkable acumen that accompanies the critic-in-exile's perception, as Dante's divine performance attests to. Said notes that exiles occupy not so much a *privileged* position in the society or culture in which they find themselves (and, of course, the irony associated with the word would be quite pronounced), as an *alternative* position.[28] That is, they can see in ways that non-exiles perhaps could not, and this allows for a powerful form of criticism. Said's exemplar in this regard is Theodor Adorno, whose flight from Nazi Germany eventually made possible one of the century's most potently original critiques of mass culture, industrial civilization, and rationalized or administered society. As Alex Thomson has noted, Adorno's own time in exile in North America profoundly influenced his peculiar brand of cultural criticism—including, of course, the critique of culture itself—even as it caused him a great deal of psychic, emotional, and even physical anguish. But in his distance from his native soil and in his often unpleasant encounters with an all-too-foreign civilization, Adorno refined his critical force.

Adorno's idea of cultural criticism is certainly stamped by his experience in the United States, but what he learns is not to reject that which is outside his idea of culture; rather the opposite, he seeks to make space in his thought for that which might come from the outside. American democracy may be the mere equivalence of everyone without hierarchy. Unlike many of Nietzsche's heirs, including Heidegger and those American Nietzscheans who follow Leo Strauss, who see this as the triumph of herd mentality over aristocratic virtues which make true dwelling on the earth impossible, Adorno hopes for a rather different sort of future, neither home-coming or disaster, but something more like the release from the dialectics of culture altogether.[29]

Of course, one could hardly call Adorno's return to Frankfurt after the war a "homecoming" in a traditional sense, as postwar Germany was quite different from the country of his youth or the *Reich* that he had fled. In many respects, Adorno remained an exile, and a proponent of a kind of intellectual or critical exile, throughout his life.

The experience of exile also helped to confirm Adorno's suspicions concerning the jargon of authenticity, with its quasi-romanticism of home and homeland that carried with it the discernible stench of fascism. He knew that one cannot "go home again," and—observing that the rustic ideals of Heideggerian thought found their real-world counterparts in the data showing "the worst atrocities in the concentration camps were committed by the younger sons of farmers"—Adorno averred that the "spirit" longing for this mythic homeland "hires itself out as the lackey of what is evil."[30] The desire for home, whether in terms of nation-state or of native land, carried with it a dark particularity that invariably casts others into the shadow. In Adorno's view, the duty of the critic is to be always *not at home*, to feel one's estrangement even in one's putative homeland. As he put it in a phrase also quoted by Said, "it is part of morality not to be at home in one's home."[31]

Adorno's embrace of exile, or his refusal to find any value in the nostalgic or positive imagery of home or homecoming, is related to his view of the critic in general. The critic must maintain a defamiliarizing distance from the culture, as well as from the society or social relations represented in works of culture, such as art and literature. This requires a double-distancing, as the critic stands separate from both the arts and from the subjects represented in the works of art. From this outside-the-outsider's perspective, the critic may engage with the dynamics of culture and society...critically. This is in no way the romanticization of the critic, who is somehow to be cast as a kind of Baudelairean *poète maudit*; on the contrary, for Adorno, this alienation of the critic is essential to the function of criticism, as crucial to his or her work as the use of mathematics is to the physicist.

Many of the critics I have been discussing are, of course, not only theorists of exile, but themselves exiles, in various ways. As noted, Erich Auerbach, expert in "the worldly world," was forced to flee his native Germany and wrote what is generally considered his magnum opus while living in Turkey, before emigrating to the United States after the war. Edward Wadie Said, whose very name registers the English-Arabic border-crossings and a sense of being "between worlds," was born to Christian parents in British-controlled Palestine, lived in Jerusalem and Cairo before attending school in Massachusetts, Princeton, and Harvard, then becoming a professor at Columbia University. Theodor W. Adorno—who dropped his Germanic last name "Wiesengrund," reducing it to a middle initial, and adopted his Italian mother's maiden name (although of Jewish descent, Adorno's father was a Protestant and his mother was Catholic)—shifted from Frankfurt to Vienna and back, from Berlin to Oxford and back, and on to New York and Los Angeles, before returning to a postwar Frankfurt transformed. Georg (or György) Lukács was born in Budapest to a prominent Jewish family, studied in Berlin and Heidelberg, served in the short-lived Hungarian Soviet Republic before fleeing to Vienna where he wrote *History and Class Consciousness*, and then moved to Berlin before relocating to Moscow in 1933; returning to his "home-town" only after the war, Lukács became involved in that region's entanglements in the decades that followed, where his own personal displacements included a brief deportation to Romania for his part in the failed revolution of 1956. Steiner notes that Lukács's own wander-ings, from Budapest to Berlin then onto Moscow, made him an exile as well, not just in his person but also in his writing: "German is Lukács's principal language, but his use of it has grown brittle and forbidding. His style is that of exile; it has lost the habits of living speech. More essentially: Lukács's entire tone, the fervent, at times narrow tenor of his vision, mirror the fact of banishment."[32] Indeed, Steiner himself is a "grateful wanderer," who was born in Paris to Viennese Jewish parents, emigrated to New York in 1940, studied in Chicago, Paris, Oxford, and has taught in many more places still. "Trees have roots and I have legs; I owe my life to that."[33]

There are also those ways in which a critic might be exiled with-out leaving home. As Gilles Deleuze has pointed out, "the nomad is not necessarily one who moves: some voyages take place *in situ*."[34] Indeed, for all of their physical movements, one could certainly make the argument that many European Jewish intellectuals, writing in French or German or English in countries that are largely non-Jewish if not downright anti-Semitic, are participating in a form of minority discourse that is itself akin to the language of the exile. Similarly for a Hungarian Marxist writing in German in Moscow, or for a Palestinian-born secular Christian Arab writing in English in New York. As Deleuze and Guattari argue in their book on Franz Kafka, the Jewish writer of German literature living in Prague, this creates a "minor literature" using a "deterritorialized language" within the larger literary tradition.[35] The critic, in viewing the entire world as a foreign land, also may make nomadic movements, deterritorializations and reterritorializations, in drawing and interpreting the literary maps produced by poets, novelists, and other writers.

Concluding my reflections on reflections on exile, then, I return to the site at which I began. In the lesson of the twelfth-century philosopher quoted at the outset, recall that while the "tender beginner" may find his own country sweet, and the "strong" can feel at home in any land, only for the "perfect" individual is the whole world like a foreign land. As Said points out, Hugh of Saint Vincent "twice makes it clear that the 'strong' or 'perfect' man achieves independence by *working through* attachments."[36] It is not enough to simply reject one's love of country, but to press on through the love and loss that characterizes the condition of exile in order, eventually and with effort, to embrace that condition. It is a process, and not necessarily a smooth or easy one. Perhaps this accounts for why the struggle takes so much time, and often finds itself fulfilled only later in life. Said, referring to Adorno who was in turn referring to Beethoven (another double-distancing), notes that the "late style" of an artist itself becomes a sort of exilic form: "a moment when the artist who is fully in command of his medium abandons communication with the established social order of which he is a part and achieves a contradictory, alienated relationship to it. His late works constitute a form of exile."[37] So too with the critic, who strives to become intimate with culture while also maintaining a profound distance, becoming an alien presence in the most homely places, wherever such places may be. *Mundus totus exilium est.* As Auerbach had asserted, the critic who would have a proper love for the world's literature must also view the entire world as a foreign land. In the secular criticism of the exile Edward W. Said, we may detect such a love of the world and, perhaps, we can glimpse the contours of that perfection toward which the worldly critic strives.

NOTES

1. See Walter Benjamin, "The Task of the Translator," in *Illuminations: Essays and Reflections*, ed. Hannah Arendt, trans. Harry Zohn (New York: Schocken Books, 1969), 76.

2. Goethe, "On World Literature," in *Essays on Art and Literature*, ed. John Geary, trans. Ellen von Nardhoff and Ernest H. von Nardhoff (Princeton: Princeton University Press, 1994), 224.

3. See Jerome Taylor, *The Didascalion of Hugh of Saint Victor: A Medieval Guide to the Arts*, trans. Jerome Taylor (New York: Columbia University Press, 1991).

4. Erich Auerbach, "Philology and *Weltliteratur*," trans. M. and E. W. Said, *Centennial Review* 13.1 (1969), 17.

5. Edward W. Said, "Reflections on Exile," in *Reflections on Exile and Other Essays* (Cambridge: Harvard University Press, 2000), 186.

6. See, e.g., my "Mapping Narratives," in *Literary Cartographies: Spatiality, Representation, and Narrative*, ed. Robert T. Tally Jr. (New York: Palgrave Macmillan, 2014), 1–12; *Spatiality* (London: Routledge, 2013), especially 44–78; and *Melville, Mapping, and Globalization: Literary Cartography in the American Baroque Writer* (London: Continuum, 2009).

7. Frank Kermode, *The Sense of an Ending: Studies in the Theory of Fiction* (Oxford: Oxford University Press, 1966), 3.

8. For an example of one such approach to the spatial peculiarities of literary texts, see Bertrand Westphal, *Geocriticism: Real and Fictional Spaces*, trans. Robert T. Tally Jr. (New York: Palgrave Macmillan, 2011).

9. Auerbach, "Philology and *Weltliteratur*," 17.

10. See Taylor, *The Didascalion of Hugh of Saint Victor*, 101.

11. Auerbach, "Philology and *Weltliteratur*," 17.

12. For an excellent account of just how much the experience in Istanbul influenced Auerbach's work, see Kader Konuk, *East West Mimesis: Auerbach in Turkey* (Stanford, CA: Stanford University Press, 2010).

13. Georg Lukács, *The Theory of the Novel*, trans. Anna Bostock (Cambridge: The MIT Press, 1971), 29.

14. Ibid., 88.

15. See Heidegger, *Being and Time*, trans. J. Macquarrie and E. Robinson (New York: Harper and Row, 1962), 233.

16. Lukács, *The Theory of the Novel*, 152.

17. Ibid., 121.

18. See Yi-Fu Tuan, *Space and Place: The Perspective of Experience* (Minneapolis: University of Minnesota Press, 1977), 161.

19. Steiner, *Extraterritorial: Papers on Literature and the Language of Revolution* (New York: Atheneum, 1976), 11.

20. Eagleton, *Exiles and Émigrés: Studies in Modern Literature* (New York: Schocken Books, 1970), 9.

21. Ibid., 18.

22. Jameson, *Postmodernism, or, the Cultural Logic of Late Capitalism* (Durham: Duke University Press, 1991), 411.

23. Ibid.

24. Said, "Reflections on Exile," 181.

25. Ibid.

26. Auerbach, *Dante: Poet of the Secular World*, trans. Ralph Mannheim (Chicago: University of Chicago Press, 1961), 133.

27. Said, "Reflections on Exile," 182.

28. Ibid., 184.

29. Alex Thomson, *Adorno* (London: Continuum, 2006), 31.

30. Adorno, *The Jargon of Authenticity*, trans. K. Tarnowski and F. Will (Evanston: Northwestern University Press, 1973), 26–27.

31. Adorno, *Minima Moralia: Reflections on a Damaged Life*, trans. E. F. N. Jephcott (London: Verso, 2005), 39.

32. George Steiner, *Language and Silence: Essays on Language, Literature, and the Inhuman* (New Haven: Yale University Press, 1998), 329.

33. See Myra Jaggi, "George and His Dragons," *The Guardian* (March 17, 2001). Retrieved April 10, 2010.

34. Gilles Deleuze, "Nomad Thought," trans. David Allison. *The New Nietzsche*, ed. David Allison (Cambridge: The MIT Press, 1977), 149.

35. Gilles Deleuze and Félix Guattari, *Kafka: Toward a Minor Literature*, trans. Dana Polan (Minneapolis: University of Minnesota Press, 1986), 17.

36. Said, "Reflections on Exile," 185.

37. Said, *On Late Style* (New York: Pantheon, 2006), 8.

CONTRIBUTORS

Cameron Bushnell is an associate professor of English at Clemson University. Her current research focuses on global politics and its expression in aesthetic forms and in the humanities. She is the author of *Postcolonial Readings of Music in World Literature: Turning Empire on Its Ear*. Bushnell has published essays in in *Contemporary Literature* and *South Asian Review*, as well as chapters in *Counterpoints: Edward Said's Legacy* and in *Resounding Pasts: Essays on Literature, Music, and Cultural Memory*.

Jeffrey Hole is an assistant professor of English at the University of the Pacific where he teaches courses in American and world literatures. He is the author of recent essays appearing in *American Literature*, *Criticism*, and *Review of International American Studies*. His current book project, *Cunning Inventions and the Force of Law*, examines the concomitances between fugitive and literary intelligence in the wake of the 1850 Fugitive Slave Act and gives particular attention to the international reach of US regulatory power.

Kristine Kelly is a lecturer in English at Case Western Reserve University. Her teaching and research interests focus on British colonial and contemporary Anglophone literature, with particular attention to colonial travel and emigration. Her publications include "Speaking Up: Caroline Chisholm's Rhetoric of Emigration Reform" in *Nineteenth Century Studies* and "Aesthetic Desire and Imperialist Disappointment in Trollope's *The Bertrams* and the Murray *Handbook for Travellers in Syria and Palestine*" in *Victorian Literature and Culture*.

Sobia Khan is a member of the English faculty at Richland College, Dallas, Texas. Her current project, titled "Transnational Identity in Crisis: Self-Writings of Edward Said, Jacques Derrida, and Theresa Hak Kyung Cha," focuses on issues on belonging and displacement. She is also an active creative writer. Her most recent short story "The Fallen" appears in *Her Texas: Story, Image, and Song* (Wing Press, 2014), an anthology on Texas women artists.

Daniel Rosenberg Nutters, a PhD candidate at Temple University, is working on a dissertation entitled "The Man of Imagination: Transformations of Romanticism in Late Henry James." His research focuses on post-Enlightenment literature, theory, and criticism, and he has published essays and reviews in the *Henry James Review*, *Journal of Modern Literature*, and the forthcoming edited volume *A Power to Translate: New Essays on Emerson and International Culture*.

Elizabeth Syrkin is a Marie Curie Research Fellow at the University of Muenster as part of the EU-funded "Diasporic Constructions of Home and Belonging" (CoHaB) Initial Training Network. She has published an essay on Ben Okri's fiction in *Commonwealth Essays and Studies*, and she is the co-editor (with Khachig Tölölyan) of a special issue of *Diaspora: A Journal of Transnational Studies*. Her other research interests include postcolonial literature, empire, modernism, and theories of space, place, and the city.

Robert T. Tally Jr. is an associate professor of English at Texas State University, where he teaches American and world literature. His books include *Fredric Jameson: The Project of Dialectical Criticism*; *Poe and the Subversion of American Literature: Satire, Fantasy, Critique*; *Spatiality (The New Critical Idiom)*; *Utopia in the Age of Globalization: Space, Representation, and the World System*; *Kurt Vonnegut and the American Novel: A Postmodern Iconography*; *Melville, Mapping and Globalization: Literary Cartography in the American Baroque Writer*; and, as editor, *Geocritical Explorations: Space, Place, and Mapping in Literary and Cultural Studies*; *Kurt Vonnegut: Critical Insights*; and *Literary Cartographies: Spatiality, Representation, and Narrative*. The translator of Bertrand Westphal's *Geocriticism: Real and Fictional Spaces*, Tally also serves as the general editor of the Palgrave Macmillan book series *Geocriticism and Spatial Literary Studies*.

Emel Tastekin is a lecturer in English Language and Literature at Yasar University. She previously taught at the Arts Studies in Research and Writing program at the University of British Columbia, where she completed her doctoral studies in English. Her research interests are nineteenth- and twentieth-century histories of literary criticism in relation to the interpretation of monotheistic scriptures and religious minorities. Tastekin's dissertation examined the work of a German-Jewish scholar of Islam, Abraham Geiger, through Derrida's concept of Abrahamic hospitality and through postcolonial theories on diasporic identities. Her current project deals with the literary aspects of religious discourses, particularly narratives by Western converts to Islam and the Qur'anic commentary of Muslim figures within modernity, to explore the rise of global Islamic discourses.

Darwin Tsen is a dual-degree PhD candidate in the Department of Comparative Literature and Asian Studies of Penn State University. His dissertation project, "Under Institutional Eyes: The Search for Collectivity in the Postsocialist Transpacific Novel," examines how collectivity is imagined in the novels of Mo Yan, Luo Yijun, and Karen Tei Yamashita.

Charlie Wesley is an assistant professor of English at Daemen College whose scholarly interests include modern British literature, exile literature, and magical realism. He has published in *The Chronicle of Higher Education* and *Modern Language Studies* as well as the collections *Education and the USA* and *Indian Writers: Transnationalisms and Diasporas*. His most recent article is entitled "Inscriptions of Resistance in Joseph Conrad's *Heart of Darkness*" in *Journal of Modern Literature*. Currently he is coediting a collection of essays on Salman Rushdie with Ana Mendes.

Russell West-Pavlov is a professor of English at the University of Tübingen, Germany, and a research associate at the University of Pretoria, South Africa. His recent books include *Temporalities* (Routledge, 2013), *Imaginary Antipodes* (Winter, 2011), and *Fictions of Space/Spaces of Fiction* (Palgrave Macmillan, 2010).

INDEX